Work and Labour in Canada

Work and Labour in Canada

Critical Issues

Andrew Jackson

Canadian Scholars' Press Inc.
Toronto

Work and Labour in Canada: Critical Issues
Andrew Jackson

First published in 2005 by
Canadian Scholars' Press Inc.
180 Bloor Street West, Suite 801
Toronto, Ontario
M5S 2V6

www.cspi.org

The chapters in this volume are based on papers originally published by the Canadian Labour Congress.

Photographs are from the Health Canada Website and Media Photo Gallery, Health Canada, http://www.hc-sc.gc.ca. Reproduced with the permission of the Minister of Public Works and Government Services Canada, 2004.

Every reasonable effort has been made to identify copyright holders. CSPI would be pleased to have any errors or omissions brought to its attention.

Canadian Scholars' Press gratefully acknowledges financial support for our publishing activities from the Government of Canada through the Book Publishing Industry Development Program (BPIDP) and the Government of Ontario through the Ontario Book Publishing Tax Credit Program.

Library and Archives Canada Cataloguing in Publication

Jackson, Andrew, 1952-
      Work and labour in Canada : critical issues / Andrew Jackson.

Includes bibliographical references and index.
ISBN 1-55130-271-3

      1. Labor--Canada--Textbooks. 2. Working class--Canada-- Textbooks. 3. Labor movement--Canada--Textbooks. I. Title.

HD8106.5.J32 2005   331'.0971   C2004-906137-2

Cover design by Susan Thomas/Digital Zone
Text design and layout by Brad Horning

05 06 07 08 09   5 4 3 2 1
Printed and bound in Canada by AGMV Imprimeur, Inc.

Canadä

This book is dedicated to

Karen, Caitlin, and Emma

Table of Contents

List of
Tables and Figures

List of Boxes

Preface

Almost all of the material in this book was originally produced, often in a very different format, as research papers for the Canadian Labour Congress (CLC). The CLC is the major trade union federation in Canada, representing some 3 million workers who belong to its affiliated unions.

The CLC has consciously tried for a number of years to contribute to and shape the public debate on work, employment, and incomes through a close factual analysis of trends in employment and unemployment, wages and working conditions, incomes of working families, the situation of equality-seeking groups, and inequality and poverty. Some of this work has been produced in popular formats under the general theme: Is Work Working for You? Other material has been prepared for presentations to government officials, at conferences, or for publication in books and academic journals.

It would seem to be obvious that wages and the quality of work are central aspects of the economic and social well-being of Canadians and should be at the centre of public debate on how our economy is performing, but it still seems to take constant effort to push these issues to the forefront and to bring them to the attention of policy makers.

The CLC has tried to highlight forces and trends affecting all working people and not just union members, and to earn a reputation for informed analysis of current issues. Theory and experience show that the social forces behind an argument are often decisive in politics and policy making, but the force of an argument is important as well. Special thanks go to the CLC elected officers, especially current President Kenneth V. Georgetti and former President Robert (Bob) White, for their recognition of the importance of economic and social research in trade union work.

Much of the analytical work of the CLC is undertaken by the Department of Social and Economic Policy. Thanks are due to my departmental colleagues Kevin Hayes, Pierre Laliberté, Cindy Wiggins, and especially Bob Baldwin, who contributed material on pensions and older workers to this book. More importantly, Bob has held up the other side of a 20-year-long ongoing conversation on work, labour, and social and economic policy issues.

Very special thanks go to Judy Cerra for her highly skilled work in pulling my text, charts, and graphs into a comprehensible format. Penni Richmond and David Onyalo have contributed greatly to my understanding of equality issues, not least by insisting that this lens should always be part of our analysis of economic and social issues.

My research work has involved frequent collaboration with trade union colleagues. Hugh Mackenzie, Jim Stanford, and Jane Stinson deserve special thanks for grounding my work in labour perspectives on work and workers. I also owe a lot to my contact over the years with John Evans and Roy Jones of the Trade Union Advisory Committee to the Organisation for Economic Co-operation and Development (OECD).

Many of the research papers produced for the CLC, which form the basis for chapters in this book, were presented to academic conferences, and some have appeared in different form in academic publications. Maintaining a link between union and academic research hopefully provides the reader with some assurance of credibility, and certainly provides for constant stimulus. Particular thanks in shaping the material in this book, either though conversation and direct input or through their own work, go to Keith Banting, Wallace Clement, Jane Jenson, Pradeep Kumar, Gregor Murray, John Myles, Lars Osberg, Charlotte Yates, Leah Vosko, and, especially, Rianne Mahon of the Institute of Political Economy at Carleton University to which I am affiliated as a research professor. Thanks to Wallace Clement for reading over the manuscript.

From the world of policy institutes, I have worked with and learned a lot from Bruce Campbell and Armine Yalnizyan of the Canadian Centre for Policy Alternatives; Ken Battle of the Caledon Institute; Andrew Sharpe of the Centre for the Study of Living Standards; and Marcel Lauziere and Katherine Scott, who were colleagues at the Canadian Council on Social Development during my sojourn there as director of research, 2000–2002.

Most of the material that follows is highly empirical, drawing heavily on data and analytical studies undertaken by Statistics Canada. The Analytical Studies Branch makes an incredibly important contribution to understanding Canadian economic and social trends, and have consistently devoted a great deal of attention to work, income, and labour (though we still badly need a national survey of working conditions, and identifiers for workers of colour on the *Labour Force Survey*!). This book draws heavily on data from the *Labour Force Survey*, much of it obtained from special tabulations by Statistics Canada or directly from public-use micro-data files. For that reason, some data tables are simply referenced to the survey rather than to published sources.

Finally, thanks to Megan Muller of CSPI for encouraging me to write this book and for so capably helping me to pull it together.

■A Note from the Publisher

Thank you for selecting *Work and Labour in Canada: Critical Issues* by Andrew Jackson. The author and publisher have devoted considerable time and careful development (including meticulous peer reviews) to this book. We appreciate your recognition of this effort and accomplishment.

■Teaching Features

This book distinguishes itself on the market in many ways. One key feature is the book's well-written and comprehensive part openers, which help to make the chapters all the more accessible to undergraduate students. These part openers include annotated related Web sites.

The chapters are unusually rich in pedagogy. Each chapter contains detailed references, questions for critical thought, and annotated recommended readings.

The art program includes provocative chapter-opening photographs, as well as numerous figures, tables, and boxed inserts.

Introduction

The central purpose of this book is to evaluate the quality of work and jobs in Canada from a critical perspective, and to open up a discussion about how conditions might be improved for working people. A substantial amount of detail is provided on recent trends in employment, unemployment, and the quality of jobs; on how the job market serves the needs of particular groups of workers; on the role of Canadian unions; and on how conditions in Canada compare to those in other countries.

Part I, "Working People and the Canadian Workplace," is divided into four chapters. These cover the importance of jobs, recent trends in the job market, and two important aspects of job quality—access to training and healthy working conditions.

Chapter 1 discusses why jobs are important from the perspective of working people, and highlights the importance, not just of wages, but also of the quality of work. It looks at some key forces shaping the nature of jobs and work. Chapter 2 provides a detailed overview of conditions in the job market and in workplaces, and key trends over the past 15 years. While Canada has done very well on some fronts and has a very high rate of employment, including in jobs requiring higher levels of education, other, more negative, trends are of concern. These include growing inequality in wages, job prospects, and family incomes, and the growing problem of low wages and unstable or precarious work.

Chapter 3 focuses on opportunities for access to training and on-the-job learning, and Chapter 4 surveys workplace conditions that have implications for both the physical and mental health of workers.

Part II, "Inequalities and Differences: Gender, Race, Ability, Age," takes an in-depth look at the labour market and work experiences of specific groups: women, minorities, and older workers. The job market is marked by deep inequalities and differences along lines of gender, race, ability, and age, all of which intersect with differences in wages and the quality of employment.

Chapter 5 details the job experiences of women and shows that there are still deep and systematic differences of pay and job quality based upon gender. Chapter

6 looks at the experiences of visible minorities (workers of colour), Aboriginal Canadians, and persons with disabilities. Despite huge differences, all these groups have some vulnerability to discrimination in the job market. Chapter 7 looks at the situation of older workers and paths from work to retirement, also highlighting some differences between generations and what has come to be known as the changing life-course.

Part III, "Contemporary Canadian Unions," looks at the role of unions in Canada and in other advanced industrial countries, and at the potential future of unions as a force for improving pay and working conditions and promoting greater equality in the job market. Chapter 8 examines union impacts on wages, low-wage jobs, benefits, and access to training, and discusses how unions affect the way in which the economy and the labour market operate. Chapter 9 looks at changes in union membership, and challenges facing unions in attempting to organize and represent workers in today's job market.

Part IV, "Canada in a Global Perspective," looks at how Canada's greater integration into the global and North American economy has changed the labour market and the world of work, and the extent to which the forces of free trade and global economic integration may limit our choices in terms of shaping how the labour market works. Chapter 10 focuses upon the impacts of globalization and the Free Trade Agreement with the U.S., and Chapter 11 compares and contrasts Canada's labour market and workplace institutions to those of some European countries.

This final chapter encourages the reader to think about the ways in which Canada's labour market model might be changed in order to improve the quality of jobs, and to address some of the many problems of work outlined in the book as a whole.

Relevant Web sites are identified in the introductions to each part of the book, and suggested readings as well as questions for critical discussion follow each chapter.

Working People and the Canadian Workplace

THIS PART OF THE BOOK PROVIDES AN OVERVIEW OF CONDITIONS IN THE JOB MARKET and in workplaces today, and a summary of trends over the past 15 years. It focuses on wages, unemployment, forms of employment, opportunities for education and training, and workplace conditions. Differences in the experience of different groups of workers, particularly by gender and age, and of Canadian workers compared to those in other countries are briefly noted, setting the stage for further analysis later in the book.

Chapter 1, "Why Jobs Are Important," sets out some of the key characteristics of jobs that are important to working people, including not just wages but also the quality of work along a number of dimensions, such as stability of employment, working conditions, and opportunities for promotion and training. Some key forces shaping the nature of jobs and work, such as government economic policies, industrial restructuring, and unions, are also highlighted.

Chapter 2, "Work, Wages, and the Living Standards of Canadian Working People," provides a detailed, statistically based analysis of trends in wages, employment, unemployment, and the quality of new jobs created over the past 15 years. Canada has done well on some fronts. We have a very high rate of employment, and there has been a shift toward better jobs requiring higher levels of education. However, there are some negative trends as well. The chapter highlights inequality in the job market, and the growing problem of low wages and precarious work—that is, the problem of low-paying and insecure jobs. Links are drawn from trends in the job market to a disturbing trend toward greater inequality in the wider society. This chapter also draws some attention to the different experiences of women and men, providing some background for the more detailed analysis in Part II.

Chapter 3, "Taking Lifelong Learning Seriously," focuses on one key aspect of job quality: opportunities for access to training and on-the-job learning. This is increasingly seen as crucially important to both individual workers and to the economy in a knowledge-based economy. A key dimension of precarious jobs is that they provide limited, if any, access to training and ladders to better jobs. It is disturbing that most opportunities for on-the-job training and career development go to higher-paid managers and professionals, compounding their relatively advantaged position in the job market.

Finally, Chapter 4, "The Unhealthy Canadian Workplace," surveys workplace conditions that have implications for both the physical and mental health of workers. The focus here is on physical hazards at work, and on work and stress. Work can be and often is very stressful because of the pace and demands of the jobs and the low degree of control exerted by employees, and also because of conflict between work and family and community life.

Related Web Sites

- The Canadian Labour and Business Centre <http://www.clbc.ca>. Canada's major joint business-labour organization conducts many studies related to training and future skill needs. All work is undertaken on the basis of advice from both employers and unions.
- Canadian Labour Congress <http://www.clc-ctc.ca>. The national umbrella organization for 3 million unionized Canadian workers. The Social and Economic Policy subsite (located under "Issues") contains many research papers on labour market issues. The site links to the Web sites of many unions in Canada and around the world.
- The Canadian Policy Research Networks <http://www.cprn.ca> is an Ottawa-based policy think-tank that involves academics and others in policy-related research work. The Work Network is one of the major streams of activity, and literally scores of articles and research papers are available on trends and changes in Canadian work and workplaces. Many papers produced by the Family Network are also relevant to understanding change in work and workplaces.
- The Department of Human Resources and Skills Development <http://www. hrsdc.gc.ca>. The department charged with responsibility for Canada's skills agenda and for labour market and labour issues provides information and research papers on a wide range of issues, including changes in the job market, what kinds of training are needed for different careers, government programs, and trends in workplaces and collective bargaining.
- Job Quality <http://www.jobquality.ca>. A subsite of the Canadian Policy Research Networks that contains a wealth of current data on the quality of jobs in Canada.
- Statistics Canada <http://www.statcan.ca>. The Web site of Statistics Canada, Canada's national statistical agency, has a wealth of free data and research papers on a huge range of employment, income, and social issues, almost all of which provide separate data for women and men. Many free Internet publications are listed under "Our Products and Services" under the subhead "Labour." Also, the latest *Labour Force Survey* data are readily available on *The Daily* subsite.

CHAPTER ONE

Why Jobs Are Important

▦ Introduction

This chapter describes the fundamental importance of good jobs to well-being, flags some major changes in the Canadian workforce and the nature of work over recent decades, and summarizes some key forces shaping the quality of jobs.

▦ Jobs and a Changing Workforce

The vast majority of Canadian families and households depend upon jobs and the labour market for their well-being. Almost eight in ten (78%) people aged 15 to 64 participate in the paid workforce, meaning that they are either working, or unemployed but actively seeking work. This is one of the highest participation rates among the advanced industrial countries, a bit higher than in the U.S., and only slightly below the very high rates in the Scandinavian countries. Among the so-called core working-age population aged 25 to 54, the participation rate in 2003 was 86% (92% for men and 81% for women). It was 79% for young adults aged 20 to 24, and 57% for older adults aged 55 to 64. Participation is understandably lower for teens and older workers, but very few Canadians have no attachment at all to the job market.[1]

Earnings from employment make up the lion's share of all Canadian household income. In 2003, Canadian households had a total income of $928 billion, two-thirds (67%) of which came from employment, with another 8% coming from small business earnings. Income transfers from governments—mainly public pensions, Employment Insurance, and welfare payments—contributed 13% of total income, with most of that amount going to retirees as Old Age Security and Canada Pension Plan payments. Just 11% of household income came from investments.[2] Some very affluent Canadians do collect very large amounts of dividend, capital gains, and interest income from their investments, but even the very affluent rely very heavily on employment and self-employment income for their livelihood.

In the 1950s and into the 1960s, the Canadian norm was for families to depend on the wages of an adult male breadwinner who worked upon leaving school until retirement at age 65 to support his wife and children. A lot has changed, and several chapters in this book focus on the changing workforce.

The importance of paid work over the life-course has shifted forward and backward. More than half of all young people now complete some kind of post-secondary education. This has delayed entry into the permanent workforce for many young adults. (However, the great majority of students work part-time and/or for part of the year, and increasingly rely on earnings to finance their studies.) Meanwhile, the normal age of retirement has fallen from 65 a generation ago to just above age 60 today. "Freedom 55" remains the dream of many. In 2000, just 36.5% of people aged 60 to 64 were still in the workforce, but this rate had jumped to 42.0% by 2003, probably reflecting big losses to RRSP investments in the stock market collapse of 2000. More older women work today than was the case a few years ago, simply because more women have been in the paid workforce for most of their lives. The situation of older workers and the role of pensions are discussed in Chapter 7.

By the mid-1970s, half of all women with employed spouses were working, and by 2003, that figure had risen to 78.7%. The vast majority of women now want to participate in the paid workforce—perhaps with some time out for maternity and parental leaves—and their incomes make up a high and rising proportion of family incomes. Women have made substantial progress, but there are still huge gaps between women and men in terms of earnings and the quality of jobs. The nature of women's work and differences between the work experiences of men and women are explored in Chapter 5.

Today, Canada has one of the most diverse populations in the world, and one of the highest rates of immigration. Workers of colour and new immigrants make up a high proportion of the workforce, and will—with Aboriginal Canadians—account for virtually all job growth in the years ahead. New immigrants are more highly educated than the Canadian-born, yet their earnings and job chances fall far short of equality. These issues are discussed in Chapter 6.

To summarize, the great majority of Canadians work for a living, and paid work is absolutely central to the economic well-being of individuals and families. Some of our income comes from government transfers, and some of our basic

> ### Box 1.1: Young People and the Transition to Work
>
> The transition from school to work is taking place later in life, and is also much more complex than in even the recent past. Statistics Canada's *Youth in Transition* survey has found that many people who were high school dropouts in their late teens eventually complete their studies, and that many young adults move back and forth between work and post-secondary studies.
>
> A survey of 22-year-olds at the end of 2001 found that just 11% of the group (14% of men and 8% of women) had not completed high school, and about one-third of these dropouts had nonetheless participated in some form of post-secondary education.
>
> At age 22, 76% of young people had participated in post-secondary education at some time, and just one in four had not participated at all. Almost half of the age group (40% of men and 48% of women) were still in school at age 22.
>
> At this age, just 34% of young people were out of school and working full-time (about the same proportion of women and men) and another 7% were not in school and working part-time. Thus, at age 22, about the same proportion of young people are in school as are in work and not studying.
>
> About one in seven 22-year-olds (14% of women and 15% of men) were not working and not studying at the end of 2001 (Statistics Canada, *The Daily*, June 16, 2004).
>
> Source: Statistics Canada, "Young People and the Transition to Work," *The Daily*, Catalogue 11-001, June 16, 2004.

needs—such as education for school-age children and health care—are met through government programs, but the fundamental reality is that we live in a market society. We must work to live, and our income from work determines our standard of living. This is true in both absolute terms and as compared to our fellow citizens. The kinds of jobs we hold and the wages we earn largely determine the kind of homes and neighbourhoods in which we live, the extent to which we can buy the goods and services we want, the extent to which we can provide our children with opportunities, and our ability to balance work with family and community life and opportunities for leisure.

Without devaluing in any way the contribution and importance of unpaid work in the home and in the community, paid work is also a critical source of meaning and purpose in the lives of most Canadians, and a major source of personal identity. Jobs connect us to the wider society, and provide us with a sense of participation in a collective purpose. Many people define themselves largely by what they do at work. Good jobs in good workplaces are needed if individuals are to develop their individual talents and capacities to the full, to actively participate in society, and to enjoy a broad equality of life chances. On the other hand, unemployment and bad jobs give rise to poverty and low income, stress, ill health, and alienation from the wider society in which we live.

Despite the central importance of paid work to our lives, Canada's progress as a country tends to be measured mainly on the basis of two key indicators: growth of Gross Domestic Product or GDP, and the unemployment rate. GDP is the sum total of all income in the country, and the sum total of all output. The unemployment rate is the proportion of people in the labour force who want to work, but cannot find any work at all. The level of GDP is certainly important, and economic growth will usually lower unemployment and raise incomes, and thus directly benefit working people. But, it is important to go beyond the economic growth and unemployment numbers to ask the question: How is work working for people?

Box 1.2: "Work: The 21st-Century Obsession"

Jobs Used to Put Food on the Table. Now They Feed Our Heart, Soul, and Ego
By Mark Swartz

10,440. That's the number of days we put in at work over a typical 40-year career. Not surprisingly then, how we feel about our jobs spills over into just about every other facet of our lives. Which leads us to the all-important question: just what is it that we really want from our employment?

Before addressing this, consider the role that work has come to play in our society. As recently as a generation ago, people regarded their livelihoods simply as a means to an end. A job provided pay and security—anything more was a bonus.

Today we are a culture obsessed with our occupations. "The reality is that we define ourselves by what we do," says Ann Coombs, thought leader and author of *The Living Workplace: Soul Spirit and Success in the 21st Century* (HarperBusiness).

Longer work weeks, the need for dual-incomes, the erosion of extended families, and decreasing use of social outlets such as religious associations make workplaces the new town hall. In addition, "our increasing reliance on materialism to satisfy our needs means that we are more inclined to let our employers own our souls," according to Coombs.

The result is that our jobs have a tremendous impact on the rest of our lives.

On the personal front, employment satisfaction can increase our feelings of self-confidence and optimism about the future. It frees us up to pursue outside interests and reduces our overall stress levels.

The effect on our workplace performance is significant as well.

"Satisfaction at work helps employees become engaged, motivated, and productive," says Tim Arnill, president and COO of Verity International, a leading Canadian career management firm.

On the flip side, not getting your needs met at work can have far reaching effects.

When people are frustrated in their jobs, morale can plummet and loyalty may all but disappear.

According to Arnill, that's when you often see absenteeism and turnover rates shoot up, along with an upswing in healthcare costs for stress-related illnesses. Which brings us back to the original question: what is it then that people truly want from work these days? It seems that, when it comes to the basics, not a lot has changed since 40 years ago. Pay and security are still crucial, according to the 2000 Canadian survey, "What Is a Good Job?"

Dr. Graham Lowe, a University of Alberta professor and co-author of the study (which can be viewed at www.cprn.com), notes that "Those who are unhappy with their level of pay have been found to exhibit lower levels of job commitment and often have less faith in management." They are also more likely to be chronically tardy.

Interestingly though, the issue of money comes up relatively low on many surveys about workplace needs. In a 2000 study by Randstad, one of the world's largest temporary and contract staffing organizations, "getting raises" ranked fifth over-all in definitions of success in the workplace.

Atop the list was being trusted to get the job done, followed by getting the opportunity to do the kind of work you want, having the power to make decisions that affect your own work, and finding a company where you want to stay for a long time. Flexibility followed closely behind raises in 6th position.

So what does this say about compensation? "Receiving satisfactory pay and benefits are definitely important factors in promoting employee well-being," according to Lowe.

However, since almost three quarters of respondents in the CPRN study were reasonably content with their salaries, this suggests that they are able to focus on other wants and needs.

It should be noted that a person's age or stage strongly influences what is sought. For instance, security tends to be more pressing for those aged 45 plus. This makes sense when you take into account the financial and family responsibilities often associated with this period in life.

Beyond a salary and the desire for continuity, what we want from work varies as widely as the range of our individual values.

Penny Balberman, CFO of a mid-sized software company, seeks out variety and challenge in her jobs. "I think of myself as a high achiever who is motivated by solving problems and making a difference," she says.

In her case, the rewards are in producing tangible results. Autonomy is essential as well. "I derive great satisfaction from being able to choose my responsibilities."

Balberman is among the growing ranks of professionals who enjoy being paid for performance. Her compensation consists of a base salary plus bonus, hinged on her contribution to the company and her business units.

Naturally this injects an element of risk. Yet it also provides the stimulus to go above and beyond the norm in terms of involvement. The desire for personal fulfillment is another feature that people are seeking more of. Roman Plawiuk, a financial services marketer, says that he is happiest "when my skills and talents are being utilized to the fullest, and I feel as if I am adding personal value."

For him, recognition from peers for a job well done and a sense of fitting in to a workplace that appreciates his efforts are major drivers. An understanding boss who supports his goals is vital as well. Beyond that, he looks for an environment where he can just be himself on a daily basis. "It's great when you can find an open, honest company where people can drop their personal shields." Both Balberman and Plawiuk have children, and they strive for a sense of balance between work and home. This doesn't necessarily mean that the two elements must always be at odds. "I find that our clients are expressing a need for work/life integration, as opposed to mere balance," says Arnill, whose company helps downsized employees from all ranks and industries. "They want to know that their job supports their outside commitments, and that they don't always have to trade off one for the other." This is especially true for Generation X and Generation Next.

What else are people searching for these days? Quite a bit, according to the Web site that is based on Lowe's study, www.jobquality.ca. Factors covered are influence, rewards, security, job design, environment, schedules, relationships, job demands, pay and benefits, training and skills, and special indicators such as union arrangements and the impact of technology.

With all of these permutations of values, needs, and workplace configurations floating around, how do you choose what's best for you? "Start by listening to what your gut tells you," says Coombs. She adds that there is a stiff price to pay when you ignore your internal compass.

This thought is mirrored in the words of Balberman. "I'm at a stage now where I know where I stand in life, and where my job fits in. I refuse to settle for less than I deserve." Plawiuk completes the thought. "What's out there will obviously influence what you get, but the truth is that it all begins inside of you."

Source: Mark Swartz, "Work: The 21st Century Obsession," *The Toronto Star*, April 5, 2003.

GDP growth and low unemployment tell us nothing about the adequacy of wages or how earnings are distributed among households and families. One disturbing trend from the 1990s into the first few years of this century has been increasing inequality in the distribution of earnings. Wages and incomes from employment have risen for those at the top, stagnated for those at the middle, and fallen for those at the bottom. Many Canadians work in very low-wage jobs. These trends have increased income gaps between families, and kept poverty at high levels even in an economic recovery. Trends in employment and earnings also raise important issues of equality between women and men, between the majority and racial minorities, and between generations.

Economic growth and unemployment numbers also tell us little about the security of employment and earnings. Many jobs are short-term and unstable, and government supports for frequently unemployed and lower-paid workers have been cut back. Low unemployment is obviously a good thing, but a low unemployment rate can hide the fact that many people are working in low-wage jobs, or are working in temporary jobs, or are working in part-time jobs even if they want to work full-time. Just having a job is a good thing, but there is a big difference between having a survival job and a job that offers a real ladder to better jobs. Economic growth and unemployment numbers also tell us nothing about the quality of jobs in terms of the pace and intensity of work, access to training and career ladders, and the consequences of jobs for our health. This book reviews all of these issues.

Box 1.3: What Is a Good Job?

Most of us would agree that a good job is defined, in part, by the level of pay. However, other dimensions are actually much more important. Prospects for promotion and learning are likely to be particularly important to younger workers, and lower-paid jobs may be taken in preference to higher-paid jobs if they are more interesting, provide greater security, more acceptable hours, better working conditions, and so on. International survey evidence suggests that job security, having an interesting job, opportunities for advancement, and being allowed to work independently—cited by 59%, 49%, 34%, and 30% of respondents respectively—rank well ahead of high pay (Clark 1999).

An Index of Job Desirability was developed for the U.S. in the late 1980s based upon the weights given to different characteristics of jobs by workers. Non-monetary characteristics of jobs were, in combination, found to be twice as important as earnings, with access to training, low risk of job loss, and characteristics of the job (non-repetitiveness and autonomy) ranking particularly highly and in that order. Other characteristics of jobs examined were hours of work, control of hours, and whether the job was "dirty." The ranking of desirable job characteristics was found to differ little between men and women or by age.

A striking finding of this study was that occupation is a limited indicator of job quality, since variation within occupational groupings was found to be as great as that between groupings. It was also found that job quality differences between women and men are much greater than earnings differences (Jencks et al. 1998).

Source: Jencks, C., Perman, L., and Rainwater, L., "What Is a Good Job? A New Measure of Labour Market Success," *American Journal of Sociology* 93(5).

Key Forces Driving the Quantity and Quality of Jobs

Macroeconomic Conditions

In a market economy, the great majority of jobs are created by private-sector employers. Workers are hired in order to produce goods and services, and workers are hired or laid off depending upon demand at home and outside Canada for those goods and services. In a downturn, many workers lose their jobs, but the biggest impact comes from the fact that employers stop hiring. In Canada, deep recessions resulted in very high unemployment in both the early 1980s and the early 1990s. To some degree, these downturns are part of the normal workings of the business cycle. However, government economic policies have also contributed to periodic high unemployment and ongoing slack in the job market.

Most economists believe that there is a natural or non-accelerating inflation rate of unemployment. The basic idea is that, if unemployment falls too low, below about 7% in the case of Canada, wages will increase too fast, driving up the rate of inflation. In both the early 1980s and early 1990s, the Bank of Canada raised interest rates very sharply to deliberately slow down the economy, fearing that inflation was rising or about to rise too fast because of low unemployment. Critics argue that central banks tend to move too fast, too soon, and that the deliberate use of unemployment to fight even low rates of inflation is very costly (Maclean and Osberg 1996).

A wider issue at stake is how to make sure that very low unemployment does not result in wage-driven inflation. Virtually all economists would agree that, over time, the growth of wages should reflect improved worker productivity or higher output per hour.[3] Mainstream economists think that this will result if labour markets are highly flexible. They take a critical view of the role of unions, minimum wages, and government income supports for the unemployed, all of which are seen to be possible sources of wages that are too high and too rigid. Other economists argue that some countries with strong unions have been able to achieve low inflation and low unemployment, basically because businesses and unions are able to agree on the right level of wages.

The important point in the case of Canada is that our job market usually runs with a bit of deliberate slack—that is, with an unemployment rate of at least 7%—and often with a lot more slack. At any given time, there are more workers looking for jobs than there are available jobs. This means that jobs are hard to find, particularly for workers whose skills and education are not in very high demand and for young people and new immigrants who lack Canadian job experience. When unemployment is high, many workers are underemployed—for example, working in part-time jobs or setting up their own very small businesses when they really want full-time jobs. The degree of slack in the job market is a huge influence upon employer investment in training for the unskilled, attention to the unrecognized skills and credentials of new immigrants, relative pay levels by skill, and employer willingness to balance demands of work and family. The very low unemployment rates reached in the U.S. after 1995 significantly reduced low pay and earnings inequality, as well as pay and opportunity gaps based upon race (Mishel et al. 2003), and there is no doubt that falling unemployment since the mid-1990s has also had positive impacts in Canada.

Economic and Industrial Restructuring

Capitalism thrives on what the famous economist Joseph Schumpeter called "creative destruction." The Canadian economy is always adapting to changing economic circumstances. Some sectors and regions expand, while others shrink. This means that many workers must change jobs, often having to move in search of new work, and it means that workers must often gain new qualifications and learn new skills. Constant change and flux is disruptive for people and communities, but it is probably a good thing, contributing to economic growth and higher productivity. But, it is better if labour adjustment measures and income supports are in place to help workers adapt. Employment security—continued employment through a series of job changes—is a more realistic social goal than job security in the sense of holding a job for life.

Canada was highly dependent upon international markets long before anyone coined the term "globalization." Our resource industries, the auto industry, and most of the manufacturing sector were driven by export markets long before the Canada–U.S. Free Trade Agreement and the North American Free Trade Agreement (NAFTA), and we have long imported a huge share of what we consume. Nonetheless, trade deals in North America and the global shift of manufacturing to developing countries have posed significant adjustment challenges. Some of the impacts are examined in Chapter 10. Our economy was also restructured in the 1980s and 1990s by the ongoing shift from goods production to services, and by technological and organizational changes in how both goods and services are produced. Chapter 4 looks at some of the implications of change in workplaces for employees, and Chapter 5 examines some of the differences between jobs of women and men that have been shaped by economic restructuring.

Over time, there have been major shifts in the structure of occupations, with some movement toward jobs requiring higher levels of formal education and skills. However, the new economy hype glosses over the fact that change is not new or even more rapid, and that many jobs are not very different from those of a generation ago. New occupations and new industries have certainly been produced by the information technology revolution and by growth in professional occupations. Between 1989 and 2003, the share of all jobs in professional occupations rose from 18% to 22%. (This includes professional occupations in business and finance; jobs in the natural and applied sciences; professional occupations in health; teachers and professors; jobs in social sciences and government; and jobs in arts, culture, and recreation.) But, more than 40% of men still work in blue-collar manufacturing, resource utilities, and construction jobs, and almost one-third of women still work in pink-collar clerical, secretarial, and administrative jobs in offices. One in five men and almost one in three women work in sales and service occupations—mainly lower-paid and often part-time jobs in stores, hotels, restaurants, and jobs as security guards, building cleaners, and so on.

Education and Lifelong Learning

Almost everybody seems to agree that education and skills are at an increasing premium in today's knowledge-based economy. Many of the working poor lack the skills sought by employers, or, in the case of recent immigrants, their credentials and skills are unrecognized. People who leave the education system early face a high risk of being trapped in low-wage and insecure jobs. While the public education system is absolutely key, employees who face restructuring or who just want to gain the skills needed to climb job ladders need access to workplace training and lifelong learning. These issues are discussed in Chapter 3.

Unions and Labour Market Institutions

In Canada, about one in three employees is covered by a union agreement, double the level in the U.S. Union coverage in the private sector has been slowly falling, but collective agreements still play a major role in shaping wages and other dimensions of employment of many workers. The role of Canadian unions is examined in Chapters 8 and 9.

All of the advanced industrial countries are, with small differences in degree, exposed to the big structural forces of technological change and globalization, but they differ profoundly in terms of the ways in which the job market is regulated or shaped by governments, employers, and unions. In most of continental Europe, wages and employment conditions of most workers are still set by collective bargaining between unions and employers, with some government intervention in the form of minimum wages and employment standards legislation. These labour market rules make a big difference in the distribution of earnings and in the quality of jobs (OECD 1996). For example, about one in four full-time workers in Canada in the mid-1990s was low paid—defined as earning less than two-thirds of the average national wage—compared to just one in twenty in Sweden, and only one in eight in Germany and the Netherlands. Differences in the distribution of earnings, in turn, have big impacts on differences in income inequality and poverty between countries. In the United States, the top 10% of the population are, at a minimum, more than five times better off than the bottom 10%, but in Sweden, the incomes of the top 10% begin at less than three times better than the bottom 10%.

It is commonly argued that more regulated job markets come at the price of economic growth and job creation, resulting in major differences in the economic performance of North America and Europe. It is true that unemployment has been very high in some of the major European economies for much of the past 20 years, which is a very serious problem. But, some smaller European countries, such as the Netherlands and Denmark, have been able to achieve low unemployment along with higher job quality and more income equality than in North America. The main factors at play have included a strong tilt toward job creation in social services, high levels of training for unemployed and low-wage workers, and close partnerships among governments, employers, and unions. This experience, which may hold some lessons for Canadians, is discussed in the final chapter.

■Conclusion

The quality of employment along a number of dimensions is critical to our individual and collective well-being, yet insufficient attention is usually paid to job quality issues. The quality of jobs is shaped by many forces, including the overall state of the economy and industrial restructuring. It is also strongly influenced by the role of governments and unions.

● ●

■Questions for Critical Thought

1. What dimensions of a job are most important to you personally?
2. To what extent do you think the definition of a good job is influenced by age, gender, and occupation?
3. How do you think the employment prospects of young adults today compare to those of previous generations, such as the baby boom generation who entered the workforce in the mid-1970s?
4. How much influence do you think governments and unions can have in shaping the quality of jobs?
5. Do you think jobs and the quality of work vary greatly between advanced industrial countries such as Canada, the United States, Japan, and the countries of the European Union?

■Recommended Reading

Brisbois, Richard. 2004. "How Canada Stacks Up: The Quality of Work: An International Perspective." Canadian Policy Research Networks <http://www.cprn.org>. This paper compares workplaces in Canada, the U.S., and the member nations of the European Union in terms of four dimensions of job quality: work-life balance, health and well-being, skills development, and career and employment security. An additional indicator on overall satisfaction with working conditions is presented separately.

The Canadian Labour Congress. "Is Your Work Working for You?" <http://www.working4you.ca>. This is an annually updated report on some key quality of work indicators.

Clark, Andrew. 1999. *What Makes a Good Job? Evidence from OECD Countries* <http://www.csls.ca/events/oct98/clark.pdf>. This paper reports on what is known about the subjective perceptions of workers on what they want from work in different countries.

Lowe, Graham S. 2000. *The Quality of Work: A People Centred Agenda*. Toronto: Oxford University Press. As director of the Work Network at the Canadian Policy Research Networks, Canadian sociologist Graham Lowe was active in promoting a policy agenda for higher-quality jobs, and quantitative indicators of job quality. Chapter 3 of this book summarizes evidence on what Canadians want from work, and Chapter 1 provides a broad overview and reflection on the future of work.

Osberg, Lars. 1997. "Changing Realities, Enduring Needs." Chapter 2 of the *1997 Report of the Human Resources Development Canada Advisory Committee on the Changing Canadian Workplace* <http://is.dal.ca/~osberg/uploads/chap2_e.pdf>. This paper, prepared by one of Canada's leading economists, discusses continuities and changes in what workers need from work.

Notes

1. Except as otherwise indicated, all data on work and employment in this book are from Statistics Canada's *Labour Force Survey*.
2. Data from the National Accounts.
3. Productivity is often seen, quite misleadingly, as a measure of worker effort. But, it is mainly driven by employer investment in machinery and equipment, in research and development, and by employee education and skills.

References

Clark, Andrew. 1999. *What Makes a Good Job?* Paris: Organisation for Economic Co-operation and Development (OECD).

Jencks, C., L. Perman, and L. Rainwater. 1998. "What Is a Good Job? A New Measure of Labor Market Success." *American Journal of Sociology* 93 (May): 1322–1357.

Maclean, Brian, and Lars Osberg, eds. 1996. *The Unemployment Crisis: All for Nought?* Montreal and Kingston: McGill-Queen's University Press.

Mishel, Larry, Jared Bernstein, and Heather Boushey. 2003. *The State of Working America 2002–03*. Washington: Economic Policy Institute and M.E. Sharpe.

Organisation for Economic Co-operation and Development (OECD). 1996. "Earnings Inequality, Low Paid Employment and Earnings Mobility." *OECD Employment Outlook*, Chapter 3, 59–108. Paris: OECD.

CHAPTER TWO

Work, Wages, and the Living Standards of Canadian Working People

Introduction

This chapter surveys some of the most important developments in the job market and in the quality of jobs from 1989 to 2003. It looks at trends in wages and in the kinds of jobs that have been created, highlighting the significance and growth of precarious (insecure and low-paid) forms of employment. Links are drawn from how the job market works to rising income inequality and poverty among Canadian families.

The Record of the Long Decade of the 1990s

By some measures, Canada has done very well on the job front for the past decade. After a brutal recession in the late 1980s and early 1990s when the unemployment rate shot up to almost 12%, an economic recovery began in earnest around 1993. The proportion of the Canadian population with jobs reached an all-time high in 2003, and was one of the highest in the world. Unemployment could and should be considered to be far too high at a bit above 7% in 2003 and 2004, but this is still well below the double-digit levels of the early 1990s. The rate of long-term unemployment is very low, and employment has increased in relatively highly skilled occupations, particularly for women. There is a lot of myth and rhetoric about the new economy, but the fact remains that, over time, there is a shift toward jobs requiring higher levels of education, which often provide higher pay and greater job satisfaction.

All that said, the overall job picture is marred by some very serious flaws. Working families have increased their incomes mainly by working more weeks in the year as unemployment has fallen. While this is a positive development, average real wages—that is, hourly or weekly wages adjusted for inflation—have been stagnant. Many workers have very unstable and low-paid jobs. Canada has relatively few workers who are unemployed for very long stretches of time, but we have large numbers of workers who are regularly employed in a series of precarious jobs and survive on low annual earnings. Large inequalities in the job market continue to exist between women and men, and have grown sharply between recent immigrants and other Canadians. The level of income inequality among families and rates of poverty are disturbingly high, particularly if we compare them to those of European countries rather than to the U.S. Earnings inequality has significantly increased when account is taken of the overall state of the economy. Redistributive economic transfers from government, economic security, and access to public and social services have all been undermined by government policy changes. As shown later in Chapter 4, many people are working in very demanding or very boring jobs, both of which are extremely stressful. In short, the labour market and jobs fall far short of meeting the needs of many working people.

In this chapter the record of the long decade of the 1990s is examined. Analysts of labour market and income trends generally try to disentangle structural from cyclical developments. Over time, the economy tends to swing between periods of strong growth and low unemployment, and periods of recession and high unemployment. Structural changes are those between similar economic periods, while cyclical changes are those over periods of recovery and recession. In the 1980s, the Canadian economy reached a cyclical high point in 1989 when the unemployment rate fell to 7.5%. The low point was in 1992 and 1993 when the unemployment rate rose above 11%. By 2000, the unemployment rate had fallen below 7%, and it remained a bit above that level through to the end of 2003. Changes between 1989 and today can be seen as structural, while changes between 1993 and 2003 partly reflect the recovery in the economy.

The Rising Corporate Share

From 1993 through 2002, the Canadian economy grew quite rapidly, indeed, just as rapidly as in the U.S. Real (that is, inflation-adjusted) Gross Domestic Product or GDP per person rose by a cumulative total of more than 25% over this period. However, income in the hands of working families failed to grow at anywhere near the same pace. Real personal income—the total of all before-tax wage, investment, small business, and government transfer income going to households adjusted for increases in consumer prices—rose by only half as much. One reason for the shrinkage in labour's share of national income has been that corporate pre-tax profits have grown as a share of the total economic pie. As a proportion of GDP, corporate profits peaked in the 1980s expansion at 10.6% in 1988. They bottomed out at just 4.7% of GDP in 1992, but rose to a new, higher peak of 12.6% in 2000 and remained above 12% in 2003. There has been a significant increase in corporate profitability, and corporate tax rates have been cut to add even more to returns to shareholders.

Reasonable people can differ about the right level of corporate profits, which are very important as a source of funds for private investment in the economy, and thus for creating more and better jobs. But, it is clear that the balance of bargaining power in the economy has tilted over time against workers. Productivity or output per worker was traditionally closely linked to the rise of real wages, but the two have tended to become de-linked. This same trend has been seen in most other advanced industrial countries since the late 1980s. It probably reflects, in part, the impacts of greater international trade and investment links with the rest of the world, which are explored in Chapter 10. Companies are mainly free to shift investment and jobs to countries where profitability is higher, and this is certainly a factor when it comes to setting wages.

Stagnant Wages

While job growth over the past decade has been healthy and has certainly benefited working families, it is striking that, on average, there were no real wage gains whatsoever for workers in the recovery period from 1993 through 2003. Average weekly and average hourly earnings for all workers just about matched the increase in prices. At the end of 2003, the average hourly wage was $17.48 per hour compared to $17.70 per hour (adjusted for inflation) a decade earlier.[1] Private-sector unionized workers saw a very modest real wage gain of just over 2% over the whole period, but real public-sector union wages fell by a bit more than 1%. Average annual earnings have increased by about 10% more than inflation, but this has been the result of lower unemployment and working more weeks in the year, not because of higher wages per hour.

Of course, averages hide the fact that some workers have experienced real wage gains while others have seen a decline in their real wages, as detailed below. Also, women have done a little better than men. Median earnings are the earnings of someone in the exact middle, that is, half of all workers earn more and half earn less. Between 1989 and 2001, median annual earnings rose only marginally, from $25,031 to $25,387, but median earnings of women rose from $18,310 to $19,865, while median earnings of men fell from $32,697 to $31,450.[2]

Low Pay

About one in four Canadian workers is low paid, defined as earning less than two-thirds of the national median hourly wage (or less than about $11 per hour in today's dollars). Half of all workers earn more than the median, and half earn less. About one in five men and one in three women are low paid, and about one in ten core working-age men aged 25 to 54 and one in five core working-age women are low paid. Data for Canada reported by the Organisation for Economic Co-operation and Development (OECD 1996) show that the incidence of low pay among full-time workers (also defined as less than two-thirds the median) is 30% or more in clerical, sales, service, and labouring occupations, and generally quite low outside these clusters. The incidence of low-paid work has been stable since 1997, despite falling unemployment. At the other end of the scale, the incidence of high pay—defined as two times the median hourly wage—increased from 7.5% to 8.3% between 1997 and 2002.

As shown in Chapter 11, the proportion of workers who are low paid in Canada is about the same as in the U.S., and very high compared to many other advanced industrial countries. Pay gaps between low-, average-, and high-paid workers are much smaller in the Scandinavian countries than in North America, with many European countries standing somewhere in between. The high incidence of low-paid work in North America helps explain why rates of poverty are also much higher than in most European countries (Smeeding 2002).

Good Jobs, Bad Jobs, No Jobs

Compared to some Western European countries, Canada has long had a job market in which many workers are employed in precarious jobs—that is, in jobs that are either insecure or low paid. Good jobs are often considered to be jobs that are full-time and permanent, involving an ongoing relationship between a worker and an employer. Such jobs are often referred to as standard jobs as opposed to non-standard jobs, which are part-time, temporary, or come in the form of self-employment. About two in every three Canadian workers are currently employed in full-time, permanent jobs, down a bit from 1989 (Vosko et al. 2003). About 15% of the workforce are self-employed, and another 11% are temporary employees. The distinction between part-time and full-time work (part-time means working less than 30 hours per week) cuts across all of these categories. A little over 10% of all permanent employees work part-time.

The decline of standard, full-time, permanent jobs since the 1960s and 1970s has been closely associated with the entry of women into the workforce. Women are much more likely to work part-time than men, partly out of choice, and partly because they find it harder to find full-time jobs. Of the 16% of adult women who work part-time, about one-third report that they would prefer to work full-time, and this proportion would likely be higher if child care and elder care were more widely available and expanded their choices in balancing work and family. The shift to temporary jobs has been driven more by employers' increased desire to have a more flexible workforce, which can be increased or decreased in size on short notice, than by workers' desires. Similarly, increased self-employment can partly be explained by the desire of larger companies and governments to contract out work to outside suppliers. Also, some people prefer to be self-employed.

The distinction between standard and non-standard jobs is not always one between good jobs and bad jobs. Entry-level, temporary, and part-time jobs for youth can be a good source of job experience. Many people, particularly students and some parents, want to work part-time. A layer of self-employed professionals and skilled workers—doctors, lawyers, accountants, architects, building contractors, artists, and so on—do very well. But, some forms of non-standard work do carry a very high risk of providing insecure and low incomes. Part-time jobs are not necessarily bad, but on average, they pay less than comparable full-time jobs, provide less health and pension benefits, and offer much more limited access to progressive career ladders. Many part-timers don't even have much control over the hours that they work, and frequently work at nights and on weekends. Most temporary workers would rather have permanent jobs. And a layer of self-employed workers—the so-called own-account self-employed who work by themselves and have no employees—tend to have very low annual earnings.

Restructuring in both the private and public sectors, driven by globalization, technological change, contracting out, and government spending cuts, has underpinned labour market segmentation. At one pole, we see a high level of insecure and/or low-paid precarious work among youth and young adults, recent immigrants, Aboriginal Canadians, persons with disabilities, and adults with limited education or in-demand skills. Women are more likely to be in precarious jobs than men, but the jobs of many men have become increasingly like the jobs traditionally held by women. Precarious work can be permanent, full-time employment that is low paid and/or frequently interrupted by unemployment; employment in temporary jobs; underemployment in involuntary part-time jobs; or employment in low-income, own-account self-employment.

Precarious work involves much more than low pay, limited access to benefits such as pension and health benefits, and a high risk of unemployment. It also carries a high risk of not being developmental; not leading to the development of skills and capacities that increase workers' abilities to access better jobs or to start and proceed on lifetime career ladders, and to better handle labour market risks such as permanent layoffs due to economic change. Job experience and on-the-job training are sources of human capital that enable workers to make upward progression in the job market and better deal with economic uncertainty.

Many low-wage and short-term jobs are traps rather than stepping stones to better jobs. Almost by definition, precarious workers are excluded from the internal labour markets of large companies and government organizations where the norm is for permanent workers to climb job ladders through promotion from within. Research shows that there was a significant widening of longer-term or life-cycle earnings differentials and life chances in the 1990s, particularly among men (Beach et al. 2003). Being trapped in a low-wage job usually also means being unable to derive some meaning and fulfillment from work. Workers value jobs not only for purely economic reasons, but also to the extent that they provide interesting work and opportunities for self-development.

At the other end of the job spectrum, core jobs—reasonably secure, full-time, full-year jobs in larger workplaces—generally require higher levels of education and skills (particularly when routinized work can be contracted out to small firms employing peripheral workers). These jobs often involve the use of skills and discretion on the job, and provide access to lifetime career ladders. For professionals and skilled workers, work reorganization and new technology can produce more interesting and developmental jobs. But, there was also a lot of old-fashioned work intensification in the 1990s in the form of greater demands and longer hours. Surveys indicate high and rising levels of stress from very long hours, demands to do more with less in the wake of downsizing, the intrusion of paid work into the home, and reduced ability to balance the demands of paid work with those of family and community. Some of these issues are explored in Chapter 4.

Table 2.1 provides some basic labour market data for 1989, the lowest unemployment year of the 1980s; for 1993, the year when unemployment peaked; and for 2003. Again, changes between 1989 and 2003 can be seen as structural changes in the job market, as opposed to the cyclical changes that took place between 1993 and 2002.

The national unemployment rate rose from 7.5% in 1989 to a 1990s high of 11.4% in 1993, to a low of just 6.8% in 2000, and has since bumped back up to just over 7.5%. As defined by the *Labour Force Survey*, being unemployed means that a person is not working at all and is actively seeking work. The headline unemployment rate is lower than alternative measures that count people who have recently worked but have given up looking for a job (known as discouraged workers), and count the lost hours of people working part-time who want to work full-time, but can't get the hours that they want.

While unemployment has fallen, it has to be borne in mind that the average duration of an unemployment spell is fairly short, and that many workers cycle in and out of jobs over the year. In 2003, 7.6% of workers were unemployed in any given month of the year, but they were unemployed for an average of just under four months (16 weeks). Unemployment is experienced by a higher proportion of the total workforce over an entire year than the apparently low monthly unemployment rate suggests. In recent years, about one in eight workers has been unemployed at least once in the year.[3] Despite eligibility provisions that limit access to Employment Insurance (EI) for many seasonal, part-time, and temporary workers, more than one-quarter of all regular EI claims, or more than 500,000 claims per year, are filed

Table 2.1: Labour Market Trends

	1989	1993	2003
Unemployment rate			
All	7.5%	11.4%	7.6%
Men	7.4%	12.0%	8.0%
Women	7.8%	10.6%	7.2%
25+	6.7%	10.2%	6.4%
Youth 15-24	11.0%	17.1%	13.8%
Average number of weeks unemployed	18.0	25.1	16.1
Employment rate			
Age 15–64	70.70%	66.50%	72.10%
Youth 15–24	63.2%	53.5%	57.8%
Men 25–54	87.6%	81.7%	85.6%
Women 25–54	68.8%	68.2%	75.7%
Part-time rate			
Youth 15–24	34.9%	45.7%	45.7%
Men 25–54	2.9%	4.8%	4.8%
Women 25–54	15.9%	17.5%	15.6%
Composition of employment			
Public sector employees	20.8%	22.0%	18.9%
Private sector employees	65.3%	62.3%	65.9%
Self-employed	13.9%	15.8%	15.2%
"Own-account" self-employed	7.2%	8.7%	9.8%

Source: Statistics Canada, *Labour Force Historical Review* CD-ROM (Ottawa, 2003).

Box 2.1: The *Labour Force Survey*

Every month, Statistics Canada releases the results of the *Labour Force Survey* based upon a large-scale survey of households. Results of the most recent release are available from <http://www.statcan.ca> in *The Daily*. Each report provides up-to-date information on participation, employment, and unemployment for men and women and different age groups for Canada and the provinces, as well as changes in employment by industry. A comprehensive view of changes in the job market over long periods of time can be gained from the annual *Labour Force Historical Review*, now released on a CD-ROM.

by workers who have filed three or more times over the previous five years.[4] Many workers are in short-term jobs. About one in seven (15%) of adult full-time workers in 2003 had been in his or her current job for less than one year. In short, even excluding young people who may want temporary jobs, there is a lot of movement into and out of employment and unemployment.

Unemployment is generally a bit higher for men than for women. This reflects the fact that proportionately more men work in very seasonal industries, such as construction, and industries subject to frequent layoffs, such as manufacturing. The rate of long-term unemployment is, overall, quite low, but highest among older men displaced by industrial restructuring. But, women are much more likely than men to be working involuntarily in part-time jobs. The biggest gap in unemployment rates is between younger and older workers. While core-age workers were less likely to be unemployed in 2003 than in the previous peak year of 1989, the unemployment rate among youth has jumped—at 13.8% in 2004, it was more than double the rate for workers aged 25 and over.

Between 1989 and 2003, the employment rate for all people aged 15 to 64 (or the proportion with jobs) rose from 70.7% to 72.1% after bottoming out at just 66.5% in 1993. The employment rate rose very strongly in the recovery period from 1993 for women aged 25 to 54, and is now well above the level of 1989. Employment rates for men aged 25 to 54 have, by contrast, fallen a bit since 1989, probably reflecting a mix of very early retirement, more older students in their late twenties, and difficulties faced by some near elderly men in escaping unemployment. The youth employment rate in 2003 was well down from the rate in 1989. Clearly, the divide between older and younger workers has opened up even further.

Looking at the kinds of jobs held by Canadians, the part-time rate (or the proportion in part-time jobs) rose from 1989 to 2003 among young workers, almost half of whom now work part-time. The part-time rate also rose (from very low levels) among men aged 25 to 54. One in six women aged 25 to 54 works part-time, down slightly from 1989, and well down from 1993. Roughly one in three core-age women part-timers wants, but can't find, a full-time job.

Since 1989, the proportion of self-employed workers has increased a bit from 13.9% to 15.2% of all workers, and within that category, the proportion of all workers who are own-account self-employed workers has risen from 7.2% to 9.8%. The proportion of temporary workers has also risen from 7% to 11% of the workforce (Vosko et al. 2003).

The recession of the early 1990s saw the loss of many permanent, full-time jobs, particularly for men in manufacturing. As the unemployment rate rose, the employment rate fell, and the proportion of part-timers, temporary workers, and self-employed increased. As the economic recovery gathered steam after 1993, job creation began to shift back to full-time jobs. Still, over the whole period since 1989, there has been a modest tilt toward more precarious forms of work. This has had disproportionate impacts on women workers and workers of colour, who are much more likely to hold these precarious jobs (see Chapters 5 and 6). There has also been a small decline in the proportion of workers who are in the public sector.

Growing Income Inequality among Families

Table 2.2: Family Income Trends in the 1990s

	1989	1993	2001	% Change 1989–2001	% Change 1993–2001
Market income					
Bottom quintile	$8,969	$5,307	$8,362	-6.8%	57.6%
Second quintile	$33,729	$29,896	$32,362	-4.1%	8.2%
Middle quintile	$53,144	$47,235	$54,127	1.8%	14.6%
Fourth quintile	$73,844	$68,720	$78,389	6.2%	14.1%
Top quintile	$124,953	$118,241	$145,580	16.5%	23.1%
Shares of market income					
Bottom quintile	3.0%	2.0%	2.6%		
Second quintile	11.5%	10.1%	10.2%		
Middle quintile	18.0%	17.7%	17.0%		
Fourth quintile	25.1%	25.8%	24.6%		
Top quintile	42.4%	44.4%	45.6%		
After-tax/Transfer income					
Bottom quintile	$20,258	$18,891	$20,721	2.3%	9.7%
Second quintile	$35,979	$32,717	$36,830	2.4%	12.6%
Middle quintile	$48,064	$44,738	$51,074	6.3%	14.2%
Fourth quintile	$62,247	$58,886	$67,878	9.0%	15.3%
Top quintile	$97,242	$91,683	$113,615	16.8%	23.9%
After-tax/Transfer income shares					
Bottom quintile	7.7%	7.7%	7.1%		
Next quintile	13.6%	13.3%	12.7%		
Middle quintile	18.2%	18.1%	17.6%		
Next quintile	23.6%	23.9%	23.4%		
Top quintile	36.9%	37.1%	39.2%		

(Data are for economic families of two people or more.)
(Constant $ 2001)

Poverty (Post-tax LICO)					
All persons	10.0%	12.9%	10.4%		
Children	11.5%	15.7%	11.4%		
18–64	9.3%	12.3%	10.6%		
65 plus	10.9%	10.8%	7.3%		

Source: Statistics Canada, *Income in Canada* CD-ROM (Ottawa, 2001), Table T802.

Increased Earnings Inequality

The past decade saw an increase in income inequality from already high levels as the gains of the economic recovery went mainly to higher-income families. Table 2.2 provides data on trends for families of two people or more. The data are in constant (inflation-adjusted) dollars. Data are shown for quintiles, each of which represents one-fifth of the total population, ranked from the lowest to the highest by income.

The table first shows the distribution of market income for 1989, 1993, and 2002—that is, income before tax, and before the addition of government transfers. This consists mainly of employment income, plus small amounts of investment income. It is clear that earnings gains have been strongly tilted to higher-income families. The top 20% of families, with average market incomes of $145,580 in 2001, took 45.6% or almost one-half of all market income in that year, up from 42.4% in 1989. In inflation-adjusted dollars, the market incomes of the top one-fifth of families rose by 23.1% from 1989 to 2001. This is much more than the gains of the other income groups. (The share of the bottom 20% rose as well, but this group receives very little earnings, and is disproportionately made up of retirees.) A family in the middle of the income distribution saw only a 14.6% increase in real market income over the eight years of recovery from 1993 to 2001, and only a very small gain over the whole period from 1989 to 2001.

How do we explain rising market income inequality among families? This is partly driven by changes in the way in which people form families. Higher-income men and higher-income women are more likely to live with each other than in the past, but the main reason is increased inequality in the job market itself. Two big factors are at play. Families low on the income scale are more likely to be made up of people in lower-paid jobs, and they are also more likely to be hit by unemployment at some time in a year.

Box 2.2: Top Incomes Take Off

The recent rise in market income inequality among families has been driven, in significant part, by a major increase in the incomes and income share of the very top segments of the workforce (Saez and Veall 2003). Between 1990 and 2000, the share of all income reported on annual income tax returns by the top 10% of individual taxpayers rose from 35.5% to 42.3% of the total. (These data exclude students and capital gains income.) The top 10% in 2000 were those making more than $59,000 per year. Even within this top group, it was the very top that made the biggest gains. The top 1% of taxpayers increased their share of all income reported on tax return forms from 9.3% to 13.6% between 1990 and 2000. The average income of this group in 2000 was $171,728. The share of the top 1% was even higher in the 1920s and 1930s. It fell sharply in the 1940s, then fell gradually to a low of 7.5% in the mid to late 1970s, and began to rise again from the mid-1980s.

Popular accounts of the growing gap between chief executive officers and average workers illustrate the same trend.

The rising share of very high incomes in the 1990s is probably explained, in part, by increased economic integration. Senior corporate executives can move to the U.S., where the share of the top 1% is even greater than here. But, a report on trends in income inequality in the recent Report of the World Commission on the Social Dimension of Globalization (ILO) shows that the share of the top 1% in gross national income of five industrial countries varies. It has remained almost unchanged in some European countries. Leading British economist Tony Atkinson speculates that the high-income share is less driven by globalization, technological change, and big structural factors than by changes in norms and values. Once large income gaps emerge and become slowly accepted, a tipping point is reached and very high incomes rapidly start to grow away from the rest.

Box 2.3: "The Rich Got Richer ..."

The Little Economic Growth There Was in the '90s Was Concentrated among High-Income Earners, Statscan Finds
By Gloria Galloway

Incomes in Canada's largest cities stagnated during the 1990s and the already wide gap between rich and poor neighbourhoods was stretched even further, a trend that experts say will inevitably lead to greater fragmentation and indifference among Canadians.

A study released yesterday by Statistics Canada found that the median income of Canadians living in larger cities increased by just 1 per cent between 1990 and 2000. During the 1980s, it rose 5 per cent.

There was economic growth during the past decade, but the study found it was concentrated among high-income earners. While the poorest 10 per cent of families in most cities saw their income fall during the 1990s, those in the top 10 per cent saw increases of between 5 and 10 per cent.

And even though the number of low-income people living in low-income neighbourhoods—areas where more than 40 per cent of families make less than the low-income cutoff—is still quite small because they tend to be dispersed across a city, their concentration has increased since 1980.

The polarization of a city into neighbourhoods based on income produces a situation where there are several cultures living parallel to each other but not interacting, said Engin Isin, a professor of social sciences at York University.

"Just imagine a city that is caught in that cycle, that the rich only sees its own kind and poor only sees its own kind," Prof. Isin said.

"If we increasingly insulate people into their own, they are less and less willing to see and encounter people who are not their own ... [and yet] the fundamental premise of a city is openness to others."

The increasing gap between rich and poor neighbourhoods is best illustrated in places such as Toronto, where, between 1980 and 2000, family income in the poorest 10 per cent of neighbourhoods rose by 2.6 per cent while the richest 10 per cent of neighbourhoods saw average increases of 17.4 per cent.

But William Strange, a professor of urban economics at the University of Toronto, said the situation may not be quite as bleak as it seems. That is because certain disadvantaged groups, including immigrants, aboriginals, and single-parent families, are disproportionately represented among low-income earners. And, for some of them—immigrants in particular—their relatively poor economic status may be temporary.

An apparent stagnation of the median income has also occurred in the United States, Prof. Strange said. "It turns out in the U.S., if you take [recent] immigrants out of the picture, median incomes have gone up a lot," he said.

In fact, the Statistics Canada study found that, in 2000, the recent immigrants in Canada's large cities were nearly twice as likely as the rest of the population to be living below the low-income cutoff. And the proportion of newcomers in this country's metropolitan areas increased to 9 per cent from 6.1 per cent during the 1990s.

In Vancouver and Toronto particularly, the low-income rates were increasingly concentrated among new immigrants.

That's actually encouraging, Prof. Strange said, because it means those people who have been in the country for longer periods of time are doing better than the statistics suggest. And, although the issue of poverty among new arrivals to Canada is serious, "they are doing better than they would have been" in their home countries, he said.

As for the polarization of the poor into certain neighbourhoods, he said people living in low-income areas don't necessarily stay there.

On the other hand, Prof. Strange said, there is much evidence to suggest that concentrated poverty can breed more poverty. "It can result in a vicious-circle situation where you start with a poor neighbourhood, people are born into that neighbourhood and grow up in that poor neighbourhood and all they learn is how to be poor."

Source: Gloria Galloway, "The Rich Got Richer ..." *The Globe and Mail*, April 8, 2004, A10.

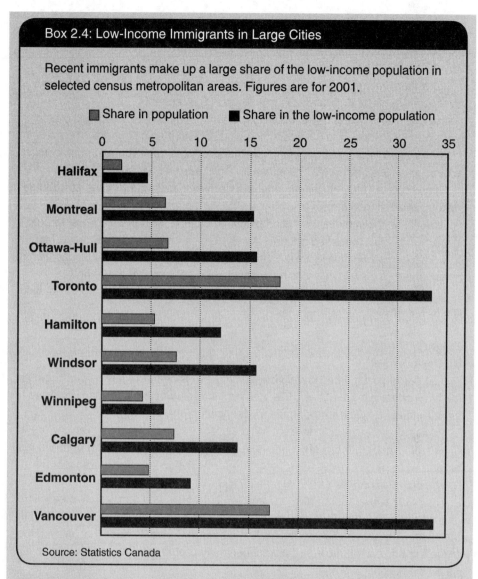

Box 2.4: Low-Income Immigrants in Large Cities

Recent immigrants make up a large share of the low-income population in selected census metropolitan areas. Figures are for 2001.

■ Share in population   ■ Share in the low-income population

Source: Statistics Canada

Vancouver

By Jane Armstrong

Perched between sea and mountain, Vancouver is viewed as the land of milk and honey for immigrants—especially by those coming from the Asian side of the Pacific. But new figures show that more than one-third of the city's newcomers are barely scraping by.

Worse, the statistics show that the number of poor new immigrants is on the rise.

More than 37 per cent of new immigrants in Vancouver are considered poor, according to statistics released yesterday from the 2000 Census. A decade earlier, less than 27 per cent of new immigrants there were poor.

The low-income threshold for a family of four was pegged by Statistics Canada at $33,600. By contrast, the percentage of low-earning new immigrants in Toronto by the year 2000 was 32.8 per cent, a 4.6-per-cent increase from the previous decade.

"I see them struggling," said Shashi Assanand, executive director of the Vancouver and Lower Mainland Multicultural Family Support Services.

A sluggish economy and high housing costs in the Vancouver area could explain in part why new arrivals have a harder time getting ahead than elsewhere, she said.

Ms. Assanand also noted that many immigrants complain that educational credentials and expertise acquired in their countries of origin aren't recognized in Canada.

As a result, doctors, engineers, and other professionals can wind up as cabbies, janitors, and fast-food employees.

Lillian To, of the immigrant services group, SUCCESS, said new immigrants aren't to blame for their narrowed options. As a group, recent immigrants have higher education levels than those born in Canada. And current professional and educational requirements for new immigrants have never been as strict as they are now.

But if credentials from the old country are not always recognized, "we're wasting talent," Ms. To said.

Calgary
By Dawn Walton

The scores of young urban professionals who have flooded Calgary helped boost its median income in the 1980s and 90s, making it the only western Canadian city to see a sizable increase, a Statistics Canada study shows.

Median income—the point at which half of all incomes are higher and half are lower—is considered a good indicator of economic well-being. It measures the ability of individuals or families to pay for necessities, including food, clothing, housing, transportation, education, and child-care.

The study shows that median income for individuals and families alike saw little change in major urban centres during the 1990s, but there was a period of growth in the 1980s. And over the 20-year period, it was cities in Central Canada that enjoyed the biggest bounce, while those in the west generally posted marginal increases and fell below the national average.

Calgary was the exception, benefiting from the influx of young professionals seeking high-paying jobs in the energy sector. Even poorer families in Calgary saw their income rise 7 per cent over the 20 years. The highest-earning families saw a jump of 19 per cent.

Ottawa-Hull, Oshawa, Toronto, Calgary, and Windsor, in that order, reported the highest median family incomes in 2000. Between 1980 and 2000, Edmonton even reported a 1-per-cent drop; Vancouver and Saskatoon reported no gains.

The median pretax income for Canadian families was $62,300 in 2000. In constant dollars, that's a 1-per-cent rise since 1990, a 7-percent increase from 1980.

The same five cities, but in a different order—Ottawa–Hull, Oshawa, Windsor, Calgary, and Toronto—had the highest median income for individuals between 1980 and 2000. Vancouver reported a 1-per-cent drop.

The median adult pretax income in 2000 was $33,600—a 2-per-cent rise from 1990 and a 9-per-cent jump, compared with 1980.

Toronto
By James Rusk

Low-income people in Canadian cities became more reliant on the government for their income from 1980 to 2000— except in Ontario in the later years, according to a Statistics Canada study.

The study found that in 2000, 51.1 per cent of the family income of low-income people in Canada's 27 census metropolitan areas came from government transfers rather than earnings. That compares with 42.7 in 1980.

But Statistics Canada found that in Ontario's cities, government support for low-income families fell sharply between 1995 and 2000, a period when the Progressive Conservative government cut welfare rates.

That drop in Ontario more than offset increased government assistance for low-income families between 1992 and 2000 in the other major Canadian cities, except Halifax and St. John's, where it fell slightly.

In the Toronto CMA, 48 per cent of income for low-income families came from government sources in 1995, compared to 45.3 per cent in 2000.

Frances Lankin, president of the Toronto United Way, which this week published a detailed study of poverty in the city, said that most of the low-income people in the city who can work do so.

But circumstances have squeezed the working poor in 1990s, she said. Minimum wages were frozen for 10 years, a period when inflation increased by 15 per cent, and average rents by 30 per cent. "There are many more people who are working and living in poverty in this city than ever before."

Kerry Wilson, a single mother with two sons, who juggles two jobs as she tries to support her family, said that for people like her, the choice between work and welfare is tough. If a family is on welfare, it has access to benefits, such as drugs and dental payments and fully paid child care, for which the working poor are not eligible.

Montreal
By Ingrid Peritz

Montreal has always had a famous district downtown called the golden square mile, where 19th-century captains of industry built their mansions. Nowadays, one could almost talk about a golden square central city.

Gentrification and booming condo development have spread into Montreal's older neighbourhoods such as tile Plateau Mont-Royal, once working-class, now home to artists and professionals.

The flip side, however, is that the kind of $250-a-month apartment that used to make central Montreal a low-rent heaven is turning into a distant memory, and low-income tenants are being pushed out.

Unlike most other cities in Canada, Montreal no longer has its poorer neighbourhoods in the central city, but concentrated in clusters "surrounding a relatively affluent downtown," Statistics Canada says.

"Gentrification has squeezed some people out," said Jack Jedwab of the Montreal-based Association for Canadian Studies. "The downtown cores are expanding and squeezing some people, more so in Toronto and Montreal than in Vancouver and Winnipeg."

The Plateau Mont-Royal is one of two neighbourhoods that have boosted themselves out of low-income categories, according to researchers at Statistics Canada.

The other is Old Montreal, where a number of fashionable condominiums have risen overlooking the harbour.

Not everyone is pleased by the metamorphosis. A 20-year-old self-styled anti-gentrification activist was arrested in January after placing fake bombs at construction sites in modest sections.

Conversely, Statistics Canada has identified three clusters of poor neighbourhoods outside Montreal's downtown core: Hochelaga-Maisonneuve in the impoverished east end, and the bustling immigrant areas known as Côte-des-Neiges and Park Extension.

Source: *The Globe and Mail*, April 8, 2004, A10.

Increased Family Income Inequality after Tax

Income inequality in Canada is quite pronounced (see Table 2.2). In 2001, the top 20% of families had average incomes, after income taxes and government transfers, of almost $114,000. This was more than five times higher than the average income of about $21,000 for the bottom 20%. The top 20% of families increased their share of after-tax/after-transfer income between 1989 and 2001, from 36.9% to 39.2% of the total, while the share of all other income groups fell. In the economic recession and recovery of the 1980s, by contrast, the income share of the top 20% of families remained rock steady. The share of the top 20% rose from 1989 to 1993, which is not surprising because the more affluent are usually in steady jobs and better protected against rising unemployment, but the fact that their share rose again between 1993 and 2001 is more unusual. Falling unemployment usually provides a big boost to lower-income families.

Between 1989 and 2001, the after-tax/transfer income share of the bottom 80% of families fell. The higher the income of a family, the more they gained in income in the 1990s. The incomes of lower-income families did rise in dollar terms in the recovery from 1993, but they gained rather little over the decade as a whole, and their share of all income fell.

Increasing income inequality reflects two big forces pushing in the same direction. Market income—mainly income from employment—has become more unequally distributed because of trends in unemployment and wages. At the same time, the equalizing impact of government social transfers has been reduced. Taxes and transfers still make a big difference to income gaps, but the difference is not as large as it once was (Heisz et al. 2001).

Box 2.5: Does Income Inequality Matter?

Some people argue that we should worry about poverty rather than income inequality, that we should not worry if some people have more than others so long as everyone gets the essentials of life. But, it is hard to argue that people don't care about their relative income, that is, where they sit in the income ladder compared to others. Consider the following thought experiment. Would you be happier with a job paying $10 per hour in a workplace where other people in the same job get $12 per hour, or with a job paying $9.50 per hour in a workplace where everybody gets the same wage? Would you be happier moving to the U.S. for a slightly higher income, even if you fell on the overall income ladder?

It is hard to believe that there can be genuine equality of opportunity—something that most people think is a good thing—if there are very large differences in economic circumstances. Research has shown that life expectancy and health are closely linked to relative, and not just absolute, income. It is not just that poor people are less healthy than people with average incomes; people in the middle of the income spectrum are also less healthy than those at the top. In relatively equal countries such as Sweden, the differences in life expectancy, health, literacy, education, and other key indicators of well-being between different sections of the population are much narrower than those in Canada, and gaps in Canada are narrower than in the U.S. (Jackson 2000). The life chances of a person are much more strongly determined by the family circumstances into which he or she is born in high-inequality countries. The chances of a person from a lower-income family climbing the income ladder are lower in the U.S. than in Canada (Fortin and Lefebvre 1998).

It is also often argued that earnings inequality is the necessary price we pay for providing incentives to work and to effort. No one argues that all jobs should pay the same. It is reasonable to pay people more if they take on extra responsibilities, or put in extra effort. But, it is far from clear that pay really reflects the demands of a job. Does a senior manager really have a more demanding and difficult job than a worker on an assembly line or in a high-volume call centre? And, how big should pay gaps be? Do senior executives really need to be paid huge multiples of what an average worker earns? It is striking that gaps between higher- and lower-paid workers vary a great deal between countries, and that high-equality countries such as Sweden do not necessarily do worse in terms of economic growth and job creation than do high-inequality countries such as the U.S.

While economic growth was strong in the 1990s and raised incomes from work as unemployment fell, the impact on incomes of many working-age households was significantly offset by cuts to Employment Insurance (EI) and social assistance programs. These cuts were made partly to balance government budgets, but also to counter supposed rigidities and disincentives to work by increasing worker dependence on wages and jobs. From 1993 to 2002, the total of all government transfers to people fell quite a lot, from 13.5% of GDP to 10.5% of GDP—the equivalent of $35 billion in 2002. Seniors' benefits were largely unaffected by policy changes, and rose due to the aging of the population, but government transfers to working-age households—mainly Employment Insurance and social assistance benefits—fell sharply. Both EI and welfare benefits fell in dollar terms because of falling unemployment, which is a good thing, but the cuts to EI benefits brought about through new legislation in 1994, raising the number of hours of work needed to qualify for benefits, also had a big impact. In 1993, there were 1.6 million unemployed workers on average over the year, 57% of whom collected regular EI benefits. By 2002, the number of unemployed had fallen to 1.3 million, but just 38% of the unemployed now qualified for benefits. The dollar saving was much greater than that justified by the fall in unemployment, and the cost was borne by the unemployed (who tend to live in lower- and middle-income households).

Changes in the proportion of the unemployed eligible for EI benefits reflect to some degree a change in the makeup of the unemployed population, such as more young workers and new immigrants looking for a first job. But, the sharp decline in the proportion of the unemployed collecting benefits mainly reflects the shift to an hours-based system with higher qualifying periods of work. This heavily penalizes many (mainly women) seasonal, casual, and part-time workers compared to the 1993 system.[5]

The redesign of the federal child benefits system in the 1990s resulted in higher benefits for low-income working families with children. However, by design, it did not provide an income supplement for the many low-income families with children who rely mainly on provincial social welfare programs. No province increased welfare rates at anything near the rate of inflation after the mid-1990s, resulting in deep income cuts to Canada's poorest households. Welfare cuts affected not just individuals and families outside the workforce, but also the many working poor families who move between low-wage jobs and social assistance.

■The Working Poor

Poverty can be defined in many ways, but the most usual measure in Canada is by using Statistics Canada Low Income Cut-offs which varies by the size of a family and the size of the community in which they live. The cut-off line in 2003 for a single person in a big city (after tax) was about $16,000, and it was about $31,000 for a family of four. As shown in Table 2.2, the poverty rate increased for working-age people between 1989 and 2001 while falling for the elderly. The fact that the child poverty rate was about the same in 2001 as in 1989 is no reason for great celebration given that the Parliament of Canada resolved in 1989 that the 1990s was to be the decade for the elimination of child poverty. Some individuals and families fall well below the poverty line, and remain there for long periods. This is certainly true of long-term welfare recipients, many of whom are outside the workforce for long periods of time because they have disabilities or are single parents with young children. Welfare rates in all provinces fall well below poverty lines, such that to be a person or household permanently without work almost certainly means living on a very low income.[6]

Individuals and families move in and out of poverty for two main reasons. Changes in families due to the breakdown or establishment of relationships are important, especially for women with children who often fall into poverty after a separation. The second major factor is the quality of jobs. A significant proportion of working families cycle in and out of poverty depending upon how many weeks of work they get in a year and at what wage. The working poor tend to move from welfare to work, and back from work to welfare after a job ends, perhaps after a period of using up savings and drawing support from Employment Insurance. In round numbers, a single person had to be working more or less full-time in a full-year job and earning about $10 per hour to escape poverty in 2003. The threshold is obviously higher if a single earner has to support a child or a non-working spouse. A two-adult family with children has to put in about 75 weeks of work a year at $10 per hour to get above the poverty line.

Minimum wages are far too low in all provinces to put working families with even full-time jobs above the poverty line (Battle 2003). Detailed calculations by the National Council of Welfare show that even low-wage (below two-thirds of the median, or less than $10 per hour), full-time, full-year jobs, supplemented by government income supports, put most families in larger cities only very modestly above poverty lines in 2000. Family incomes from low-wage work barely even exceed the new Market Basket Measure of poverty developed by the federal and provincial governments to measure basic costs of living. As noted above, among core-age workers aged 25 to 54, about one in ten men and more than one in five women are in low-wage jobs, and two out of three young people (many of whom have left home) are in low-wage jobs.

The chances of being unemployed at some time in the year are high for low-wage workers. Throughout most of the 1990s, between one-quarter and one-third of Canadian families experienced at least one spell of unemployment in a given year, and the risk of unemployment is concentrated among the relatively uneducated and unskilled. Adults with less than a high school education have about double the unemployment risk of high school graduates, and three to four times the unemployment risk of college and university graduates. The risk of periodic unemployment is highest among youth, single adults, recent immigrants, Aboriginal Canadians, and persons with disabilities.

Over the six years between 1993 and 1998, one in five Canadians aged 25 to 54 lived in poverty at least once, but less than one in 10 lived in poverty for more than four years.[7] About half of all movements of working-age adults in and out of poverty are due to changes in jobs and wages. Most adult low-paid workers (particularly women and those with low levels of education) remain low paid, sometimes moving a bit above the poverty line, and sometimes falling below, depending upon the state of the economy and their luck in finding a steady job. At least half of all adult low-wage workers seem to be more or less permanently trapped in low-wage jobs that would keep them barely above the poverty line (Beach et al. 2003; Drolet and Morrissette 1998; Finnie 2000; Janz 2004). Vulnerability to poverty among adult low-wage workers is particularly great for single adults and single parents who must rely on one income and one wage, as opposed to two-person families, which can usually combine two wages. Vulnerability is also greater for recent immigrants who tend to have larger-than-average families to support. Many adult low-wage workers do not live in poverty because they are cushioned by family incomes, but low earnings are clearly a major source of poverty. Vulnerability to being part of the working poor is significant and increasing due to the changing quality of jobs.

Conclusion

Jobs clearly matter a lot to the well-being of Canadians. The record from 1989 to 2003 has been good in many ways. The proportion of Canadians with jobs is at an all-time high, and many jobs are of reasonably high quality. Still, there are many very low-paid and insecure jobs; the proportion of such jobs has been rising a bit; and the earnings gains of recent years have been highly concentrated. Canada has a major and growing problem of working-poor families.

● ●

Questions for Critical Thought

1. Based on your own experience and that of your family and neighbours, are you surprised at the incidence of low-paid and precarious work?
2. How aware do you think people generally are of the problems of low-wage and frequently unemployed workers?
3. To what extent do you think growing inequality of earnings and after-tax incomes is inevitable?
4. Do you think income inequality and poverty should be issues of greater public concern?
5. Do you think we should deal with poverty and low income by spending more on social programs or by improving the quality of jobs?

Recommended Reading

Freiler, Christa, Laurel Rothman, and Pedro Barata. 2004. "Pathways to Progress: Structural Solutions to Address Child Poverty" <http://www.campaign2000.ca>. This report from the anti-child poverty group Campaign 2000 draws particular attention to the role of the job market in creating child poverty, the situation in Canada compared to other countries, and the need for new policy directions.

The National Council of Welfare Report #120. 2004. "Income for Living?" <http://www.ncwcnbes.net>. This report crunches the numbers to detail the links from pay and hours of work to living in poverty for different family types in different cities.

The Review of Economic Performance and Social Progress. 2001. Jointly published by the Centre for the Study of Living Standards and the Institute for Research on Public Policy (<http://www.csls.ca>), this provides an excellent overview of key Canadian economic and social trends in the 1990s. See in particular the Introduction, "The Longest Decade," and "Trends in Economic Well-Being in Canada in the 1990s" by Lars Osberg and Andrew Sharpe.

Vosko, Leah, Nancy Zukewich, and Cynthia Cranford. 2003. "Precarious Jobs: A New Typology of Employment." *Perspectives on Labour and Income*. Ottawa: Statistics Canada. This paper defines precarious jobs along several dimensions, and draws a useful distinction between non-standard jobs and low-quality jobs. It also stresses differences in the quality of jobs held by women and men.

Notes

1. Data from *Survey of Employment, Earnings and Hours.*
2. Data from Statistics Canada, *Income in Canada* CD-ROM (Ottawa: Statistics Canada).
3. Data from Statistics Canada, *Survey of Labour and Income Dynamics* (Ottawa: Statistics Canada).
4. *Employment Insurance Monitoring and Assessment Report* 2002.
5. For details, see *Falling Unemployment Insurance Protection for Canada's Unemployed* at <http://www.clc-ctc.ca>.
6. See National Council of Welfare, *Income for Living?* (2004), Report #120.
7. Data from Statistics Canada, *Income in Canada* CD-ROM (Ottawa: Statistics Canada).

References

Battle, Ken. 2003. *Minimum Wages in Canada: A Statistical Portrait with Policy Implications.* Ottawa: Caledon Institute of Social Policy.

Beach, Charles, Ross Finnie, and David Gray. 2003. "Earnings Variability and Earnings Stability of Women and Men in Canada: How Do the 1990s Compare to the 1980s?" *Canadian Public Policy* XXIX, Supplement: 541–565.

Drolet, Marie, and Rene Morrissette. 1998. *The Upward Mobility of Low Paid Canadians, 1993–1995*, Cat. 75F0002M. Ottawa: Statistics Canada.

Finnie, Ross. 2000. *The Dynamics of Poverty in Canada.* Toronto: C.D. Howe Institute.

Fortin, Nicole, and Sophie Lefebvre. 1998. "Intergenerational Income Mobility in Canada." In *Labour Markets, Social Institutions and the Future of Canada's Children*, edited by Miles Corak, Statistics Canada Cat. 89-553. Ottawa: Statistics Canada.

Heisz, Andrew, Andrew Jackson, and Garnett Picot. 2001. "Distributional Outcomes in Canada in the 1990s." *Review of Economic Performance and Social Progress*, edited by Keith Banting, Andrew Sharpe, and France St-Hilaire. Ottawa and Montreal: Institute for Research on Public Policy and Centre for the Study of Living Standards.

Jackson, Andrew. 2000. *The Myth of the Equity-Efficiency Trade-Off.* Ottawa: Canadian Council on Social Development.

Janz, Teresa. 2004. *Low Paid Employment and Moving Up.* Statistics Canada Income Research Paper, Cat. 75F0002MIE2004009. Ottawa: Statistics Canada.

Organisation for Exonomic Co-operation and Development (OECD). 1996. "Earning Inequality, Low Paid Employment and Earnings Mobility." *OECD Employment Outlook.* Paris: OECD.

Saez, Emmanuel, and Michael Veall. 2003. *The Evolution of High Incomes in Canada, 1920 to 2000.* National Bureau of Economic Research Working Paper <www.nber.org/papers>.

Smeeding, Timothy. 2002. *Globalization, Inequality and the Rich Countries of the G-20: Evidence from the Luxemburg Income Study.* Luxemburg Income Study Working Paper no. 320 <www.lisproject.org>.

Vosko, Leah, Nancy Zukewich, and Cynthia Cranford. 2003. "Precarious Jobs: A New Typology of Employment." *Perspectives on Labour and Income* (October): 16–26. Ottawa: Statistics Canada.

CHAPTER THREE

Taking Lifelong Learning Seriously

■ Introduction

This chapter discusses the importance of lifelong learning to the creation of better jobs and higher living standards for Canadian workers. It draws attention to the importance of education and skills to individual workers and to the functioning of the economy as a whole, and to the problem of lack of access to workplace-based training for many workers, especially non-managers and professionals.

■ Learning and Workplaces

It is now almost universally recognized that education and skills are the foundations for both a healthy society and a healthy economy, and that learning is an ongoing process that must take place over the whole life-course. Education, skills training, and lifelong learning (or what economists call investments in human capital) are seen as the key to success for individuals, firms, and countries in the new and rapidly changing global economy. The basic argument is that individuals with low skills will do badly in the job market, and that the Canadian economy will not thrive unless we create highly skilled jobs.

Ideally, people would participate in early childhood education programs and arrive at school ready to learn. They would receive a first-class school education that provides them with basic skills, such as literacy and numeracy, and the capacity to learn and work with others, as well as the knowledge needed to proceed to a post-secondary education appropriate to their particular skills and capacities. Post-secondary education is increasingly needed to acquire reasonably well-paid jobs that also provide career ladders to better jobs. It can span a wide range, from short-term vocational and technical training directly tied to entry-level requirements of jobs, to apprenticeship programs combining classroom and on-the-job instruction, to co-op and advanced technical and business education programs in college, to general and career-oriented professional programs in university.

Learning should be seen as a process that continues rather than ends with employment in a steady job, and the workplace should be seen as an important site for lifelong learning. In a fluid job market marked by constant industrial and firm restructuring, and by rapid technological and organizational change within workplaces, workers need to periodically upgrade their skills. Many will need training to switch jobs and careers. And, climbing up job ladders over a working lifetime almost always involves learning new skills.

The good news for Canadians is that our children do relatively well at school, scoring above average in internationally comparable tests of basic competencies, including math, science, and literacy and numeracy. Moreover, the proportion of children and youth with very low scores is relatively low compared to many other countries, including the U.S. The proportion of youth who do not complete at least a high school education is too high, at a bit under one in ten, but it is falling. Improving public education is obviously important, but it is an area where we have done reasonably well. The same is true to a degree of participation in post-secondary education. About one-quarter of 25- to 29-year-olds have graduated from university, and another quarter have graduated from college. By some measures, we have the most highly educated generation of young adults in the world, and one of the most well-educated workforces overall.

The bad news for Canadians is that our workplace-based training system is relatively underdeveloped, and falls far short of producing the kind of results we get from public education. Despite all of the rhetoric on the importance of skills and learning in the new knowledge-based economy, our performance leaves much to be desired. Indeed, in *Knowledge Matters*, the federal government acknowledged this weak Canadian performance in terms of lifelong learning and access to training and retraining, and called for a 1 million increase in the number of adult learners over five years within a broad-based, accessible, and comprehensive adult-learning system.

While individuals can and do seek training, it is mainly employers who determine access. Unfortunately, employer-sponsored training is directed very disproportionately to already highly educated professional and managerial employees. Many average employees with formal qualifications and the willingness to learn more do not get access to the further training that they need to upgrade their skills and qualifications. Perhaps most importantly, if we take equality of opportunity seriously, there is little in the way of a second chance for people who leave the educational system with limited qualifications, or made early career choices that turned out to offer poor job and career prospects.

Many working people are caught in a low-skills trap. A little under one-half of all young adults have not completed a post-secondary qualification and, like the many older workers who left formal education early, are vulnerable to being trapped in low-wage, dead-end jobs. An estimated four in ten working-age Canadians have limited literacy and numeracy skills, which makes it very difficult for them to take skills training. Many new immigrants to Canada have high formal qualifications, but often they also need further training to gain Canadian equivalencies and credentials recognition. Most of these vulnerable workers are on their own when it comes to the difficult task of upgrading their skills to find better jobs and to deal with a changing job market.

> **Box 3.1: What Are the Jobs of the Future?**
>
> Projecting what jobs will look like a decade or more from now is extremely difficult. Past projections have often been wrong. After the mid-1990s, for example, many more jobs were created in blue-collar jobs than had been expected, partly because of a major boom in new housing construction.
>
> Forecasts on the future Canadian job market can be found by looking at *Job Futures* at <http://www.hrsdc.gc.ca>. This provides information on wages by detailed occupations, together with some idea of how strong demand will be for workers in each occupation.

Skills, the Economy, and a Changing Job Market

Investment in education and skills and the fostering of an advanced knowledge-based economy are critical to maintaining and increasing the living standards of Canadian workers. We live in a world of abundant cheap labour and cheap transportation costs, and many jobs producing goods and services that can be easily moved are being transferred to countries that can combine relatively low wages with a reasonably high level of skills. Labour-intensive industrial production has already decisively shifted to developing countries such as China and Brazil. Workers in developing countries employed by transnational and domestic corporations with access to modern machinery and equipment are quite capable of producing standardized, high-quality industrial goods, from clothes and autos to planes and computers. New communications technologies also now permit the outsourcing of a range of services jobs from data processing to software development. In the longer term, the jobs that will remain in the traded sectors of the advanced industrial countries—that is, in those sectors where production can be moved elsewhere—will have to be based on high productivity or on high value. Usually, this means jobs in operations that are very capital-intensive, or in operations that produce unique, sophisticated, or very high-quality products that can command a price premium in global markets to support decent wages. If Canadian-based companies are to successfully participate in very competitive global markets while maintaining good wages and working conditions, they must be highly productive and highly innovative. This, in turn, requires a highly educated and skilled workforce.

Technological change, especially change that is driven by the use of information and communications technologies, has been pervasive over the past 20 years and more. It has often been accompanied by major changes in the organization of production, such as automation, or the use of work teams and the devolution of more decision-making authority to frontline workers. Many routine clerical and blue-collar production jobs have been eliminated or radically changed, and many new occupations have appeared. There has long been a debate among social scientists as to whether these ongoing technological and organizational changes have fuelled a demand for higher worker skills, or have been introduced so as to deliberately deskill the workers whose jobs survive automation and outsourcing. In practice, there has been change in all directions, depending upon the sector, the occupation, and the characteristics of individual companies. There are many very boring, routine, and stressful jobs working with new technology, such as work in many call centres, but also many interesting new jobs, such as running computer systems, or writing complex software, or running advanced diagnostic equipment in hospitals. The concept of skill is itself not neutral, and refers to a range of characteristics of jobs, from the need for vocational and educational credentials, to cognitive complexity, to the level of responsibility in the job.

The consensus among most researchers, supported by the Canadian evidence, is that the skill content of jobs has been slowly rising over time. There has been faster-than-average job growth in professional and technical occupations that usually require advanced qualifications, and a rising skill content in jobs within a wide range of other occupations (Applebaum et al. 2003; Betcherman et al. 1998). Change, however, is probably not much more rapid than was the case in earlier periods. Back in the 1950s and 1960s, there was a huge scare that automation would eliminate factory jobs. Since that time, but long before the computer revolution, there was indeed a big shift out of relatively unskilled but reasonably well-paid factory jobs into jobs in the service sector. The shift to services has produced many more skilled jobs in some sectors—such as health care, finance, and business services—but also many less skilled jobs in personal and consumer services, such as in restaurants and retail trade. Many low-wage, low-skills services jobs are not vulnerable to relocation to lower-wage countries, and many are also not terribly subject to elimination through technological change. The shift to services, combined with technological and organizational change and greater international competition in manufacturing and some high-end service industries, has helped divide the workforce between skilled workers with good jobs and relatively unskilled workers with poor jobs.

The major point is that there is a rising ante. It is getting harder and harder for workers with less than a post-secondary education to find a steady, well-paid job, and the skill requirements in good jobs in both the private and public sectors will probably continue to grow. The relatively uneducated and unskilled are increasingly consigned to precarious and marginal jobs that provide low levels of employment security, low pay, limited career progress, and a high risk of poverty. The increased premium upon education means that there is an increased risk of marginalization. Without broadly based, equitable access to education and skills training, many workers will be left behind. This is especially true of young people who leave school with limited education and skills, of women who leave the workforce for extended periods, of older workers who fall victim to industrial restructuring that devalues their existing skills, and of new immigrants whose skills and credentials are frequently not recognized.

Skills and Better Jobs

Going one step further, there is some evidence that investment in education and skills can help produce more good jobs. Investment in worker training, in conjunction with changes in work organization that take full advantage of those higher skills, has been found in numerous Canadian and international studies to have positive, if hard to quantify, impacts on firm level productivity and profitability (Arnal et al. 2001; Betcherman et al. 1998; Gunderson 2002; Lowe 2000). While it is hard to separate out the impacts on productivity of new capital investments, technological change, changes in work organization, and investment in workers skills, it seems clear that the largest productivity payoff comes from a bundling together of all of these elements as part of a coherent, high value-added business strategy. Knowledge-based firms that adopt these kinds of strategies will tend to grow and expand, replacing good jobs eliminated in the process of technological and organizational change.

Investment in skills and learning has the potential to expand the economy. Countries that have invested most heavily in education and worker training have achieved higher rates of job creation and economic growth. Relative economic success in the new global economy depends, among other factors, on creating a knowledge-based economy. Beyond investment in public education at all levels, investments in the skills of employed workers through on-the-job training are particularly critical to the success of new forms of work organization based on employee involvement. Higher productivity can be gained through greater worker autonomy and latitude in decision making. It is generally recognized, as in recent reports from the Organisation for Economic Co-operation and Development (OECD) and the International Labour Organization (ILO), that work reorganization and skills investments need to go hand in hand to maximize the potential productivity benefits of the new information and communication technologies (Arnal et al. 2001; ILO 2001).

All that said, there is strong evidence that companies, particularly Canadian companies, tend to under-invest in on-the-job training. A comprehensive study of Canadian firms in the mid- to late 1990s found that, at most, only about one in 10 firms had become serious learning organizations (Betcherman et al. 1998). Many firms do provide some training, particularly training for new employees, and occasional computer, marketing, and management training, but this is not the same thing as being systematically committed to constant upgrading of the skills of all employees as part of a comprehensive strategy. There are many reasons why Canada lacks a strong workplace training culture. Traditionally, high levels of immigration of skilled workers have kept down the need to train from within. High unemployment for much of the 1990s meant that firms could easily hire from outside for needed skills, rather than train and promote from within. And, there has been less of an expectation in Canada that firms will train and retrain workers than is the case in some other countries. In Germany and many other European countries, most companies accept that they have an obligation to provide apprenticeship training, and there is a highly formalized system of vocational training for young people who do not go on to an academic education. Canada lacks the works councils that are mandated by law in many European countries to help plan and deliver training. Restrictions on layoffs in many European countries have also encouraged companies to train during downtime when business is slow.

There are more general factors that limit firm investment in skills. Training is costly, particularly for smaller firms, and the gains from training are uncertain and often unknown. It is often easier to pursue a cost-cutting strategy than it is to fundamentally rethink how production is organized. Many companies complain, perhaps with good reason, that too many of their employees lack the basic skills needed to learn. Perhaps, most importantly, firms that do train risk losing the newly trained workers to other firms, thus losing out on their investment. Poaching skilled workers is particularly widespread in countries with no training culture, where free-riding firms can get away with behaviour that is damaging to the economy as a whole. Investment in training is thus likely to be greatest in large firms that provide steady employment at decent wages and, as result, experience low worker turnover. Firms' widespread adoption of outsourcing strategies has driven the growth of more precarious employment relationships in smaller firms that are much less well equipped to invest in training.

Skills, the Needs of Workers, and Human Development

In Canada today, employer support for training of employed workers on the job, or through paid courses and leaves, goes disproportionately to managers and professionals with relatively high levels of formal education. Far from equalizing opportunities, the workplace training system thus increases rather than minimizes inequality of income and opportunity based on class background and educational attainment, and the lack of a good training system thwarts human development. We may have the most highly educated generation of young adults in the world, but many Canadians are seriously underemployed (Livingstone 2002; Lowe 2000). At least one in five jobs requires education and skills far below those of the workers who hold them. Underemployment in precarious jobs affects many young people as well as highly educated and skilled recent immigrants. There is evidence that skills gained in the educational system often atrophy and rot from lack of use in the workplace.

Training is an essential ingredient in human development. Workers want to develop their individual capacities and capabilities, and to work in jobs that allow them to exercise and develop their skills. The workforce has become more highly educated, and has justifiably higher expectations of what work will provide in terms of the ability to use an education and continued opportunities to learn. Higher levels of education and skills are generally associated with higher levels of autonomy at work, more varied and interesting jobs, and higher levels of job satisfaction. Investment in skills is also needed to promote the kinds of work reorganization that create more interesting and less stressful jobs, and give workers more control over the pace and content of work. Management and labour objectives are not always the same when it comes to work reorganization, which too often results in high levels of stress. But, investment in training is a major ingredient in jointly determined work reorganization processes that can satisfy the interests of both parties.

Education and training is about much more than meeting the skill needs of employers alone. Workers will usually want to gain general rather than highly firm-specific skills, and skills that are recognized through formal certificates or credentials. These will give them much more leverage as individuals in the job market, and the option of either climbing a job ladder with their current employer, or looking around for a new job. Workers with a high level of general, certified skills are much less likely to experience prolonged unemployment or a deep pay cut if they lose their current jobs and are forced to seek other ones.

Training programs are likely to be most developed and most likely to meet the different needs of workers and employers when they are developed jointly. This can take place through collective bargaining, European-style works councils established by law to deal with training and other issues, joint training committees, or similar institutions (ILO 2001, 2002). A major, recent OECD study concludes that joint employer-employee approaches promote more equitable access to training, increase worker involvement in training activities, and increase the training intensity of firms (Arnal et al. 2001, 48). Close employee involvement in the design and delivery of training can facilitate the introduction of new technology and new work practices by ensuring that the current workforce is provided with the tools to adapt to, and to benefit from, change.

New technologies and new forms of work organization can be introduced in very different ways, with very different implications for the skill content of jobs and the quality of work (Applebaum 1997). Joint approaches to workplace change and related training are much more likely to generate positive outcomes in terms of both higher productivity and worker well-being. Certainly, joint approaches to training are a key feature of the industrial and labour relations systems of some European countries with highly productive and innovative economies, notably Germany and the Scandinavian countries. Joint approaches are also common in unionized workplaces. In the U.S. and Canada, productivity gains from the introduction of new forms of work and new technologies have been greatest where there has been a comprehensive, negotiated process of workplace change (Black and Lynch 2000). The key reason for this outcome is, not surprisingly, that worker buy-in into work reorganization is far greater when workers have an independent voice, and when firms respond to their needs.

Joint approaches are also more likely to result in training programs that develop portable, as opposed to very narrow and firm-specific, skills. Such joint programs are often developed at the sectoral rather than firm level, raising the skill level of the workforce as a whole while spreading the costs across all employers in a sector. Recently, the advantages of a joint approach to training have been demonstrated in Canada through the successes of some sectoral skills councils, such as in the steel industry. Some unions and employers have negotiated access to training through collective agreements and joint training committees, as in the automotive assembly sector. Unions representing workers in the skilled trades have traditionally played a major independent role in the design and delivery of training, especially through apprenticeship programs. Many construction unions run their own training centres. In Canada, unionized workers enjoy greater access to employer-sponsored training because unions have pushed employers to take on the task of upgrading skills and providing current employees with better jobs, rather than just hiring from the outside to meet new needs (Sussman 2002).

Joint training programs can have a big impact upon the working lives of people employed in traditionally low-wage sectors of the economy. Often, supposedly low-skill and low-wage jobs can be made into better jobs with greater responsibilities if training is provided. The employer often benefits from job enrichment through lower turnover. Most often, job ladders are few and far between in sectors such as hotels, restaurants, building services, and support jobs in health care and social services. This is partly because the better jobs requiring higher skills, including supervisory positions, are filled by hiring people with higher skills or formal qualifications, rather than by training current employees to take the better jobs when they open up. In hotels and hospital kitchens, for example, supervisors tend to be hired from college programs, but other approaches are possible. In some grocery stores in Ontario, employers and unions have agreed to training programs for cashiers that allow them to move into better-paid jobs as meat-cutters. In Las Vegas, there is a large union-run training institute that now does almost all of the training for the hotel industry, allowing workers to gradually climb up the job ladder (Applebaum et al. 2003). In summary, good joint training programs can be a significant force for better jobs.

Who Gets Access to Training?

Statistics Canada's *Adult Education and Training Survey* regularly gathers information on adult (aged 25 to 64) participants in formal job-related learning. Formal activities are defined as structured courses or programs leading to a certificate or qualification. Courses are much shorter than programs, and include seminars and workshops. Overall, in 2002, just over one in three adults participated in formal, job-related training, up slightly from 1997. Participation is about the same for women and men, declines with increasing age, and rises with the person's level of education. The average amount of time spent in formal job-related training over the year was 25 days per participant, spent mainly in courses rather than programs (Peters 2004). A lot of this learning effort is undertaken by individuals without the support of employers. In addition, about one-third of all adults engage regularly in self-directed, job-related learning.

Table 3.1 and Figure 3.1 provide information on participation in formal, job-related training that is supported by employers. Either they directly provided the training, or they provided a paid leave, or, more minimally, they just provided some contribution of time or money. Employer-supported training obviously makes access for the employee much easier, and is likely to be related to the current job and immediate career prospects of workers. As shown, just one in five adults participated in such training in 2002, about the same as in 1997. Participation rates are similar for women and men. Participation rises a lot with the level of education of the employee—from 9.5% for those with high school or less, to almost one-third for university graduates, and the participants with higher education also receive many more hours of training. In line with the pattern by level of education, professional/managerial workers are more than twice as likely to receive employer-supported training than are blue-collar workers.

Table 3.2 provides information from a different survey (*Workplace and Employee Survey*) on employer-supported training. Here, the definition of training is not restricted to formal activities leading to a certificate or diploma, but includes informal, on-the-job training. Participation rates of all employees in all forms of on-the-job learning are, as one would expect with this broader definition, quite high at 55%, though they are lower (at 37%) in formal classroom training. Again, participation increases with the level of education. Also, it is striking that employees in larger firms are much more likely to receive training, particularly classroom training, than are employees of small- and medium-sized firms. Employees in firms with more than 100 employees are almost twice as likely to get some classroom training as employees in firms with less than 20 employees. Unions make a difference, particularly in small firms.

Table 3.1: Participation in Formal Employer-Supported Training in 2002

Adult (Aged 25–64) Participation in Formal Employer-Supported Training in 2002

	Employer-Supported	Mean Annual Hours
All	20.2%	120
Men	20.2%	132
Women	20.3%	109
High school or less	9.5%	86
Post-secondary, Non-university	23.5%	115
University	31.8%	145
Full-time	27.4%	100
Part-time	17.2%	189
Professional / Managerial	34.0%	117
Other white-collar	18.9%	99
Blue-collar	14.9%	123

Source: Statistics Canada. *Working and Training, First Results of the 2003 Adult Education and Training Survey,* (Ottawa, 2003), (Cat. 81-595-MIE2004015).

Figure 3.1: Participation in Formal Employer-Supported Training in 2002

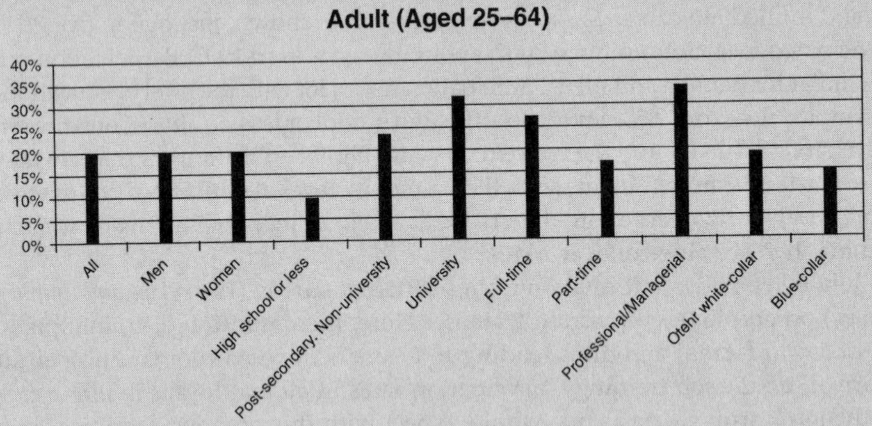

Adult (Aged 25–64)

Source: Statistics Canada. *Working and Training, First Results of the 2003 Adult Education and Training Survey,* (Ottawa, 2003), (Cat. 81-595-MIE2004015).

In summary, employer-provided training is highly concentrated on the higher layers of the shrinking core workforce in larger firms and the public sector. The concentration of formal training on well-educated professionals and managers in large firms reflects the fact that such firms are not only more likely to be pursuing

Table 3.2: Proportion of Employees Participating in Employer-Supported Training in 1999

	Classroom or On-the-Job	Classroom
All employees	55%	37%
Men	53%	37%
Women	56%	37%
Part-time	47%	25%
Union	58%	41%
Non-union	53%	35%
Education		
Less than high school	40%	21%
High school only	48%	28%
College diploma	57%	38%
University degree	64%	49%
Establishment Size		
<20	44%	26%
20–49	51%	31%
50–99	59%	37%
>100	64%	48%

Source: Statistics Canada. *Guide to the Analysis of Workplace and Employee Survey, 2001*, Catalogue 7-221, August 2003.
Note: Many people receiving classroom training also receive on-the-job training.

high-productivity strategies that require skills, but are also still committed to promoting the skills of their core workers. Even blue-collar workers in large firms get more training than average. Also, larger firms are much more likely to be unionized, and the presence of unions makes a difference to training efforts.

There is good evidence that many workers want more training than they are getting from the current system. Twenty-eight percent of adults report that they want more job-related training, but face significant barriers in terms of either time and/or money (Peters 2004). Many people may just have low expectations of their employer, or have given up. Training participation and desire for even more participation are both greatest among younger workers who want to embark on developmental job and career ladders.

The weaknesses of the employer-based adult training system have not been adequately compensated for through public policy. Governments do provide some support to adult learning for a small proportion of unemployed workers, mainly funded from the *Employment Insurance Act*. The fact that eligibility is restricted to current or recent EI recipients, however, means that many of the working poor, as well as recent immigrants, do not qualify. Classroom training for the unemployed was cut back over the 1990s. There are no programs in place to provide paid training leaves for adult workers who want to upgrade their skills or qualifications by returning to school, though some very modest support is provided through the tax system. Over the years, many reports have called for paid educational and training leaves to facilitate the goal of lifelong learning, but individuals are still pretty much on their own. Governments have also been very reluctant to intervene in employers' training decisions. Of the provinces, only Quebec mandates a minimum employer effort on worker training. Here, an employer who does not spend at least 1% of payroll on training must pay that amount to the provincial government. This has had some positive impacts on the overall level of employer training (Peters 2004).

Canada in International Perspective

Countries differ greatly in terms of the extent to which they invest in active labour market policies to promote lifelong learning and labour adjustment, and Canada is a relatively poor performer.

While it is hard to compare the training systems of different countries, the Organisation for Economic Co-operation and Development or OECD finds that the Canadian annual participation rate in adult worker training is, at 35.7%, below the industrial country average, and that (at just over 1%) we also lag behind the

Table 3.3: Canadian Job-Related Training in International Perspective

	Canada	U.S.	Denmark	OECD Average
Employed age 25+				
Participation in year				
All	35.7%	42.1%	53.7%	37.2%
Men	36.4%	41.8%	51.5%	36.6%
Women	34.9%	42.5%	56.5%	37.9%
Mean number of				
hours per participant				
(Firm size 100–499)	128	122	127	120

Source: A. Tuijnman and E. Boudard, *Adult Education Participation in North America: International Perspectives* (Ottawa: Statistics Canada and Human Resources Development Canada, 2001), Cat. 89-574-XPE.

average in terms of employer spending on training as a percentage of payroll costs (OECD 1999; Tuijnman and Boudard 2001). We lag behind not only European countries where there is a very strong emphasis on training, such as Germany and the Scandinavian countries, but also the United States.

Canada also lags well behind many European countries—but not the U.S.—when it comes to training programs for unemployed workers. As a share of the economy, we spend less than one-third as much as the Scandinavian countries, which are strongly committed to active labour market policies to get the unemployed into jobs. Research by the OECD suggests that it is particularly important for governments to invest in the basic skills of unemployed and low-wage workers, such as literacy and numeracy (Martin 2000).

■Conclusion

The importance of lifelong learning to better jobs and higher living standards has been widely recognized, but Canada falls well short of providing adequate access to training opportunities for both employed and unemployed workers.

• •

■Questions for Critical Thought

1. Do you think all the talk of the need for education and skills to succeed in the job market is overblown, or an accurate reflection of what it takes to find and keep a good job today?
2. How do you think the needs and interests of employers and workers differ when it comes to how much and what kind of on-the-job training should be provided?
3. Are some jobs intrinsically and inevitably low-skill jobs?
4. Can you think of specific examples of the kinds of jobs where more investment in skills might turn a low-wage, dead-end job into a better job?
5. If education and skills are the key to better jobs, why are there so many examples of higher-educated people being underemployed in dead-end jobs?

■Recommended Reading

Applebaum, Eileen, Annette Bernhardt, and Richard J. Murname, eds. 2003. *Low Wage America*. New York: Russell Sage Foundation. This important book provides several case studies of low-wage industries in the U.S., and how low-wage jobs can be improved through a combination of work reorganization and training.

Betcherman, Gordon, Kathryn McMullen, and Katie Davidman. 1998. *Training for the New Economy: A Synthesis Report*. Canadian Policy Research Networks. Available from the CPRN Web site <http://www.cprn.org>, this remains the most comprehensive report on training in Canada.

Livingston, D.W. 2002. *Working and Learning in the Information Age: A Profile of Canadians*. Ottawa: Canadian Policy Research Networks. David Livingstone has long drawn attention to the great efforts made by many Canadians to learn in the face of great obstacles, and the very real differences between the learning needs and strategies of working people and the resources that are available in workplaces.

Sussman, Deborah. 2002. "Barriers to Job-Related Training." *Perspectives on Labour and Income* (Summer): 5–12. A useful summary of what we know about access to training in Canada.

Organisation for Economic Co-operation and Development (OECD). 2004. "Improving Skills for More and Better Jobs. Does Training Make a Difference." *OECD Employment Outlook*, 183–222. Paris: OECD. Summarizes the most recent research, which shows that greater employer and public investment in skills is indeed a major factor in creating more and better jobs.

References

Applebaum, Eileen. 1997. *The Impact of New Forms of Work Organization on Workers*. Washington, DC: Economic Policy Institute.

Applebaum, Eileen, Annette Bernhardt, and Richard J. Murname, eds. 2003. *Low Wage America*. New York: Russell Sage Foundation.

Arnal, Elena, Wooseok Ok, and Raymond Torres. 2001. *Knowledge, Work Organization and Economic Growth*. Labour Market and Social Policy Occasional Paper no. 50. Paris: OECD.

Betcherman, Gordon, Kathryn McMullen, and Katie Davidman. 1998. *Training for the New Economy: A Synthesis Report*. Ottawa: Canadian Policy Research Networks.

Black, Sandra, and Lisa Lynch. 2000. *What's Driving the New Economy: The Benefits of Workplace Innovation*. National Bureau of Economic Research Working Paper no. 7479.

Gunderson, Morley. 2002. *Rethinking Productivity from a Workplace Perspective*. Ottawa: Canadian Policy Research Networks.

International Labour Organization (ILO). 2001. *World Employment Report*. Geneva: ILO.

_____. 2002. *Learning and Training for Work in the Knowledge Society*. Geneva: ILO.

Livingstone, D.W. 2002. *Working and Learning in the Information Age: A Profile of Canadians*. Ottawa: Canadian Policy Research Networks.

Lowe, Graham. 2000. *The Quality of Work: A People Centred Agenda*. Toronto: Oxford University Press.

Martin, John P. 2000. *What Works among Active Labour Market Policies: Evidence from OECD Countries*. OECD Economic Studies no. 30. Paris: OECD.

Organisation for Economic Co-operation and Development (OECD). 1999. "Training of Adult Workers in OECD Countries." *OECD Employment Outlook*, 133–175. Paris: OECD.

Peters, Valerie. 2004. *Working and Training: First Results of the 2003 Adult Education and Training Survey*. Ottawa: Statistics Canada.

Sussman, Deborah. 2002. "Barriers to Job-Related Training." In *Perspectives on Labour and Income* (Summer): 5–12.

Tuijnman, A., and E. Boudard. 2001. *Adult Education Participation in North America: International Perspectives*, Cat. 89-574-XPE. Ottawa: Statistics Canada and Human Resources Development Canada.

CHAPTER FOUR

The Unhealthy Canadian Workplace

▪ Introduction

The purpose of this chapter is to provide a broad overview of the state of employment and working conditions to set a context for an analysis of the impacts of the working environment on health. The focus is on the quality of work as opposed to wider conditions in the labour market, and on working conditions as opposed to wages.

The links from employment to health are not examined here in detail, though they implicitly frame the selection of topics. Suffice it to say at the outset that research has established strong links from unemployment and precarious employment to poor health outcomes, and from poor employment conditions to poor physical and mental health. Poor employment conditions include: dirty and dangerous jobs, including exposures to harmful substances that pose risks to physical health in terms of injuries and occupational disease; jobs that are stressful by virtue of the pace, demands, or repetitive content of the labour process; jobs that are stressful because of the exercise of arbitrary power in the workplace; jobs that are stressful because they do not meet human developmental needs; and jobs that are stressful because they conflict with the lives of workers in the home and in the community.

■ Work and Health

In recent years, health researchers have increasingly emphasized the links between work stress and physical and mental health. Stress can arise from many sources, including job insecurity, the physical demands of work, the extent of support from supervisors and co-workers, work-life conflict, and job strain (Wilkins and Beaudet 1998). High job strain—a combination of high psychological demands at work combined with a low degree of control of the work process—and other sources of workplace stress have been linked to an increased risk of physical injuries at work, high blood pressure, cardiovascular disease, depression and other mental health conditions, and increased lifestyle risks to health.

The well-established linkage from income and social class to physical and mental health outcomes is probably, in very significant part, a product of the work conditions associated with income level and class position. Work poses physical risks, and is clearly a major source of psychosocial stress, which has been identified as one major cause of increased morbidity and mortality. Gender is, of course, a major intervening variable.

It is ironic, not to say tragic, that the shift to a post-industrial society with an increasingly well-educated and skilled workforce is associated with rising levels of stress rather than increased well-being at work. Research has shown some negative consequences for health to date, but the full impact of current conditions is likely to be slow to appear. Many of today's older workers and retirees were workers in the Golden Age of post-war capitalism when working conditions were more closely regulated, and conditions were improving. The health impacts of 21st-century work may be just appearing.

This chapter seeks to provide a general overview of current conditions and the overall direction of change, to look at some important cleavages among workers in terms of access to good jobs, and to place the situation in Canada in a comparative context. Comparisons are made with the European Union because better working conditions in the EU along some dimensions do suggest that improvement of the quality of the Canadian work environment is not incompatible with having a highly productive economy.

■ What Is a Good Job?

An appropriate starting point is to consider what constitutes a good job from the perspective of workers. For all of the emphasis (rightly) placed on the fundamental importance of waged employment as the critical source of working-class income and well-being in a capitalist society, other dimensions of employment are at least as important to workers. On the economic front, non-wage benefits, job security, and opportunities for advancement are as important as wages. The content of work and the nature of the labour process are less tangible and measurable, but count for a lot as well. A major international survey in 1989 found that having an interesting job and being allowed to work independently rank very high as desirable features of employment in all countries. The recent EKOS/CPRN survey of changing employment relationships in Canada confirmed that a large majority of workers place a high value on having interesting and personally rewarding work, enjoying some autonomy on the job, and having the ability to exercise and develop their skills and capacities. Jencks et al. (1988) found that there is much more unequal distribution of quality jobs along valued dimensions other than pay, indicating that even large pay differences are an imperfect proxy for large class differences in the quality of employment.

The statement that quality of employment involves much more than pay will come as a surprise only to economists who have been trained to view work as a disutility endured in order to gain income. Work is better seen as a potential sphere for the development of individual human capacities and potentials. Production is also a social process. Good workplaces are those in which there are valued relationships with co-workers and some degree of active participation and democratic control of the work process. Bad workplaces, by contrast, are alienating and authoritarian.

Recognizing that there is considerable overlap between categories, seven key dimensions of employment with relevance to well-being and health are considered:

- Job and employment security
- Physical conditions of work
- Work pace and stress
- Working time
- Opportunities for self-expression and individual development at work
- Participation at work
- Work-life balance

Before these dimensions are considered in detail, it is useful to briefly summarize some of the wider economic and social forces affecting Canadian workplaces.

■ Forces Shaping Workplace Change in Canada

The terms of employment—wages and benefits, hours, working conditions—reflect the relative bargaining power of workers and employers, and the related willingness of governments to establish minimum rights and standards. Over the 1980s and 1990s, the context has been one of high unemployment and underemployment, increased employer ability to shift production and new investments to lower-cost regions and countries, and an ideologically driven decrease in state intervention on behalf of workers.

There has been a pervasive and ongoing restructuring of the labour market and of employment relationships intended to promote productivity and competitiveness, as opposed to promotion of a worker-centred agenda of good jobs (Lowe 2000). The basic direction of change is best understood as a simultaneous intensification and casualization of work by employers. The most common forms of organizational change have been downsizing, contracting out of non-core functions, and securing greater flexibility of time worked through a combination of increased overtime and increased part-time and contract work.

The restructuring of work has been driven by employers. Governments have been, at best, mostly passive bystanders, but countervailing forces do exist. The unionization rate was remarkably steady in the 1990s at about 30% of paid workers, though it has been modestly declining in the private sector.

Dimensions of Job Quality

Job Security

In considering the linkages from labour market conditions to health, researchers have studied both the availability of work and the nature of work. It is well established from studies of laid-off workers that the state of unemployment is bad for health for both material and psychological reasons. However, the relatively well-studied transition from stable employment to long-term unemployment is less frequent than alternation between short-term unemployment and precarious employment. Frequent short-term unemployment is also a source of stress and anxiety due to lack of income, uncertain prospects for the future, and its potential to undermine social support networks (World Health Organization 1999). Workers who must move from one short-term job to another are also likely to derive less satisfaction and meaning from their paid work.

Most Canadians are familiar with the national unemployment rate, which is reported monthly and stood at just above 7% in 2003. Taken at face value, this number considerably understates the true extent of employment insecurity. To be counted as employed, one need only have worked for a few hours in a week, so employment includes temporary employees, part-time workers who want more hours, and people who are working in low-wage survival jobs while looking for regular jobs that match their skills. To be counted as unemployed, a person has to have been unable to find any work at all, and to have been actively seeking work even if he or she knew that no suitable jobs were available.

In 1999, when the national unemployment rate averaged 7.6%, just 71% of people aged 16 to 69 in the workforce were employed all year, and 12% of men and 13% of women who worked at some time in the year were unemployed at least once in the same year. The others worked for part of the year and were not in the workforce for another part of the year.[1] Earlier in the 1990s, about one in five workers was unemployed at least once in any year. And, Statistics Canada reports that no less than one in three Canadian families had at least one member of the family unemployed each year in the 1980s and 1990s.[2]

Long-term unemployment in Canada is much lower than in other advanced industrial countries. In 2001, just 17% of unemployed workers had been out of work for more than six months compared to a 42% average in Organisation for Economic Co-operation and Development (OECD) countries, and 60% in the European Union (EU). However, many Canadians cycle between precarious jobs and unemployment, and precariously employed workers tend to be trapped in low-wage jobs.

> **Box 4.1: Fear of Job Loss**
>
> As one would expect from the unemployment data, many working Canadians worry about losing their jobs. The Personal Security Index (PSI) of the Canadian Council on Social Development (CCSD) tracks the proportion of people who think there is a good chance they could lose their jobs over the next two years. This stood at 28% in 2001, down from a recent high of 37% in 1998. Fear of job loss is slightly higher among men than women, and much higher in lower-income households. The PSI also tracks the proportion of workers who are confident they could find an equivalent job within six months if they lost their current job. Thirty percent were not confident in 2001, down from 38% in 1998. Confidence declines significantly with age.

Precarious work in Canada is not only widespread, it is much more precarious than in many other countries. In the EU, a binding policy directive establishes that there should be limits on renewals of temporary contracts and notification of vacancies to temporary workers. National laws in EU countries commonly provide for non-discrimination against temporary and part-time workers in terms of pay, benefits coverage, and access to training (EIRO 2000a). Minimum pay laws and widespread collective bargaining provide a wage and benefit floor to the job market. As a result, there are far larger pay gaps between precarious and core workers in Canada than in most EU countries, though gaps here are somewhat smaller than in the U.S. (Jackson 2000).

Job insecurity in the precarious labour market is heightened by lack of supports and services to promote access to better employment. The dominant ethos is that heavy sticks are needed to drive the unemployed into available low-wage jobs; hence, our minimal and deeply punitive social welfare system, which makes even minimum wages look attractive, and the recent cuts to the EI program in the form of higher qualifying hours requirements, which effectively cut off the precariously employed workers who need income support the most.

A key difference between core and peripheral workers is access to employer-sponsored health benefits. As shown in Table 4.1, less than half of non-union workers have access to medical, dental, and disability coverage compared to about

80% of unionized workers. Access to health-related benefits is much lower for non-professional/managerial non-union workers, particularly in smaller private-sector firms. Under the current health care system in most provinces, lack of employer coverage generally means that the costs of prescription drugs outside of hospitals, dental care, and many disability-related supports and services must be paid for from family budgets. There are also large gaps between core and peripheral workers in terms of access to paid sick leave, though here there is at least entitlement to a modest floor through the EI program. Many precariously employed workers thus face directly higher risks to health because of the quality of their employment.

Table 4.1: Benefits Coverage—Union vs. Non-Union

	Medical Plan	Dental Plan	Life/ Disability Insurance	Pension Plan
All employees	57.4%	53.1%	52.5%	43.3%
Unionized	83.7%	76.3%	78.2%	79.9%
Non-union	45.4%	42.6%	40.8%	26.6%

Source: Ernest Akyeampong, "Unionization and Fringe Benefits." Statistics Canada, *Perspectives on Labour and Income*, Catalogue 75-001, 3(8), August 2002.

Lack of employer-sponsored pension coverage for many precarious workers combined with a relatively ungenerous public pension system implies longer working lifetimes. Many low-wage older workers are significantly better off after they retire at 65 and qualify for the combined Old Age Security pension and Guaranteed Income Supplement, which at least provides an income close to the poverty line.

To summarize, a large minority of workers experience continuing precarious employment and high risks of unemployment. The risks of precarious employment in terms of low income, stress, and anxiety are compounded by lack of access to benefits.

■Physical Conditions of Work

One might have thought that dirty and dangerous work was a thing of the past, banished along with the dark satanic mills of the Industrial Revolution, but occupational diseases and injuries rooted in the physical conditions of work are very much a feature of the contemporary workplace.

In 1998, there were 793,000 officially recorded workplace injuries, more than three times the total number of traffic injuries. There were 375,000 injuries involving time loss reported to Workers' Compensation Boards, and 798 workplace fatalities. For every 100 workers in 1998, there were 5.5 injuries, and 2.6 time-loss injuries: 3.4 for men, 1.5 for women, and 2.9 for young workers (Human Resources Development Canada 2000). The incidence of accidents and injuries is modestly falling, but still very high. And, there has been a disturbing upward trend in repetitive strain and other soft tissue injuries associated with highly repetitive machine and keyboard work. These account for an upward trend in the proportion of workplace injuries reported by women.

As one would expect, physical injuries—sprains and strains to backs and hands, cuts, punctures, lacerations, fractures, and contusions—are associated with physically demanding jobs. Manufacturing and construction account for 20% of employment but about 40% of injuries, explaining the gap between injury rates among men and women. But, injury rates are also high in sectors such as retail trade, and health and social services.

Sullivan (2000) argues that workers' compensation practices, which were designed to address physical trauma in a world of manual, blue-collar, male work, have not changed to sufficiently recognize the growing reality of less visible physical injuries that develop over a period of time. Soft tissue injuries, such as repetitive strain injuries affecting women clerical and service workers, are under-reported and under-compensated.

Table 4.2 provides some unpublished data on exposure to physical hazards at work from the *General Social Survey* of 1991. Astonishingly, no comparable recent information is available. As shown, one in three (34.1%) workers reported some negative health impacts from a workplace hazard exposure, and a significant minority of workers were exposed to dust, dangerous chemicals, loud noise, and poor quality air.

Occupational diseases are, of course, also related to workplace risks and exposures. Lung diseases and cancers are linked to physical risks, including inhalation of toxic fumes, handling of hazardous chemicals, and exposure to carcinogens. In a very limited number of cases, there is a very clear causal linkage between occupational exposure and disease onset, which has been recognized by Workers' Compensation Boards. For example, boards recognize that occupational exposure causes asbestosis among asbestos mine workers, and a range of lung diseases among other miners. A handful of highly specific cancers have been demonstrably linked to exposure to specific carcinogens at work, but the overall incidence of occupational disease compared to workplace injuries is extremely low, *if* we go by the official data.

However, a wide range of conditions have been linked to occupational exposures. The Workers' Compensation system, run by governments and funded by employers, demands high standards of scientific proof of cause and effect in order to keep down costs, but many carcinogens are present in the general environment as well as in the workplace. Experts estimate that anywhere from 10% to 40% of cancers may be caused primarily by workplace exposures, but only a tiny proportion of cancer victims qualify for Workers' Compensation. Similarly, workplace stress and heavy

Table 4.2: Physical Work Environment

	Experienced Negative Health Impact from Workplace Health Hazard Exposure	Experienced Workplace Injury in Past Year	Risk of Injury Caused Worry	Exposure to Dust in Air Most of the Time	Exposure to Dangerous Chemicals Most of the Time	Exposure to Loud Noise Most of the Time	Exposure to Poor Quality Air Most of the Time	Negative Health Impacts from Exposure to Computer Screen
All	34.1	9.2	7.6	18.8 (45.0)*	7.5 (48.4)*	15.7 (42.1)*	15.3 (70.7)*	8.5
Men	36	11.9	9.6	23	10.6	22.9	14	6.7
Women	31.3	5.9	5.1	13.8	3.8	7.1	16.8	10.6
Union	41.2	11.5	12.7	24.4	9.7	23.1	20.8	9.1
Non-union	30	8	4.8	15.9	6.4	11.8	12.5	8.1
Managerial/ Professional	35.4	5.8	5.9	14	5	8.3	17.6	12
Skilled/ Seim-skilled	33.1	10.5	7.8	20.9	8.8	20.4	14.6	6.7
Unskilled	34	11.1	10.2	21.5	9.4	17.7	14	6.8

*Figure in brackets is % of those exposed (most of the time or sometimes) reporting a negative impact on health.
Source: Statistics Canada, "Physical Work Environment," *The General Social Survey: An Overview*, Catalogue 89F0115, March 15, 1991.

physical exertion are associated with heart conditions, but only a tiny proportion of heart attack victims (e.g., firefighters) qualify. The key point is that occupational diseases due to the physical hazards of work are prevalent, but largely unrecognized. Somewhat ironically, employers end up bearing a large share of the costs anyway through employer-funded, long-term disability plans.

The European Foundation for the Improvement of Living and Working Conditions, an official European Union institution, regularly conducts surveys on European working conditions. The third survey in 2000 followed surveys for 1990 and 1995. It found that "[e]xposure to physical hazards at the workplace and conditions such as musculo-skeletal disorders and fatigue caused by intensification of work and flexible employment practices are on the increase" (European Foundation for the Improvement of Living and Working Conditions 2000, 10).

In 2000—defining significant exposure as exposure at least one-quarter of the time—29% of European workers were exposed to noise; 22% to inhalation of vapours, fumes, and dust; 37% reported having to move or carry heavy loads; and no less than 47% reported having to work in painful or tiring positions. In each case, a little under half of those reporting the hazard were exposed all of the time. Fortunately, given increasing rather than declining exposure to all of these risks (except inhalation exposure), 76% of European workers reported that they had been well informed of hazards. As one would expect, exposure is greatest in occupations such as machine operators, but the EU data also indicate quite widespread exposure to physical hazards.

The European survey also provides data on the incidence of repetitive work for which no general Canadian information is available. In the EU, 31% of workers report continuous, repetitive, hand/arm movements, and 23% report working at short, repetitive tasks with cycle times of less than one minute. One in four (24%) workers reports continuously working at high speed, with the level being highest among machine operators (35%), but still high among clerical workers (20%) and service workers (23%). The incidence of high-speed work due to tight deadlines has been modestly increasing, though there is variation between countries and between different categories of workers. The survey found that those working at high speed were much more likely to report negative health effects, such as muscular pain, stress, and anxiety. One recent Canadian survey suggests that the incidence of high-speed work in Canada and the U.S. is well above the average of all advanced industrial countries (Brisbois 2003).

To summarize, despite the transition to a post-industrial society, the risks of occupational injury and disease are still high. One-third of Canadian workers (31.3%) feel that their employment puts their health and safety at risk, a bit above the average for advanced industrial countries (Brisbois 2003). Regrettably, little hard data are available on the physical hazards of work in Canada. One aspect of work reorganization likely has been the intensification of physical demands on some groups of workers. Highly repetitive work with short cycle times is likely just as prevalent as in the EU, explaining the sharply rising incidence of repetitive strain injuries among clerical and industrial workers.

■Workplace Control, and Stress

Sources of stress at work include the pace and demands of work, and the degree of control that workers have over the labour process. Karasek and Theorell (1990) and others have stressed that jobs are particularly stressful if high demands on workers are combined with a low level of decision latitude with respect to the use of skills and discretion on how to do the job. Stress from high-strain jobs (high demands, low control) is greater among women than men, primarily because of lower levels of job control (Wilkins and Beaudet 1998).

High-stress jobs have been found to be a significant contributing factor to high blood pressure, cardiovascular diseases, mental illness, and long-onset disability, but the link between stressful work conditions and health is all but unrecognized by Workers' Compensation Boards (Sullivan 2000). There is a link from low levels of control over working conditions not only to stress but also to higher rates of work injuries. Even where work is physically demanding, there is less risk of injury if workers can vary the pace of work, take breaks when needed, and have some say in the design of work stations.

While there have been case studies pointing to high levels of stressful work in many Canadian workplaces (e.g., Lewchuk and Robertson 1996), general data are limited. Statistics Canada's *General Social Survey* provides some information. In 2000, 35% of workers reported experiencing stress at work from "too many demands or too many hours," up slightly from 33% in 1994, and up from 27.5% in 1991. Stress from this source is highest among professionals and managers, at 49% and 48% respectively, but is still high among blue-collar workers (28%) and sales and service workers (29%). By industry, the incidence of stress from "too many demands or hours" is highest in education, health, and social services at over 40%.[3] As one would expect, there is a strong relationship between working long hours and working in jobs that impose high demands.

Women are more likely than men to report high levels of stress from "too many hours or too many demands"—37% compared to 32%. This partly reflects work-life balance issues considered below, but it also reflects the high proportion of women working in the high-stress educational, health, and social services sectors, as well as in clerical positions that involve highly routinized, fast-paced work.

With respect to job control, data from the *General Social Survey* indicate that in 1994, just 40% of Canadian workers reported that they had "a lot of freedom over how to work," down sharply from 54% in 1989. Men generally exercise more control than women (43% compared to 38% in 1994). Professionals and managers predictably report that they exercise much more control than skilled workers who, in turn, have more freedom than unskilled workers (51% vs. 35% vs. 31%, respectively).

The same survey indicates that about half of all working Canadians believe that their jobs involve a high degree of skill, with self-reported levels of exercising a high level of skill being a bit higher among women than men.

Data from the *National Population Health Survey* for 1994–1995 have been used to construct a measure of decision latitude based on responses to two questions: "I have a lot to say about what happens in my job," and "My job allows me the freedom to decide how I do my job." This response is now being used as an official population health indicator. In 1994–1995, 48.8% of all respondents, 52.3% of men and 44.5% of women, reported high decision latitude, while 36.6%–30.7% of men and 44.0% of women reported low or medium decision latitude (Statistics Canada 2001).

To summarize, while we lack detailed information on changes in the overall incidence of work involving high demands and low worker control, high-stress work is common and likely on the increase.

■Opportunities for Self-Development

As noted, a valued characteristic of work is the opportunity it provides for the exercise and development of skills and capacities. Most of us welcome the chance to work in interesting, challenging jobs, and the opportunity to learn new things. The data presented above suggest that skilled workers, particularly professionals, are usually able to utilize their skills on the job, and enjoy a fair degree of control over the labour process. Educational credentials are increasingly the major requirement to access these kinds of good jobs. Access to training on the job is also an important determinant of well-being over the course of a working lifetime, since it provides opportunities for further skills development and for advancement to more challenging and rewarding work. As noted in Chapter 3, there are major barriers to training.

There is abundant evidence that many jobs are structured to minimize the need for skills rather than to further develop workers' capacities, and that overqualification is a serious problem (Livingstone 2002). More than one in four Canadian men and women—and 40% of young people under 25—feel overqualified for their current job according to a survey by Canadian Policy Research Networks.[4] Employers routinely overlook the skills and credentials of many new immigrants with the result that they are sidelined into low-paying, dead-end jobs.

■Working Time

A historic goal of the organized labour movement has been to expand free time. Important breakthroughs were the ten and then the 8-hour working day; the five-day working week and the advent of the weekend; the negotiation of paid days off; and pensioned retirement at progressively earlier ages. By the 1950s, the healthy norm of the standard, five-day, 40-hour week with paid annual vacation and retirement with a decent pension was firmly entrenched.

While progress was made through the 1970s and into the 1980s in terms of reduction of weekly hours, annual hours, and the length of a working lifetime, the recent past has seen an increase in daily, weekly, and annual hours for many core workers in full-time jobs. Long hours are most prevalent among salaried professional and managerial workers, and among skilled blue-collar workers who frequently work paid overtime. From an employer's perspective, overtime helps adjust production to changing market demand, and provides a particularly high cost-saving if the extra hours are not paid for. Even overtime pay premiums are often cheaper than the costs of hiring, training, and providing non-wage benefits to additional workers. Unpaid overtime is increasingly required not just of managers and professionals, but also of public and social services workers attempting to cope with increased workloads. Self-employed workers also tend to work very long hours.

While some workers want to work overtime for higher pay or out of commitment to the job or a career, most have limited ability to refuse demands for longer hours under employment standards legislation and under collective agreements. In most provinces, overtime in excess of 40 hours can be required up to varying maximum levels of up to 50 hours or so, provided an overtime premium is paid. Only 25% of unionized workers have some right (usually conditional) to refuse overtime.

The Statistics Canada *Workplace and Employee Survey* found that 9% of all workers and 12% of workers in firms of more than 500 in 1999 would have preferred to work fewer hours for less pay. This can be considered an underestimate of involuntary long hours to the extent that many workers would not accept a pay cut but might still choose to take part of a compensation increase in the form of reduced hours. Reduced work time has recently been emphasized by several major industrial unions. For example, the Communications, Energy and Paperworkers' Union (CEP) have limited overtime in pulp and paper mills, and the CAW have increased paid days off in the auto-assembly sector.[5]

There has been a strong trend to long (and short) working hours for both men and women in the 1980s and 1990s at the expense of the 40-hour work week norm.[6] The proportion of men working more than 50 hours per week in their main job rose steadily from 15% in the early 1980s to about 20% in 1994, and has continued at that level through 2000. Over the same period, the proportion of women working more than 50 hours per week has risen from 5% to about 7%.[7] About one in three men and one in eight women in paid jobs now work more than 40 hours per week.

As noted above, working long hours is closely associated with working in high-demand jobs. While these jobs may be interesting and challenging and give rise to opportunities for advancement, long hours and high demands can be harmful to both physical and mental health. Studies suggest that very long hours are linked to high blood pressure and cardiovascular disease. Statistics Canada has found that moving to longer working hours has some negative impacts on health, such as smoking, drinking, and poor diet.[8] Long hours also create a high risk of stress in terms of balancing work with domestic and community life.

The shift of core workers to long daily and weekly hours of work is much more characteristic of the U.S. and Canada than the more regulated job markets of continental Europe. The usual weekly hours of full-time paid workers in the EU are below 40, and falling (EIRO 2000a). Some countries, notably France, the Netherlands, and Germany, are now close to a 35-hour norm. The proportion of men working long weekly hours is generally very low. For example, just 2% of Dutch men and 8% of German men work more than 45 hours per week.[9]

Working on weekends appears to be increasing rapidly. The incidence has gone from 11% in 1991 to 15% in 1995, and to 25% in 2000.[10] Women are more likely to work on weekends than men (28% compared to 21%), reflecting high employment rates in retail and health services. More than one in three production workers work on weekends, reflecting the rising incidence of continuous industrial production.

As noted, regular hours are shorter and jobs are less precarious in most European countries. These countries also provide much more generous paid time off work. In Canada, the minimum vacation entitlement under provincial employment standards is two weeks after a minimum length of service of about one year.[11] In collective agreements, the norm is three weeks of paid vacation, rising to four weeks after 10 years.[12] By contrast, in the EU, the minimum statutory entitlement to paid vacation leave is 20 days or four weeks, and the average provided in collective agreements is 25.7 days or more than five weeks. German, Danish, and Dutch workers get six weeks of paid vacation per year (EIRO 2000a). Statutory paid holidays on top of paid vacation entitlements are comparable between Canada and European countries.

The average age of retirement in Canada has been steadily falling, but there is generally very limited provision for a phased-in retirement process that would allow older workers to voluntarily reduce their hours of work. Indeed, most defined pension plans create an incentive to maximize earnings (and, therefore, hours) just before retirement. By contrast, most European countries rely more heavily on public than on private pensions, and the tendency in many continental European countries has been to provide more flexible options for older workers.

To summarize, there is a strong trend toward longer hours for core workers, as well as toward more unsocial hours and more variable hours. Vacation entitlements and phased-in retirement provisions in Canada are quite limited compared to many European countries. These all have direct implications for stress and for physical and mental health.

Work-Life Balance

Longer and more unpredictable hours combined with high and rising job demands are particularly likely to cause stress and anxiety in families where both partners work, and for single-parent families. In both cases, women bear the brunt of the burden (Duxbury and Higgins 2002).

Increased family working time has been a critical factor in maintaining real incomes in a labour market marked by more precarious employment and stagnating wages. Family work hours obviously determine both income and the time potentially available to spend with family, children, and in the community. While long hours may result in higher incomes, work-family time conflict may affect the physical and mental health of parents and also influence the well-being of children. Much of the burden of caring for elderly parents as well as children is borne by working families.

Box 4.2: Working Families

There has been a very large increase in the total working hours of two-person families with children since the mid-1970s. This has come through increased work hours for many men, the increased entry of women into the workforce, and the shift of women into full-time jobs. About one in four (73%) two-person families with children has two earners today compared to one in three in 1975, and three in four (73%) working women in two-parent families work full-time. Thus the majority of women in two-person families with children now work full-time. Six in ten women single parents (63%) with children work, 77% of whom work full-time. Full-time employment rates for women are only slightly lower for those with preschool children, reflecting maternity and parental leaves taken after the birth of a child.[13]

Recent data from the *General Social Survey* show that time pressures are steadily increasing. Between 1992 and 1998, 25- to 44-year-old parents employed full-time put in an average of two hours more per week in paid work activities. In 1998, fathers averaged 48.3 hours and mothers averaged 38.5 hours per week of paid work and related activities—up 5% for fathers and 4% for mothers from 1992. Lone-parent mothers increased their time in paid work even more than married mothers.

Box 4.3: "'Role Overload' Makes Workers Sick"

By Wallace Immen

A decade of increasing demands from employers combined with conflicts between home and office has created a generation of frazzled Canadians who are booking more time off for mental and physical fatigue, according to a study done for Health Canada.

The effects of "role overload" are costing Canadian businesses as much as $10-billion a year in overtime and contracting out required to complete the work of absent employees, estimated Linda Duxbury, a business professor at Carleton University in Ottawa.

"We should all be concerned about this," Prof. Duxbury said. "We knew there was a problem a decade ago. Organizations throughout the '90s talked about the importance of people, but then treated them like any other commodity. It is clear we've left the decade in far worse shape in terms of the work force, in terms of their health, and in terms of how they feel about their employer."

Prof. Duxbury and Chris Higgins of the University of Western Ontario assessed the cost of absenteeism as reported by 31,500 Canadians who work in public, private, and non-profit organizations. About 55 per cent of those who responded were women, many of them in their 40s facing mid-career pressures and a "full nest" at home, with the need to care for children and elderly parents.

The study is the fourth of seven the authors are doing on aspects of work comparing the results of the 2001 National Work-Life Conflict Study to a similar poll of workers at private, public, and non-profit organizations done in 1991. The survey found 25 per cent of Canadians worked at least 50 hours a week in 2001, which was up substantially from a decade earlier, when only 10 per cent of workers reported such long hours.

The biggest pressure, what Prof. Duxbury termed "role overload," is the feeling there is not enough time available to meet the demands in the job and their personal life.

Professional women in the survey reported working as hard as the men at work but also working harder than men at home. "It's the 'super-mom' thing," Prof. Duxbury said.

The survey found 60 per cent of all respondents said they have trouble balancing their work and family demands and 28 per cent had missed at least three days of work in the previous six months because of illness. One in 10 reported taking "mental health days" because of emotional or mental fatigue.

"Elder care is going to be the next big thing," said Prof. Duxbury. A decade ago, only one in 12 reported having to deal with the care of elderly parents or relatives, but in the 2001 survey, 60 per cent said they had some form of elder care. In the survey, 10 per cent said it was causing them stress and physical fatigue every day, and another 15 per cent said it was causing stressful situations at least once a week. "That's because of the aging of the boomers. I think the point to make is: For years employers have talked about working families and really dismissed it."

While the survey found women still have primary responsibility for child care, one in three men reported having primary responsibility for elder care. "The reality is, if it's your parent you take the active role," Prof. Duxbury said.

The widespread use of cellphones, e-mail, and laptop computers have also added the expectation of instant response to work outside of office hours.

"Some organizations now expect people will be available 24/7 and that is also contributing to stress," she added.

The strain was most obvious among people in management roles. "A decade ago, people believed to be a manager was the best job to have in Canada. You got paid more, you had more status and had more flexibility."

But many organizations have seen the downsizing of middle management. "Now we enter the new decade with a group that is absolutely critical to our ability to change within the organization. And that is the group that reports it has the most workload and the heaviest demands, and that they find their jobs less interesting and increasingly demanding," Prof. Duxbury said.

Commitment among managers has declined the most precipitously in the decade, the study found. While 62 per cent of employees reported being highly satisfied with their jobs and 66 per cent felt committed to their organization in 1991, the satisfaction level dropped to 46 per cent in 2001 and commitment was down to 53 per cent.

"That is an appalling decline," Prof. Duxbury said.

For employers, the message is: "You're not going into this as an accommodation or to be nice to people, you're doing this because it makes business sense. If you can reduce work-life conflicts you can reduce absenteeism by at least a quarter, if not more." Benefits costs will also be reduced.

"And if you don't focus on balance in work-life conflicts, good luck in recruiting and retaining employees in the next decade as we move into a sellers' market because you're not going to get loyalty.

"You can pay for their presence but you can't buy their passion. The only way you can motivate this work force and get creative work and great customer service out of them is to actually focus on work-life balance."

The study suggests employers should:

- Identify ways of reducing workloads, particularly of managers and professionals.
- Start recording the total costs of understaffing and overwork.
- Hire more staff in areas overly reliant on overtime work.
- Give employees the right to turn down overtime. Saying "no" should not be a career limiting move.
- Allow time off in lieu of overtime pay.
- Offer both child care and elder care referral services.

For employees, the study recommends:

- Say "no" to overtime hours if work expectations are unreasonable.
- Limit the amount of work they take home
- Try to reduce the amount of time spent in job-related travel.
- Take advantage of available flexible work arrangements.

Source: Wallace Immen, "'Role Overload' Makes Workers Sick," *The Globe and Mail*, October 22, 2003, C3.

Work-family conflicts arise not just from longer and longer hours, but also from the frequent incompatibility of work schedules with the schedules and needs of children. While a minority of employers do offer flextime arrangements that are responsive to the needs of employees, the great majority of part-time jobs do not offer comparable pay, benefits, and career opportunities.

Reported levels of time stress and work-family stress among parents are extremely high. More than one-third of 25- to 44-year-old women who work full-time and have children at home report that they are severely time stressed, and the same is true for about one in four men. Twenty-six percent of married fathers, 38% of married mothers, and 38% of single mothers report severe time stress, with levels of severe stress rising by about one-fifth between 1992 and 1998. About two-thirds of full-time employed parents with children also report that they are dissatisfied with the balance between their jobs and home life. Fathers and mothers alike blamed their dissatisfaction on not having enough time for family, which tends to lose out in the event of time conflict.[14]

To summarize, there is strong evidence of mounting work-life conflict and stress. This is driven by mounting demands from work, the still largely unchanged division of domestic labour between men and women, and the failure of the Canadian state to provide caring services on a sufficient scale.

Social Relations and Participation at Work

Work is a social process, and the social relations of production are an important aspect of the quality of jobs and of working life, but little hard information is available on this relatively intangible dimension. In 2000, 15% of workers reported stress in the workplace from "poor interpersonal relations," down slightly from 18.5% in 1994, but up from 13% in 1991.[15] Women report higher levels of stress from this cause than do men. Less than one-half of employees feel that they have much influence on their jobs. A recent survey by Canadian Policy Research Networks shows that only 10% of workers feel that they can strongly influence employer decisions that affect their jobs, and 45% feel that they have no influence at all. There are few significant differences by age or gender.[16]

Unionized workers do have some influence through the process of collective bargaining. About one in three paid workers in Canada is covered by the provisions of a collective agreement. Coverage is highest by far in the public sector and in large private-sector firms, particularly in primary industries, manufacturing, transportation, and utilities. By definition, collective agreements give access to a formal statement of conditions of employment, such as hours and working conditions, and access to a formal grievance and arbitration process. A formal grievance system militates against the exercise of arbitrary managerial authority, and against harassment by co-workers. Collective agreements also often provide for joint processes to govern working conditions over the life of a contract, such as labour-management, training, and health and safety committees. While the great majority of agreements contain a management rights clause clarifying the power of management to assign and direct work, the majority also provide for some advance notification of, and consultation over, technological and organizational change. Many collective agreements also feature detailed job descriptions, meaning that changes in tasks are subject to joint agreement.

Most Canadian unions have adopted formal policies relating to workplace health and safety, work-family balance, work reorganization and access to training, and have paid some attention to all of these quality of work-life issues in bargaining. Improvement of the work environment has been on the agenda, and some unions have made gains. However, there are continuous pressures to increase productivity to maintain employment and wages, which tend to militate against an agenda of humanizing work and creating more healthy workplaces.

While some non-union workers also enjoy access to formalized (if non-binding) processes of dispute resolution and collective consultation, worker "voice" in the Canadian workplace is much weaker than in countries where unionization rates are much higher. Moreover, many European countries have legislation providing for joint works councils with powers to at least discuss working conditions. The EU survey shows that 78% of workers believe they have the possibility of discussing working conditions and 71% the possibility of discussing organizational change, most frequently on a formal basis.

John O'Grady (Sullivan 2000) shows that effective workplace health and safety committees effectively reduce rates of injuries and disability, but are largely absent from the precarious labour market.

To summarize, institutions of collective representation are relatively weakly implanted in Canadian workplaces, undercutting workers' ability to shape working conditions.

Conclusion

This overview suggests many grounds for concern over the potential health impacts of trends in Canadian workplaces. Workplace threats to physical health remain significant. Pervasive job insecurity is a source of stress to many peripheral workers. In core workplaces, the pace and intensity of work are on the rise, and many are working very long hours in very demanding jobs. The incidence of high-strain jobs that combine high demands and limited control is quite high, particularly among women.

One key conclusion is that we need much more and better information about the level and trends of workplace determinants of health. We lack systematic evidence of the kind collected in Europe. This could and should be remedied by providing sufficient funding to Statistics Canada to conduct regular surveys on the quality of the work environment and working conditions. The new *Workplace and*

Employee Survey (WES) provides only very limited information in this area, and the *National Population Health Survey* provides only very limited information on working conditions.

A second key conclusion is that governments must intervene to help shape and improve workplace conditions. A wide range of relevant recommendations have been made over the years, most recently in the 1990s by two Human Resource Development Canada-initiated consultations. These were the Donner Task Force (the *Report of the Advisory Group on Working Time and Redistribution of Work*, 1997) and the *Report of the Collective Reflection on the Changing Workplace* (1997). The thrust of the first was to regulate working time by limiting long hours and by making precarious work more secure. The thrust of the second—which included a very wide range of options—was to propose changes to employment standards and forms of collective representation. At the end of the day, it is unlikely that there will be significant positive changes in the workplace if everything is left to employers, and if governments do not help equalize bargaining power between workers and employers.

• •

Questions for Critical Thought

1. How important are work and working conditions as determinants of physical and mental health in a post-industrial society?
2. How would you set out to clearly establish links between work and health?
3. High-stress jobs are often defined as those with high demands but low levels of control. What kinds of jobs are most stressful by this definition?
4. Does it seem plausible to you that work is generally becoming more and more stressful and demanding?
5. What are some of the different ways in which work-related stress and conflicts affect women and men?

Recommended Reading

Duxbury, Linda, and Chris Higgins. 2002. *The 2001 National Work-Life Conflict Study*. Health Canada <http://www.hc-sc.gc.ca>. Duxbury and Higgins have conducted several major studies of conflicts between work, family, and community life over the past several years, sparking increased interest in work-related stress as a key determinant of health.

European Foundation for the Improvement of Living and Working Conditions. 2000. Report on the European Survey on Working Conditions <http://www.eurofound. ie>. Reports based on this regular European Union-wide survey provide a much more detailed picture of working conditions than is available for Canada.

Karasek, Robert, and Tores Theorell. 1990. *Healthy Work: Stress, Productivity and the*

Reconstruction of Working Life. New York: Basic Books. This is the classic study of the impacts of workplace stress on health. Stress is seen as the result of high job demands combined with low levels of control.

Lowe, Graham. 2000. *The Quality of Work: A People Centred Agenda*. Oxford: Oxford University Press. A broad overview of the importance of work to well-being, and a useful introduction to recent trends in Canadian workplaces.

Sullivan, Terrence, ed. 2000. *Injury and the New World of Work*. Vancouver and Toronto: University of British Columbia Press. Contains recent studies of trends in workplace injuries, showing how "soft tissue" injuries attributable to fast-paced work have grown compared to traditional workplace accidents.

Notes

1. Data from Statistics Canada, *Survey of Labour and Income Dynamics* (Ottawa: Statistics Canada).
2. *The Daily*, September 6, 2000.
3. For 2000 data, see <http://www.jobquality.ca>.
4. <http://www.jobquality.ca>.
5. On working time issues, see Human Resources Development Canada, *Report of the Advisory Group on Working Time and Distribution of Work*, 1997, and Andrew Jackson, *Creating More and Better Jobs Through Reduction and Redistribution of Working Time* <http://www.clc-ctc.ca>.
6. Statistics Canada, "The Changing Work Week: Trends in Weekly Hours of Work," *Canadian Economic Observer* (September 1996).
7. *Labour Force Survey* data, <http://www.jobquality.ca>.
8. Statistics Canada, "Longer Working Hours and Health," *The Daily*, November 16, 1999.
9. *OECD Employment Outlook* (Paris: OECD, 1998), Chart 5.2.
10. 1991 and 1995 data from the *Survey of Work Arrangements*; 2000 data from the *Workplace and Employee Survey* (WES).
11. Saskatchewan alone provides for three weeks after five years.
12. Seventy percent of unionized workers qualify for four weeks after 10 years, and 28% qualify after five years.
13. Statistics Canada, *Work Arrangements in the 1990s* (Ottawa: Statistics Canada), Cat. 71-535 MPB #8, Tables 3.1, 3.2.
14. Statistics Canada, *The Daily*, November 9, 1999.
15. Statistics Canada, *General Social Survey*, 2003.
16. <http://www.jobquality.ca>.

References

Brisbois, Richard. 2003. *How Canada Stacks Up: The Quality of Work—An International Perspective*. Ottawa: Canadian Policy Research Networks.

Clark, Andrew. 1999. *What Makes a Good Job?* Paris: OECD.

Duxbury, Linda, and Chris Higgins. 2002. *The 2001 National Work-Life Conflict Study.* Health Canada <http://www.hc-sc.gc.ca>.

European Industrial Relations Observatory (EIRO). 2000a. *Working Time Developments: Annual Update 2001.*

_____. 2000b. *Non-Permanent Employment, Quality of Work and Industrial Relations.*

_____. 2000c. *Working Time Developments and the Quality of Work.*

Human Resources Development Canada. 2000. *Statistical Analysis of Occupational Injuries and Fatalities in Canada* <http://www.hrsdc.gc.ca>.

Jackson, Andrew. 2000. *Why We Don't Have to Choose between Social Justice and Economic Growth: The Myth of the Equity-Efficiency Trade-Off.* Canadian Council on Social Development <http://www.ccsd.ca>.

Jencks, C., L. Perlman, and L. Rainwater. 1988. "What Is a Good Job? A New Measure of Labour Market Success." *American Journal of Sociology* 93 (May): 1322–1357.

Karasek, Robert, and Tores Theorell. 1990. *Healthy Work: Stress, Productivity and the Reconstruction of Working Life.* New York: Basic Books.

Lewchuk, Wayne, and David Robertson. 1996. "Working Conditions under Lean Production: A Worker-based Benchmarking Study." *Asia Pacific Business Review* (Summer): 60–81.

Livingstone, David. 2002. *Working and Learning in the Information Age: A Profile of Canadians.* Ottawa: Canadian Policy Research Networks.

Lowe, Graham. 2000. *The Quality of Work: A People Centred Agenda.* Oxford: Oxford University Press.

Statistics Canada. 2001. *Health Indicators.* Cat 82-221-XIE.

Sullivan, Terrence, ed. 2000. *Injury and the New World of Work.* Vancouver and Toronto: UBC Press.

Wilkins, Kathryn, and Marie P. Beaudet. 1998. "Work Stress and Health," *Health Reports* 10, no. 3 (Winter): 47–62.

World Health Organization (WHO). 1999. *Labour Market Changes and Job Insecurity.* Regional Publications/European Series no. 81. Geneva: WHO.

PART II

Inequalities and Differences: Gender, Race, Ability, Age

THIS PART OF THE BOOK TAKES AN IN-DEPTH LOOK AT THE LABOUR MARKET AND work experiences associated with specific groups: women, minorities, and older workers. The job market is marked by deep inequalities and differences along lines of gender, race, ability, and age, all of which intersect with differences in wages and the quality of employment.

Chapter 5, "Women in the Workforce," compares and contrasts the occupational distribution, forms of employment, and earnings of women and men, and shows that there are deep and systematic differences based upon gender. Women are more likely than men to be in lower-paid and precarious jobs, and the pay gap between women and men remains well entrenched. That said, it is important to emphasize that there are significant differences among the labour force experiences of different groups of women, as well as among men.

Chapter 6, "Minorities in the Workforce," examines the experiences of visible minorities (workers of colour), Aboriginal Canadians, and persons with disabilities. Despite huge differences, what these groups have in common is at least some degree of vulnerability to discrimination in the job market, which also means a failure by employers to accommodate differences.

This chapter summarizes evidence of significant pay, employment, and opportunity gaps between visible minority workers (a large proportion of whom are recent immigrants) and other Canadians. These differences are disturbing in that they cannot be explained away with reference to education and ability. It is not just new immigrants, but also workers of colour born and educated in Canada who operate at a disadvantage. This poses a real challenge to the goal of social inclusion of all Canadians.

While a layer of new immigrants and visible minorities do very well in the job market, the same cannot be said of Aboriginal Canadians. The very low level of economic well-being of many Aboriginal people and communities reflects the fact that their pay levels are very low compared to the Canadian norm, and that their jobs are often very unstable.

Persons with disabilities face a different problem—great difficulty gaining access to any kind of employment. While one would expect employment rates for persons with disabilities to be lower than average, the gap also reflects a collective failure to accommodate people with different needs in the workplace.

Finally, Chapter 7, "Older Workers, Pensions, and the Transition to Retirement," looks at paths from work to retirement, the changing fortunes of older Canadian workers, and at older people who are still active in the job market. This highlights the different experiences of different age groups and what has come to be known as the changing life-course.

■ Related Web Sites

All of the Web sites listed in Part I are also relevant to many of the issues faced by women, minorities, and older workers.

- The Canadian Council on Social Development (CCSD) <http://www.ccsd.ca>. A leading social research organization, the CCSD has produced a number of studies on the labour market experiences of visible minorities and new immigrants, and reports for the United Way of Greater Toronto that cover new immigrant issues. The Disability Research Information Page on the CCSD Web site provides access to all CCSD research on disability issues plus links to major disability research sites.
- The Canadian Race Relations Foundation <http://www.crr.ca>. The foundation is committed to building a national framework for the fight against racism in Canadian society and acts as a resource and facilitator in the pursuit of equity, fairness, and social justice. It publishes research on discrimination against both racial minorities and Aboriginal people.
- Council of Canadians with Disabilities <http://www.ccdonline.ca>. As the lead advocacy organization for persons with disabilities, the council has published a wide range of position papers, covering human rights, income supports, and other issues.
- The Organisation for Economic Co-operation and Development <http://oecd. org>. The OECD has a large subsite on "Ageing Society" with many papers on older workers, the transition to retirement, and the potential costs of an aging society.
- Status of Women Canada <http://www.swc-cfc.gc.ca>. Status of Women Canada (SWC) is the federal government department that promotes gender equality and the full participation of women in the economic, social, cultural, and political life of the country. SWC focuses its work in three areas: improving women's economic autonomy and well-being, eliminating systemic violence against women and children, and advancing women's human rights. The Web site provides access to research papers and to gender equality indicators.

CHAPTER FIVE

Women in the Workforce

◼ Introduction

This chapter provides an overview of women's work. It examines the increased participation of women in the Canadian workforce; differences in the kinds of jobs held by women and men, including the much greater likelihood of women working in part-time jobs; the segregation of women and men into very different kinds of occupations; pay gaps between women and men; and the difficulties many women face in balancing work and family.

In certain circles, it has become rather fashionable to see feminist perspectives on work as rather outdated, a relic of the 1970s, hardly in tune with the new world of opportunity that has opened up for women. Some old barriers have indeed eroded, but equality for women has still not been achieved. Indeed, there are still huge differences between the kinds of jobs held by women and men, and the size of their paycheques.

While working women have made significant progress over the years in terms of achieving equality of opportunity and outcomes with men, there are still systematic differences. Women and men are employed in very different kinds of jobs, and the level of occupational and industrial segregation between women and men is very high. Good jobs for women still tend to exist disproportionately in public and social services, rather than in the business sector of the economy. Usually, but not always, occupations where women predominate in the business sector are relatively low paid, and this helps explain the still very significant pay gap between women and men. The kinds of jobs held by women also tend to be more precarious and insecure. Systematic gaps between women and men partly reflect continued job discrimination and undervaluation of women's work compared to that of men. These gaps also reflect the fact that the burden of domestic work and child care is still mainly borne by women, and that this double burden has not been adequately addressed by employers or governments.

While this chapter makes a lot of comparisons between the experiences of women and men, it is also important to emphasize that there are also major differences in labour market experiences among women. These differences have been growing, and the progress of some women has not been experienced by all. There are large differences in the quality of jobs between women of colour, Aboriginal Women, and other women, and between women who belong to unions and other women. These differences are dealt with in greater detail in later chapters.

■Women Continue to Enter the Workforce

In almost all advanced industrial countries, the participation rate of women in the workforce has steadily climbed since the 1960s, and the gender gap in employment rates has narrowed. The participation rate of women in Canada is now one of the very highest among the Organisation for Economic Co-operation and Development (OECD) countries. In 2002, 71.9% of women aged 15 to 64 were participating in the workforce, either working or actively seeking work, compared to 70.1% in the U.S., and an OECD or industrial country average of just 59.6%.[1] In all countries, participation rates and employment in full-time jobs tend to be lower for women because women still bear the primary responsibility for child care as well as elder care and work in the home generally. Almost everywhere, the gap between the employment rates of women and men increases with the presence and number of children in a family. The low participation rates of women in many continental European countries reflect the survival of a traditional male breadwinner family model in which men still provide the main source of family income, and many married women do not participate in paid work at all. This model is eroding as more women have sought economic equality with men and as cultural norms have changed, but it is still a significant influence on the job market. The very high participation rates of women in the Scandinavian countries reflect the fact that many of the caring needs of households that were traditionally met by women in the home have now been assumed by the whole society through the government. Child care and care for the elderly is readily available at low cost, which has helped women to work outside the home and also created many good jobs for women.

Canada's very high rate of labour force participation by women certainly does not reflect a well-developed system of government-supported child care. Even in Quebec, a comprehensive system is relatively new. Outside Quebec, quality care is hard to find, and is expensive. High rates of participation in paid work undoubtedly reflect the fact that most Canadian women want to work and pursue a career, and to enjoy some measure of economic independence, rather than be full-time caregivers at home. Cultural norms have shifted much further away from the male breadwinner model of the 1950s than in many European countries, but high participation rates of Canadian women also reflect new economic realities. As men's wages have stagnated, women have entered the labour force to help maintain and increase real family incomes. The dual-earner family is now the Canadian norm. In fact, women earn more than their male spouses in fully one-third of dual-earner families, double the level of 1980, and up from one-quarter in 1990.[2] The earnings of women are, of course, the main source of income for most single-parent families and for women who live alone. The key point is that the earnings of women are hugely important to economic well-being, and are rarely just an add-on to male earnings. This makes the low earnings of many women highly problematic for both economic and equality reasons.

Women continued to enter the Canadian workforce in increasing numbers in the 1990s, though at a slower rate than in the past. The participation rate of women aged 15 to 64, which was just over one-half in the mid-1970s, had reached two-thirds by the late 1980s, and stood at almost three-quarters (73.0%) in 2003. This is still a bit below the participation rate of 83.2% for men, though the rate for men has been stable or even falling because of a trend to earlier retirement over most of the 1980s and 1990s. The domestic responsibilities of women, and the fact that many women with young children continue to take some time out of the paid workforce, still make a difference. About 40% of women with children under age three do not have a paid job. This helps explain why the participation rate of women aged 25 to 54 is very high, at 80.9% in 2003, but is well below the 91.6% participation rate of men in the same age group. The past few years have seen a big increase in the participation rate of older women. For women aged 55 to 59, the rate has jumped from just under one-half in the mid-1990s to 59.7% in 2003. More of today's older women have worked for all or most of their lives than was the case with earlier generations.

■Precarious Work

The fact that more women are working is positive from the point of view of the economic independence of women and the incomes of families, but tells us nothing about the quality of the jobs that women are finding. As was noted in Chapter 2, a significant minority of workers are employed in precarious jobs—that is, in insecure jobs that carry a high risk of unemployment and/or low pay and provide limited access to benefits such as pensions and drug and dental plans. Precarious jobs also involve limited control of working hours and conditions, and offer limited prospects for advancement in the job market. The incidence of precarious and insecure forms of work has been rising in the 1990s, and is somewhat higher for women than men. The main differences between women's jobs and men's jobs in terms of the form of employment are that women are much more likely to work part-time than are men, and are also less likely to be in the more attractive forms of self-employment, such as incorporated businesses with employees (Vosko et al. 2003).

■Unemployment

The unemployment rate of women is almost always a bit lower than that of men. In 2003, the unemployment rate for women aged 15 to 64 was 7.3% compared to 8.1% for men, and for core working-age women aged 25 to 54, it was 6.4% compared to 6.6% for men. Women also tend to be unemployed for a slightly shorter period — 15 weeks compared to 17 weeks for men in 2003. Lower unemployment rates for women mainly result from the fact that a higher proportion of men are employed in seasonal jobs such as construction and primary industries, while relatively more women are employed in steadier public and social services jobs. Also, women who lose a job are a bit more likely than men to spend a period of time outside the workforce rather than to actively look for another job right away. That said, many women have experienced unemployment in recent years. The unemployment rate for women topped 10% in both 1992 and 1993 before slowly falling over the rest of the decade. Younger women have experienced and continue to experience very high rates of unemployment. In 2003, the unemployment rate for young women aged 15 to 24 was 11.9%.

While women are unemployed a bit less often than men, they are also less likely to have very stable employment. The average woman worker has been in her job for a bit over one and one-half years, compared to two years for men. Shorter job tenure is one indicator of more precarious employment, and also reflects periods spent out of the workforce caring for children. There continues to be a significant gap between the proportion of women and men who work full-time hours for a full year — that is, who are steadily employed. In 2001, 58% of men worked full-time hours for the full year compared to 51% of women.[3] As a result, unemployed women are much less likely than unemployed men to receive regular Employment Insurance benefits. In recent years, only one in three unemployed women has qualified for benefits, about 10 percentage points lower than the proportion of men who qualify. Women working part-time often find it hard to get enough hours of work to qualify for regular and maternity leave benefits.

■Part-Time Work

The paradox of part-time work for women is that this is a form of employment that can help balance work and family roles, but one that usually comes at a high cost in terms of job quality (Duffy and Pupo 1992). Certainly women are much more likely to work part-time than men, and part-time jobs are, on average, much less desirable than full-time jobs. Some part-time jobs—usually in unionized workplaces, public services, and with some larger companies—can offer good pay and benefits, stable hours and regular shift times, and decent career development prospects. In such contexts, the flexibility of part-time work is welcomed by many, mainly women, workers who may choose to work part-time for a few months or even years before returning to full-time work.

However, most part-time jobs are low paid, and some employers deliberately create part-time jobs to keep labour costs at a minimum. In many stores and restaurants, it is not uncommon for part-time workers to be paid less than regular, full-time employees, to receive no benefits, and to have little or no control of their work schedule. Hours can be posted with little advance notice to meet the fluctuating demands on a business for goods and services, or to fill holes in the work roster. Part-time schedules are usually much more flexible than those of full-time workers who are promised 35 to 40 hours of work per week. It is not uncommon for part-time and casual workers to be obliged to sit at home and wait to be called into work, depending on whether business is good or slow. The practice of varying the hours of part-timers makes business sense, but makes a mockery of the common idea that part-time work gives the worker flexibility of hours in a way that meets the needs of women. Employment standards legislation in most provinces is all but silent on the right of part-timers to advance notice of hours, and on equal wages and pro-rated benefits between full and part-time workers (Broad and Hagin 2002).

Someone is considered to be a part-time worker if he or she works in a main job for less than 30 hours per week. More than one in four of all women work part-time compared to only about one in ten men. As shown in Figure 5.1, women at any age are much more likely to work part-time than are men in the same age group. Most male part-timers are students. In the core working-age group of people between 25 and 54, just 4.8% of men work part-time compared to 21.2% of women. Women with children, especially two or more children, are much more likely to work part-time than other women.

Working part-time can, in principle, be desirable. This form of work allows young people to earn an income while pursuing an education, and it can allow both women and men to better balance the demands of work and family and community life. However, it is clear that a substantial minority of part-timers are working part-time only because they cannot find full-time jobs. About one in four women part-timers in the core working-age group (aged 25 to 54) consistently reported through the 1990s and into 2003 that she was doing so involuntarily, either because she could not find a full-time job or had given up looking. This count of involuntary part-timers does not include the majority of women part-timers who say they have made this choice to look after children or to deal with personal and family responsibilities. This choice can be seen as socially constructed. Some of these women would likely choose to work full-time if they could find high-quality, affordable child care or

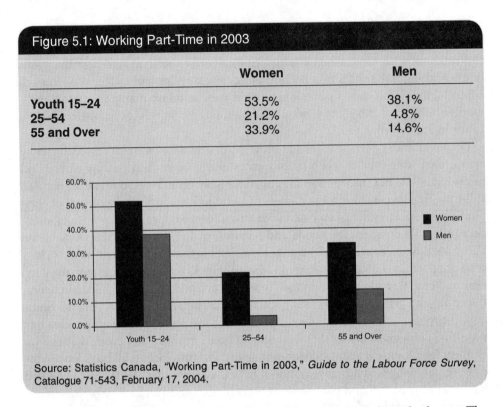

Figure 5.1: Working Part-Time in 2003

	Women	Men
Youth 15–24	53.5%	38.1%
25–54	21.2%	4.8%
55 and Over	33.9%	14.6%

Source: Statistics Canada, "Working Part-Time in 2003," *Guide to the Labour Force Survey*, Catalogue 71-543, February 17, 2004.

elder care, or if their spouses took on a greater share of work in the home. The incidence of part-time work for women tends to be much lower in countries such as Sweden and Denmark which offer organized child care arrangements, and the gap between women and men working part-time is much more modest in the Netherlands, where it is common for both partners to work part-time and to share child care responsibilities.

Part-time work is usually undesirable because pay and benefits are generally much worse than in full-time jobs. In 2003, part-time jobs paid a median hourly wage of just $10 per hour (i.e., half make more, and half less) compared to $17.32 per hour in full-time jobs. Women part-timers actually make more on average than male part-timers, but the fact remains that there is a huge hourly wage gap between the two kinds of work. Partly, this reflects the fact that many part-time jobs are to be found in relatively low-wage industries, such as retail trade and the hospitality industries, but studies have also shown that part-time jobs tend to be paid less than comparable full-time jobs. Typically, part-time jobs are also only about one-half as likely to provide benefits as full-time jobs. Thus, in 1999, just one in five part-timers (18.9%) was covered by an employer pension plan compared to 41.6% of full-timers, and 19.8% of part-timers were covered by a supplementary medical insurance plan compared to 59.5% of full-timers.[4] Opportunities for career advancement and training are much more limited than in full-time jobs.

Work schedules are often extremely variable. Four in ten (37.9%) non-union part-timers work irregular hours or are on call compared to one in four unionized part-timers.[5] Irregular part-time hours make it extremely difficult to balance work and family, and work and education.

Box 5.1: Improving Part-Time Work in Saskatchewan

Quebec and Saskatchewan stand out as two provinces that have tried to protect part-time workers to some degree through labour legislation. Amendments to the *Saskatchewan Labour Standards Act* in 1994 required employers to post part-time work schedules one week in advance, to provide rest and meal breaks to part-timers, and to provide pro-rated benefits to part-time workers (in establishments with more than 10 employees). However, very strong opposition from the business community meant that the Saskatchewan government failed to implement the most innovative section of the new Act, which would have required employers to offer available hours of work to their current part-time workforce before hiring new part-timers. This would have allowed part-timers to gradually turn themselves into full-time workers. Employers did not want to lose the control of total hours worked which comes with maintaining a predominantly part-time workforce.

For details, see studies by Dave Broad and colleagues from the Social Policy Research Unit of the University of Regina, posted at <http://www.uregina.ca/spr>.

Temporary Jobs and Self-Employment

Both corporate and public sector employers have tried to limit hiring of costly full-time, permanent employees by hiring temporary workers to meet spikes in demand, and by outsourcing or contracting out some tasks to outside suppliers. As a result, there has been an increase in contract or temporary workers, and in the number of self-employed over the past decade and more. This has come on top of a traditional layer of self-employed workers who run their own businesses.

Contract and temporary work can lead to a permanent job, and a few workers enjoy moving from contract to contract or want to work only in a seasonal job. But, such employment is rarely a first choice for adult workers, since temporary workers are typically excluded from benefit plans, training programs, and career ladders, and are paid less than permanent employees.

In 2003, 13.0% of all women employees compared to 11.9% of male employees were in temporary jobs, which are defined as jobs that are casual, seasonal, or, most often, have a defined end date. The incidence of temporary employment for women has increased from 11.7% of women in 1997, and from about 7% in 1989. Women temporary workers are much more likely to work part-time than temporary male workers.

Another form of precarious employment is self-employment. A layer of self-employed workers are high-earning professionals—such as doctors, lawyers, architects, engineers, and accountants—who usually work with professional colleagues and employ support workers. Others are owners of small- and medium-sized businesses that employ workers. These people are mainly self-employed by choice, and those who are in high demand or run successful businesses can earn high and stable incomes. However, a large and growing layer of self-employed workers are running tiny businesses of their own mainly because they cannot find stable, permanent employment. Micro-enterprises run the whole range from home and building cleaning, to household maintenance, to child and elder care, to making clothes, to working as freelance writers and editors and artists. Many self-employed workers have just a few clients and can, in some cases, be considered to be hidden employees. The legal distinction between self-employed and contract workers is not clear-cut, and can even differ from one statute to another (Fudge et al. 2002). The rapid growth of self-employment in the first half of the 1990s was mainly driven by the increasing numbers of so-called own-account workers—that is, self-employed workers who are unincorporated and employ no paid help. Much of this growth is probably explained by the difficulty of finding regular paid jobs. Though some growth is explained by the desire of some women to run their own businesses and to have some control over their working hours, about one-half of all own-account workers say that they would rather have regular jobs.[6] A lot of people are self-employed for short periods.

Self-employment among women rose in the first half of the 1990s from 9.9% of total women's employment in 1990 to 11.6% in 1997. It has since remained at about that level (11.3% in 2003). While self-employment is more prevalent among men, accounting for fully 18.9% of all men's jobs in 2003, self-employed women are much more likely to be own-account workers, running their own micro-enterprises with no employees. In 2003, more than 70% of all women self-employed workers were own-account. Women self-employed workers are much more likely to have very low earnings than are self-employed men. In 2000, almost half (45%) of all self-employed women made less than $20,000 from their businesses compared to 19% of self-employed men. Less than one-fifth of self-employed workers making more than $60,000 per year were women.

■ Occupational Segregation of Women and Men

In Canada, as in all advanced industrial countries, there is still very marked occupational segregation between women and men. In other words, men and women hold very different kinds of jobs, working in almost parallel occupational worlds. This is hugely important because jobs where women predominate tend to be lower paid than jobs where men predominate, even though the educational and skill requirements may differ very little. Traditionally, men were relatively concentrated in blue-collar industrial occupations, as well as in white-collar management jobs and in the professions, while women were relatively concentrated in low-level, pink-collar clerical and administrative jobs in offices, and in sales and services occupations. This division has broken down to a limited degree over time as women have entered professional and managerial jobs in increasing numbers. But, women in better-paid occupations are still mainly to be found in only a relatively few occupational groups, notably working in health, education, and social services jobs in the broader public sector. Women are almost twice as likely as men to work in the public sector, defined as working directly for government or in almost entirely government-funded bodies, such as schools, universities, and hospitals. One in four women work in public services compared to just one in eight men. The better-paid

Table 5.1: Employment by Broad Occupation

	Men		Women	
	1989	2003	1989	2003
Management	10.6%	10.6%	6.3%	6.7%
Professional occupations in business and finance	2.3%	2.8%	2.0%	3.0%
Natural and applied sciences	7.2%	9.6%	1.9%	3.1%
Professional occupations in health	1.1%	1.2%	4.6%	4.5%
Social science, government, religion	1.9%	2.1%	2.5%	4.2%
Teachers and professors	2.6%	2.7%	4.1%	5.2%
Art, culture, recreation and sport	2.1%	2.5%	2.8%	3.3%
Sub-total professional/ Highly skilled	17.2%	20.9%	17.9%	23.3%
Technical, assisting occupations in health	0.8%	0.8%	4.3%	5.1%
Financial, secretarial, clerical, administrative	7.8%	7.0%	30.2%	24.1%
Sales and service occupations	18.2%	19.8%	31.1%	32.2%
Blue collar	45.3%	40.9%	10.1%	8.5%
Sub-total blue-collar and pink-collar	72.1%	68.5%	75.7%	69.9%

Source: Statistics Canada, "Employment by Broad Occupation," *Labour Force Historical Review 2003*, Catalogue 71f0004, February 17, 2004.
Note: Sub-total categories are not from original source.

professional and managerial jobs in the business sector of the economy and, indeed, many of the higher jobs in the public sector are still held mainly by men.

Table 5.1 provides a fairly detailed picture of employment of women and men by broad occupational groups in 1989 and 2003. Looking first at 2003, it is striking that four in every ten men (40.9%) are still to be found in blue-collar jobs—the construction trades and labourers; equipment operators and transport jobs, such as truck and bus drivers; workers in primary occupations, such as in mining and forestry; and labourers, machine operators, and assemblers in manufacturing and utilities. While by no means all well paid, these kinds of jobs do tend to command about average pay, and are often unionized. Just 8.5% of women are employed in these blue-collar jobs, one-fifth the proportion of men, and this small minority of women are mainly to be found in relatively low-paid manufacturing jobs in sectors such as clothing rather than in the well-paid skilled trades.

By contrast, one-quarter of women (24.1%) are still to be found in non-professional office jobs—that is in financial, clerical, administrative, and secretarial jobs—compared to just 7.0% of men. Many of these jobs are quite skilled, certainly involving computer skills, but they tend to pay less than skilled blue-collar jobs.

A lot of both men and women work in usually low-paid, often part-time, sales and service jobs, a big occupational category that includes salespersons, chefs and cooks, security guards, and child care and home support workers. But, more women are employed in these lower-end jobs than are men: one in three women (32.2%) works in these occupations compared to one in five men (19.8%), and the men who work in these kinds of jobs tend to be young. Women predominate in technical and assisting occupations in health—that is, in non-professional jobs below the level of a registered nurse.

Turning to professional occupations, which usually require higher levels of formal education and qualifications, women hold a slight edge over men. One in four women (23.3%) work in these kinds of jobs, a somewhat higher proportion than for men (20.9%). But, women are significantly more likely than men to work in professional health care occupations; in social sciences, government, and religion; and in teaching. Men, by contrast, predominate by a big margin in the natural and applied sciences. Finally, men hold a big lead in management jobs. More than one in ten men (10.6%) are in management jobs compared to 6.7% of women. Moreover, men hold double the proportion of senior management jobs, which make up 0.7% of all men's jobs compared to just 0.3% of all women's jobs.

The majority of women thus still work in the traditional clerical, sales, and services categories, and very few women work in the blue-collar occupations. Many women do work in occupations requiring higher levels of education and providing better levels of pay, but these women are still relatively concentrated in public and social services.

The recent report of the federal government's Pay Equity Task Force (Government of Canada 2004) further details the fact that women are still highly concentrated

Box 5.2: The Changing Generational Fortunes of Young Women and Young Men

The past 25 years or so have seen a huge shift in the life experiences of younger adults. A generation ago, young people left home, formed marital unions, entered stable jobs, and had children at a much earlier age than is now the case. Today, it is not until age 23 that the majority of young people are working. Before that age, the majority are still at school. More than 40% of people in their twenties still live at home, up from just one in four in 1981. At age 25 to 29, close to half of young women are still single compared to just one-quarter a generation ago. The average age at which a woman has a first child has risen by four years, to age 28, and single-child families are increasingly the norm (Beaujot 2004).

Key changes in the job market help explain this delayed transition to the adult norm of a generation ago. Good jobs require higher levels of education, and there has been a significant deterioration in the quality of jobs available to young people who do not get a post-secondary education. In the 1990s, wage gaps and differences in employment and unemployment rates between young people with and without post-secondary qualifications greatly increased (OECD 2004). As a result, post-secondary enrolment has soared to one of the highest levels in the world.

On balance, young women have fared better than young men. Compared to earlier generations, families have been prepared to invest in the education of all children, and most young women now expect and want to pursue an education and a career. Not only has the education gap between the sexes closed, women aged 25 to 34 are now much more likely than men of the same age to have completed a post-secondary education (56% compared to 42%). And, compared to earlier generations, the earnings of young women have fallen far less than those of young men.

Well-educated younger women are doing very well in the job market compared to women of a generation ago, and even compared to young men. They occupy a much higher proportion of professional and highly skilled jobs. But, the fact remains that women who do well in the job market usually do so by delaying or foregoing having children, and pay a price when they eventually do have children (Lochead 2000). The employment and wage gap really opens up when women start to have children. As a society, we have equalized educational opportunities, but not opportunities in the job market.

in a small number of traditionally female occupational categories—health care, teaching, clerical, administrative, and sales and services jobs, and overwhelmingly predominate in the very lowest-paid occupations, such as child care workers, cashiers, and food services workers. Women are still greatly under-represented in most of the highest-paying professions, from specialist physicians, to senior private-sector managers, to corporate lawyers and security dealers. Even in the public sector where women predominate, men are much more likely to hold senior management jobs. In the federal public service, men are more than twice as likely to be senior managers.

All that said, there has been some continued progress made by a layer of women who have moved into professional and managerial jobs over the past decade and more. Since 1989, the proportion of women in management jobs has risen from 6.3% to 6.7%. Most importantly, the proportion of women in professional and highly skilled jobs has risen from 17.9% to 23.3%. This occupational shift has been more pronounced than for men (17.2% to 20.9%). It has been relatively greatest for women in social sciences and government jobs, but has also taken place in professional occupations in business and finance and in the natural sciences. In short, a small group of women are moving into higher-end jobs in the private as well as the public sector, though they remain a very small proportion of all women. Paralleling this shift, the proportion of women in non-professional office jobs as clerical workers and secretaries has fallen from 30.2% to 24.1% of all women's jobs. Meanwhile, the proportion of women in low-paid sales and services jobs has increased slightly.

In summary, about one in three women now works in a managerial or professional job, and this share is rising. This reflects rising levels of education among women, the growth of professional jobs in public and social services, and, to a modest degree, the movement of women into professional jobs in business and finance, and the natural and applied sciences. But, two in three women are in lower-level, pink-collar jobs, which tend to pay less than the blue-collar jobs still held by many men.

■ The Persistent—and Growing—Pay Gap between Women and Men

As noted, women are much more likely than men to be employed part-time and for only part of the year, and women are much more likely to be employed in lower-paid occupations (horizontal segregation). Within broad occupational and industrial categories, women are also less likely to be employed in higher-paid professional occupations (vertical segregation). The net result is that, on average, women earn less than men. In all OECD countries, there is a significant wage gap between women and men, with women's hourly pay averaging just 84% that of men. The wage gap in Canada is somewhat above average, with women earning an average of just 81% of what men earn. Economic research has consistently shown that the greatest part of the wage gap in Canada, as in other industrial countries, cannot be explained by objective factors such as the educational level and job experience of women, but is created by gender (Drolet 2002; OECD 2002).

Pay gaps can and do result from cultural preconceptions of the value of particular jobs, reinforced by comparisons with other employers operating on the same assumptions, rather than on an objective analysis of job characteristics. Male factory workers are still often paid more than women clerical workers, even though their jobs are neither more highly skilled, nor involve greater responsibility. Well into the 1970s, nursing and elementary school teaching were low-paid jobs mainly because these were professions dominated by women, rather than because the skill and responsibility of the work was low. Traditionally, male workers were more highly unionized than women, and greater bargaining power helped raise their relative wages. Until quite recently, the cultural norm was that men should be paid a family-supporting wage, and women were viewed as secondary income earners.

Pay gaps can also arise from the fact that women are discriminated against when it comes to accessing better jobs and promotions. Such discrimination can be overt—protection of male job preserves—or more systemic—a failure to recognize and accommodate difference. One key difference between women and men, of course, is that women still bear primary responsibility for domestic work, particularly the care of children, and often choose to work fewer hours, or to take parental and child care leaves. While differences in total work experience are not that great, the perception that a career comes second seems to be a major factor behind the glass ceiling that continues to exist in some workplaces and professions.

The struggle for pay equality for women goes back a long way. Some women have worked for pay since the days of the Industrial Revolution, and demands for better pay and equal pay for women are part of the history of the labour movement (even though unions were dominated by men until well into the 1970s). The principle of equal pay for women and men doing the same job is long standing. As long ago as the 1950s, most provinces had legislated against pay discrimination in the sense of paying women less than men performing the same work. However, expressed in this way, the principle of equality is problematic for the simple reason that women and men work mainly in different jobs rather than for different pay in the same job. The broader principle of equal pay for work of equal value gained currency only in the 1970s, and was legislated in the federal jurisdiction and in some provinces (mainly with application only to the public sector). This led to comparisons between male- and female-dominated jobs in the same establishment, and some closing of pay gaps that could not be justified with reference to effort, qualifications, responsibility, and other objective benchmarks. Pay gaps have closed in larger workplaces covered by pay equity laws, but they are still very much the reality over the whole job market today.

▌Wage Gaps between and within Occupations

Table 5.2, Average Weekly Wages by Occupation in 2003, shows average weekly wages for a range of occupations, broadly the same as those in Table 5.1, but with a bit more detail. Average weekly wages reflect both hours worked in the week and wages per hour. The earnings gap between women and men reflects both fewer hours worked in a week, on average, mainly because of part-time work, and lower hourly wages. In 2003, the median hourly wage for all workers (half make more and half make less) was $16 per hour, and the median hourly wage for women was 80% that of men ($14.43 per hour compared to $18 per hour). The average weekly wage was $663, with women earning just 71% the average weekly wage of men ($549 compared to $773).

Two major points emerge clearly from the table. First, average wages are usually higher in male-dominated occupations. Second, even within occupations, women earn much less than men.

Table 5.2: Average Weekly Wages by Occupation in 2003				
	All	Men	Women	Women as % Men
Management	$1,143	$1,261	$956	76%
Professional occupations in business and finance	$979	$1,125	$863	77%
Natural and applied sciences	$990	$1,028	$866	84%
Professional occupations in health	$872	$1,025	$852	83%
Social science, government, religion	$819	$966	$750	78%
Teachers and professors	$868	$962	$813	85%
Technical, assisting occupations in health	$567	$697	$545	78%
Financial, secretarial, administrative	$628	$835	$588	70%
Clerical	$543	$605	$518	86%
Sales and service occupations	$408	$518	$329	64%
including retail clerks	$329	$463	$267	58%
including child care and home support	$372	$473	$366	77%
Trades, transport and equipment operating	$736	$755	$454	60%
Processing, manufacturing, utilities	$643	$707	$490	69%
All occupations	$663	$773	$549	71%

Source: Statistics Canada, *Labour Force Historical Review*, Catalogue 71f0004, February 17, 2004.

Looking at wage differences between occupational groups, the average weekly wage for all occupations in 2003 was $663, translating into an annual income of close to $35,000 for full-year workers. As one would expect, professionals and managers are paid well above average, ranging from $800 to over $1,000 per week. The best-paid occupations are those dominated by men: managers; professionals in business and finance, and the natural and applied sciences. The other professional occupations where women predominate are paid a bit less.

Turning to non-professional jobs, wages of blue-collar trades, transport and equipment operators, and, to a lesser extent, of occupations in manufacturing and processing, are higher than those in the pink-collar jobs held by women—that is, in assisting jobs in health, financial, secretarial, and administrative work, and even more so in clerical work. The lowest weekly wages are in sales and services occupations—just $408 per week—where women predominate, and in some jobs, such as retail clerks and cashiers and child care and home support, workers are paid even less.

Looking at wage differences between women and men within occupational groups, the wages of women are anywhere between 58% and 84% those of men, but are always lower. Gaps tend to be a bit smaller in professional occupations, especially those such as teaching and health where women hold the most jobs. It is striking that men earn much more than women in the lower-paid sales and service occupations as well as in non-professional office jobs. This is probably because they are much more likely to work full-time, but also because they hold the better full-time jobs.

Annual Earnings of Women and Men

In 2001, women earned an average of $24,688 or 64% of the average $38,431 earned by men.[7] Women working full-time for the full year earned an average of $35,258 or 72% of the $49,250 earned by men working full-time for the whole year. The earnings gap is smallest for younger women and single women, reflecting the fact that the presence of children makes a big difference.

From 1980 until the mid-1990s, the real (inflation-adjusted) annual earnings of men were quite stagnant, while slowly rising for women.

Figure 5.2, Female/Male Earnings Ratios for Full-Time/Full-Year Workers, shows the annual earnings of women full-time, full-year workers as a percentage of those of comparable men for each year since 1980. This is the key number that has been traditionally used to chart pay gaps. The trend is clear. From 1980 until the mid-1990s, the pay gap was closing. Since that time, it has started to widen again, especially for the most highly educated women. In 2001, university-educated women earned just 67.5% as much as university-educated men, down from 75.9% in 1995. The gap for all women has widened only modestly over the same period. How can this trend for pay gaps to widen among the highly educated be explained? A key factor seems likely to have been the fact that, as shown in Chapter 2, earnings gains have been concentrated among the very highest-paid people, who tend to be men.

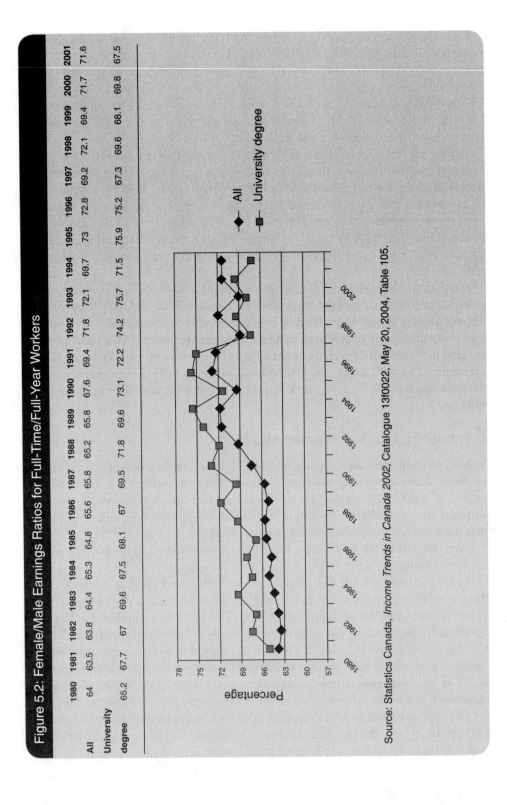

Figure 5.2: Female/Male Earnings Ratios for Full-Time/Full-Year Workers

	1980	1981	1982	1983	1984	1985	1986	1987	1988	1989	1990	1991	1992	1993	1994	1995	1996	1997	1998	1999	2000	2001
All	64	63.5	63.8	64.4	65.3	64.8	65.6	65.8	65.2	65.8	67.6	69.4	71.8	72.1	69.7	73	72.8	69.2	72.1	69.4	71.7	71.6
University degree	65.2	67.7	67	69.6	67.5	68.1	67	69.5	71.8	69.6	73.1	72.2	74.2	75.7	71.5	75.9	75.2	67.3	69.6	68.1	69.8	67.5

Source: Statistics Canada, *Income Trends in Canada 2002*, Catalogue 13f0022, May 20, 2004, Table 105.

Figure 5.3: Distribution of Annual Earnings of Women and Men in 2001

	Men	Women
Under $5,000	11.8	15.7
$5,000–9,999	8.7	13.5
$10,000–14,999	6.7	11.5
$15,000–19,999	6.8	9.5
$20,000–24,999	6.7	8.8
$25,000–29,999	6.9	8.4
$30,000–34,999	6.8	8.3
$35,000–39,999	6.4	6.1
$40,000–44,999	6.4	4.8
$45,000–49,999	5.5	3.3
$50,000–59,999	8.8	4.4
$60,000 and over	18.4	5.7

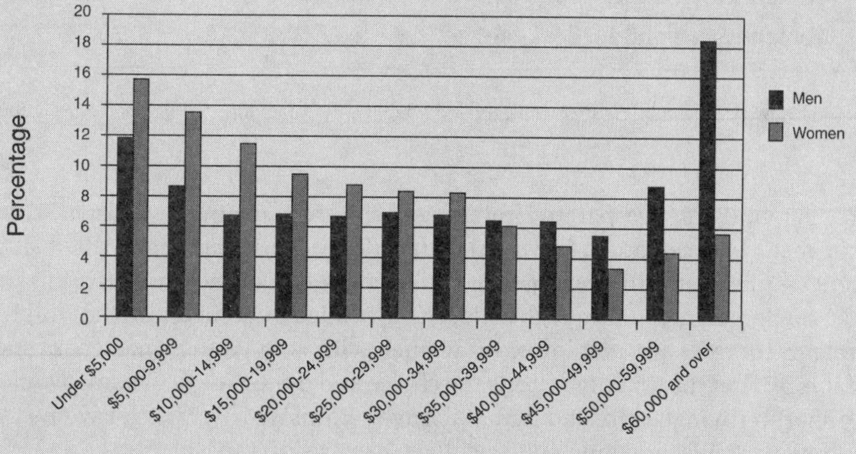

Source: Statistics Canada, *Income Trends in Canada 2002*, Catalogue 13f0022, May 20, 2004,

Low earnings of many women are a major part of the explanation for very high poverty rates among single-parent families headed by women. Low earnings for women are also a big factor behind low family incomes, since high-earning men now tend to live with higher-earning women. This is a phenomenon that has come to be called homogamy, or the tendency of likes to live together. Of course, a layer of well-paid men can support spouses who do not work or work only part-time, but this is much less common than a generation ago.

Figure 5.3, Distribution of Annual Earnings of Women and Men in 2001, indicates that there is a higher proportion of women than men in all earnings brackets until an income level of $35,000 to $40,000 is reached. At an annual earnings level of $60,000, men predominate in a proportion of three to one. Roughly one in five men earns more than $60,000 compared to only slightly more than one in twenty women. That is why the trend to higher earnings for high earners seems to be reversing the trend for the pay gap to close.

Work-Family Balance

Table 5.3: Employment of Women with Children

	1990	1995	2002	Percentage of Which Were Full-Time in 2002
Employment rate				
Women with a child < 16	63.2%	64.2%	71.5%	73.3%
Women with a child < 6	56.1%	58.3%	64.9%	70.8%

Source: Statistics Canada, *Guide to the Labour Force Survey*, Catalogue 71-543, February 17, 2004.

Three in four (73%) two-parent families with children are now two-earner families. While many women (and a few men) with children work part-time, half of all two-parent families with children have two full-time earners. And, more than six in ten (63%) single-parent families with children are headed by someone in the workforce. Employment rates are a bit lower for women with very young children, as shown in Table 5.3, but this mainly reflects the choice and opportunity of some women to take short-term maternity and parental leaves. Employment rates for women with children, particularly young children, have been rising rapidly.

Many women must deal with unstable and unpredictable work schedules. There has also been an increase in unsocial hours in the 1990s, with more women and men working at night and on weekends. More women are also now working very long hours. About one in seven works more than 41 hours per week. Unpredictable or long hours, combined with high and rising job demands, cause acute stress for many women, in large part because women still bear the major responsibility for domestic labour (child care, elder care, household maintenance, etc.). Increased family working time has been a critical factor in maintaining real incomes in a labour market marked by more precarious employment and stagnating wages, but the resulting pressures on women in terms of balancing work and family are significant and greater than in many other countries because of the relative underdevelopment of publicly financed and delivered early childhood, elder care, and home care programs.

Conclusion

Some women are making progress in the job market as professional jobs have opened up to the highly educated, but many other women are dealing with precarious and low-paid employment. Disturbingly, the pay and opportunity gap between working women and men, which had been closing until the mid-1990s, has recently started to grow. The fact that women still bear the primary responsibility for child and elder care, and are relatively excluded from some higher-paying jobs, helps account for these gaps.

● ●

Questions for Critical Thought

1. Can women ever achieve full equality with men in the job market if caregiving responsibilities are not equally divided between women and men?
2. Is it reasonable to expect that part-time jobs could provide the same pay and job opportunities as full-time jobs?
3. To what extent do you think that the high level of occupational segregation between women and men is a product of discrimination, as opposed to different choices made by women and men?
4. How do you think gender shapes the kind of choices women and men make about jobs and careers?
5. Why do you think the long trend toward a smaller pay gap between women and men may have come to an end in recent years?

Recommended Reading

Armstrong, Pat, and Hugh Armstrong. 1994. *The Double Ghetto: Canadian Women and Their Segregated Work*. Toronto: McClelland & Stewart. Now a little dated in terms of data, but a good treatment of the key differences between the jobs of women and men and of the relationship between paid work and domestic work.

Drolet, Marie. 2002. "The Male-Female Wage Gap." *Perspectives on Labour and Income* (Spring): 29–37. A Statistics Canada summary of trends in, and causes of, the pay gap between women and men.

Organisation for Economic Co-operation and Development (OECD). 2002. "Women at Work: Who Are They and How Are They Doing?" *OECD Employment Outlook,*

61–125. Provides a wealth of information that shows how Canadian women are faring in the job market compared to women in other countries.

Vosko, Leah. 2000. *Temporary Work: The Gendered Rise of a Precarious Employment Relationship*. Toronto: University of Toronto Press. Explains how gender has structured changing forms of employment and shaped the quality of jobs, with a major focus on the rise of precarious work.

Wilson, S.J. 1996. *Women, Families, and Work*, 4th ed. Toronto: McGraw-Hill Ryerson Limited. A useful source of further analysis.

■Notes

1. *OECD Employment Outlook* (Paris: OECD, 2003), Table B.
2. Statistics Canada, *Income in Canada* CD-ROM. 2001. Table T105.
3. Statistics Canada, *Income in Canada* CD-ROM. 2001. Table T101.
4. Data from Statistics Canada, *Workplace and Employee Survey* (Ottawa: Statistics Canada).
5. Data from Statistics Canada, *Survey of Work Arrangements* (Ottawa: Statistics Canada, 1993).
6. Data from Statistics Canada, *Survey of Self-Employment* (Ottawa: Statistics Canada).
7. Statistics Canada, *Income in Canada* CD-ROM. 2001. Table T101.

■References

Beaujot, Roderic. 2004. *Delayed Life Transitions: Trends and Implications*. The Vanier Institute of the Family <http://www.vifamily.ca>.

Broad, Dave, and Fern Hagin. 2002. *Women, Part-Time Work and Labour Standards: The Case of Saskatchewan*. Regina: Social Policy Research Unit, University of Regina.

Drolet, Marie. 2002. "The Male-Female Wage Gap." *Perspectives on Labour and Income* (Spring): 29–37.

Duffy, Ann, and Norene Pupo. 1992. *Part-Time Paradox: Connecting Gender, Work and Family*. Toronto: McClelland & Stewart.

Fudge, Judy, Eric Tucker, and Leah Vosko. 2002. *The Legal Concept of Employment: Marginalizing Workers*. Report for the Law Commission of Canada. Ottawa.

Government of Canada. 2004. Pay Equity Task Force Final Report. *Pay Equity: A New Approach to a Fundamental Right*. Ottawa.

Lochead, Clarence. 2000. "The Trend to Delayed First Childbirth." *ISUMA: Canadian Journal of Policy Research* (Autumn): 41–44.

Organisation for Economic Co-operation and Development (OECD). 2002. "Women at Work: Who Are They and How Are They Doing?" *OECD Employment Outlook*, 61–125. Paris: OECD.

_____. 2004. *Developing Highly Skilled Workers: Review of Canada*. Directorate for
   Science, Technology and Industry. Paris: OECD.

Vosko, Leah, Nancy Zukewich, and Cynthia Cranford. 2003. "Precarious Jobs:
   A New Typology of Employment." *Perspectives on Labour and Income*, 16–26.
   Ottawa: Statistics Canada.

CHAPTER SIX

Minorities in the Workforce

Workers of Colour and Recent Immigrants,
Aboriginal Canadians, and Persons with Disabilities

▮Introduction

This chapter reviews recent evidence on the quality of jobs, on income, and on the incidence of poverty for minorities in the workforce. Under the federal *Employment Equity Act*, four major groups are designated as likely to experience discrimination in employment: women, visible minorities (defined as non-Aboriginal people who are non-White in colour and non-Caucasian in race); Aboriginal peoples, and persons with disabilities. These are, of course, very different groups, but all experience poor labour market conditions and outcomes compared to the Canadian norm, and employment or lack of it is one of the major factors at play behind higher rates of poverty. While not explaining everything, discrimination is one of the factors at play.

In her Royal Commission on Equality report, Judge Rosalie Abella stated that discrimination ... means practices or attitudes that have, whether by design or impact, the effect of limiting an individual or group's right to the opportunities generally available because of attributable rather than actual characteristics. What is impeding the full development of potential is not the individual's capacity but an external barrier.

These barriers can be intentional, as in overt racism in hiring and promotion decisions, or they can be the by-product of discriminatory systems and procedures. The failure to properly appraise foreign skills and credentials or the job experiences of new immigrants is one example. The failure to see beyond a disability to the talents of an individual job applicant is also a barrier to equal opportunity. Barriers include a failure to accommodate differences, as in lack of provision for employment supports such as special devices for persons with disabilities, or a refusal to recognize religious beliefs that may depart from the norm. Disadvantage in the job market also flows from the frequent but more subtle practice of giving preference in hiring and promotion to job applicants from the same gender, social background, and networks as the person doing the hiring. This is particularly the case in periods of high unemployment when many qualified applicants are available to fill vacant jobs.

Often employment equity laws and practices simply require a formalized and transparent hiring and promotion process so that individual applicants are judged on their individual merits. In the case of Canada, employment equity laws are limited in scope, covering mainly only public-sector and some very large private-sector employers in a few jurisdictions. Pay equity laws, requiring equal pay for equal work of equal value, cover many more workers, but are almost always limited to differences in pay between full-time men and women workers, and do not apply to workers from other disadvantaged groups.

Chapter 8 details the impacts of unions on the pay and employment of minorities, which are positive and significant. In a more general way, minority workers probably benefit from being employed in larger workplaces and enterprises that have relatively formalized pay grids, hiring processes, and job ladders. Once hired into stable, full-time, permanent jobs, minority workers probably experience less discrimination than in the job market as a whole. This underlines one of the key problems, which is that minority workers are more likely to be employed in unstable and precarious jobs.

■ Visible Minorities and New Immigrants in the Workforce

The term "visible minority people" is used in statistical surveys and legislation, usually on the basis of the self-identification of the individual involved. The term "workers of colour" is used interchangeably in this chapter, and is preferable in the sense that minorities constitute the vast majority of the world's peoples and will soon become the collective majority in some of our big cities. Some activists prefer the term "racialized workers" to signal that race is not an objective biological fact or valid scientific concept, but a social and cultural construct.

Immigration from non-traditional source countries in the 1980s and 1990s has dramatically changed the face of Canada and the Canadian labour force. Data from the 2001 Census, the main source of information for this section of the chapter, show that 13.4% of the population now belong to visible minority groups, up from just 4.7% in 1981 and 9.0% in 1990. Their share is expected to grow to 20% by 2016. The visible minority share of the working-age population today is slightly smaller than their share of the whole population, just below 13%, because recent immigrant families tend to be younger than average and have more children. The largest visible minority communities are people of Chinese origin (26% of all visible minority people); of South Asian origin (e.g., people from India, Pakistan, Bangladesh, Sri Lanka, and Asian Africans) who make up 23% of the total; and Blacks (17%). Other visible minority people come from a very wide range of other countries, and include Arabs, Filipinos, Latin Americans, and Vietnamese and other Southeast Asians.[1] Many of these groups are themselves very diverse. For example, the Chinese communities in Canada include descendants of 19th-century immigrants, as well as recent immigrants from both Hong Kong and mainland China. The Black community includes those who escaped slavery in the U.S. 150 years ago, West Indian immigrants from the 1950s and 1960s, and new immigrants from Africa and the Caribbean. Some studies suggest that Blacks and South Asians are most vulnerable to racial discrimination.

Virtually all of the growth of the Canadian labour force now comes from immigration. According to Citizenship and Immigration Canada, 70% of the net growth of the Canadian labour force in the first half of the 1990s was the result of immigration, and all of the net growth of the labour force is expected to come from immigration by 2011. If it were not for new arrivals to Canada, we would soon see an even more rapidly aging workforce and fewer labour force entrants than retirees. New immigrants can help fill some major looming shortages of skilled workers. Clearly, our economic future as a country very much depends upon successfully integrating newcomers into the Canadian labour market. Indeed, the Conference Board of Canada calculates that the successful inclusion of visible minorities into the workforce could give a very significant boost to economic growth over the next decade and more (Conference Board of Canada 2004).

There is a large but not complete overlap between the two categories of "recent immigrants" and "visible minorities." About three in every four new immigrants to Canada since the late 1980s have belonged to a visible minority group, the result of a big shift in the traditional source countries of Canadian immigration, from Europe to Asia and, to a lesser extent, other regions of the world. Due to continuing high levels of immigration, about one in five Canadians (18.4%) was born in another country. This is the highest proportion in the world other than Australia, and much higher than in the U.S. or Europe. While new immigrants are drawn mainly from visible minority groups, about two-thirds of the visible minority population were either born in Canada (one-third) or arrived in Canada before 1990. In short, the experiences of new immigrants in the job market are not the only factors behind the experience of all visible minority workers. The great majority of both visible minority people and new immigrants live in the three largest urban centres of the country—the Greater Toronto Area, Montreal, and Vancouver, and more than 40% live in Greater Toronto alone.

Visible minority workers, or workers of colour, are, on average, paid significantly less and have less job security than other workers, despite much higher than average levels of education. While some of these workers with high levels of education have moved into good, professional jobs, many others with good qualifications are trapped in low-pay, insecure, no-future jobs. Workers of colour are disproportionately employed in jobs requiring lower levels of skills and education, despite higher-than-average qualifications. The fact that many visible minority workers (about one-third) are relatively recent immigrants is often used to explain away these large gaps in economic status compared to the native born. Advocates of the catch-up theory say that economic differences based on race will disappear as immigrants gain more Canadian job experience and move into the mainstream, just like previous White European immigrants. But, the fact of the matter is that economic gaps between immigrants and all other Canadians have widened as immigrants have been increasingly drawn from minority racial groups. Immigrants used to catch up quickly, but racialized people who came to Canada in the 1980s have still not caught up.

Recent immigrants are more highly educated than other Canadians, and more highly educated than previous immigrants. Like earlier generations of immigrants, they are younger than the general population, and have come to Canada to seek new economic opportunities. But economic gaps have still grown, and visible minority workers who are not immigrants, but were born in Canada and educated in Canada, still have lower earnings than comparable Canadian workers. Large and growing gaps of income and opportunity are at least partly explained, not by real differences in education and skills, but by racial discrimination. As Grace-Edward Galabuzi (2001) has eloquently and convincingly argued, economists and social analysts are frequently blind to the reality of racial discrimination, particularly the effects of racism, which is systemic, institutional, and cultural. He argues that the evidence of major economic gaps based upon race demands that Canadians stop denying the reality of racism and take concrete actions to counter exclusion and marginalization.

Figure 6.1: Average Annual Earnings of Visible Minorities and All Canadians in 2000

Average Annual Employment Income in 2000

	All	% Average	Men	Male % Average	Women	Female % Average
All Earners	$31,757	100%	$38,347	100%	$24,390	100%
Visible Minorities - All	$27,149	85.5%	$31,623	82.5%	$22,301	91.4%
Visible Minorities - Canadian Born	$22,781	71.7%	$25,701	67.0%	$19,737	80.9%
Chinese	$28,846	90.8%	$33,350	87.0%	$24,069	98.7%
South Asian	$28,072	88.4%	$33,222	86.6%	$21,610	88.6%
Black	$25,156	79.2%	$28,441	74.2%	$21,984	90.1%
Immigrants - 1990-94	$25,560	80.5%	$30,292	79.0%	$20,553	84.3%
Immigrants - 1995-99	$23,889	75.2%	$29,014	75.7%	$18,113	74.3%

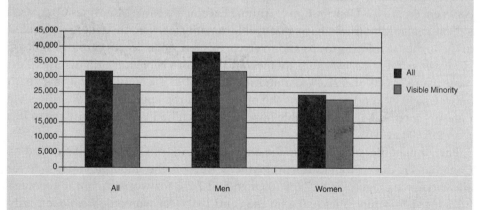

Source: Statistics Canada, *Statistical Area Classification: Highlight Tables, 2001 Counts, For Canada, Provinces and Territories*, 2001 Census, Catalogue 97f0024, February 27, 2004.

■ Pay and Employment Gaps Today

The last Census showed that the average annual earnings of all visible minority workers was $27,149 or 85.5% of the average for all earners.[2] The gap was even bigger for visible minority workers born in Canada who earned an average of $22,781 (or 71.7% of the average) and for new immigrants. Blacks fell further below the average than Chinese and South Asians (79.2% compared to 90.8% and 88.4%). The earnings gap is bigger for visible minority men (who earn 82.5% of the Canadian average) than it is for visible minority women (who earn 91.4% of the Canadian average). This may be because pay gaps are lowest in the public sector, where more women work, and, perhaps, because many women of colour are employed in underground jobs, such as nannies, cleaners, and home-based sewing, where low earnings are not reflected in the data. While the pay gap for women minority workers is smaller than for men, their earnings are still very low.

Workers of colour are also less likely to hold jobs providing pension plan coverage. In 1999, 35.3% workers of colour were in jobs with pension plans compared to 42.2% of all workers. For men, the difference was 36.0% compared to 45.3%; for women it was 34.4% compared to 38.8%.[3] More precarious jobs mean an interrupted earnings history, a reduced ability to save, and reduced Canada/Quebec Pension Plan contributions toward future benefits. In combination with low employer pension plan coverage, this means that many workers of colour will likely be more vulnerable to low income in old age.

Averages are, of course, made up of high earners, low earners, and those in between. Figure 6.2, Distribution of Annual Earnings: Visible Minorities Compared to Non-Visible Minorities, shows that visible minority workers are under-represented in the higher earnings groups and overrepresented in the lower earnings groups. However, 6.5% of visible minority men and 2.0% of visible minority women earn more than $75,000, and 22.4% of minority men and 13.4% of minority women earn between $40,000 and $75,000. At the other end of the spectrum, 31.9% of visible minority men and 42.2% of visible minority women had very low earnings of less than $15,000 in 2000.

Part of the difference between the annual earnings of visible minorities and all Canadians is due to higher unemployment. In 2000, the unemployment rate for all workers averaged 7.4% (7.6% for men and 7.2% for women), but it averaged 9.5% for visible minorities (9.0% for men and 10.0% for women). Visible minority workers are thus more likely to experience earnings interruptions, but the main factor in the pay gap is that visible minority workers are more likely to hold lower-paid jobs. Reflecting higher-than-average levels of education (discussed below), visible minority workers are actually slightly overrepresented in professional jobs, but they are under-represented in management jobs as well as in relatively well-paid skilled manual jobs, and are overrepresented in lower-paid clerical sales and services jobs.

Figure 6.2: Distribution of Annual Earnings: Visible Minorities Compared to Non-Visible Minorities

Distribution of Annual Earnings of Visible Minorities and Non-Visible Minorities

	Non-visible minority men	Visible minority men	Non-visible minority women	Visible minority women
<$15,000	25.7%	31.9%	39.4%	42.2%
$15,000–25,000	13.1%	17.1%	18.5%	20.5%
$25,000–40,000	21.1%	22.2%	22.6%	21.8%
$40,000–75,000	30.3%	22.4%	17.2%	13.4%
>$75,000	9.8%	6.5%	2.5%	2.0%

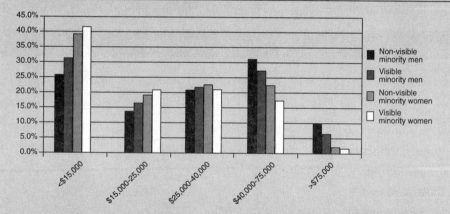

Source: Statistics Canada, *Statistical Area Classification: Highlight Tables, 2001 Counts, For Canada, Provinces and Territories*, 2001 Census, Catalogue 97f0024, February 27, 2004.

▉The Role of Education

Strikingly, the Census clearly showed that visible minority workers are more highly educated than all other Canadian workers. As shown in Table 6.1, 20.4% of visible minority people over 15 have an undergraduate university qualification compared to 13.1% of all Canadians, and 7.1% compared to 4.8% have a post-graduate qualification. At the other end of the spectrum, a smaller proportion of visible minority people in the working-age population have failed to complete high school. Higher educational qualifications than average for visible minority people reflect the

Box 6.1: Economic Security of Visible Minority Workers

Each year, the Canadian Council on Social Development (CCSD) publishes The Personal Security Index (PSI) based, in part, on the results of a nationally representative public opinion survey. The PSI measures fear of job loss by asking the question: "I think there is a good chance I could lose my job over the next couple of years." (Respondents agree or disagree on a scale of 1–7.) Among visible minority workers with jobs in late 2001, about one in three (34.0%) strongly agreed that they could lose their jobs over the next couple of years compared to one in four (25.8%) other people with jobs; 44.6% strongly disagreed that they could lose their jobs over the next couple of years, much less than 64.3% of other people with jobs. The PSI also measures confidence in employability by asking the question: "If I lost my job, I am confident that I could find an equivalent one within six months." Among visible minority respondents, 37.8% strongly disagreed they could find an equivalent job in six months compared to 28.8% of other respondents; 42.8% strongly agreed they could find an equivalent job, well below the 57.9% of other respondents who strongly agreed.

Table 6.1: Education of Visible Minorities and All Canadians, Compared

	All	Visible Minority
Less than high school	31.3%	28.0%
High school	14.1%	12.5%
Some post-secondary	10.8%	13.1%
Trades certificate or diploma	10.9%	6.6%
College diploma	15.0%	12.3%
University qualification/undergraduate	13.1%	20.4%
M.A. or Ph.D.	4.8%	7.1%

Source: Statistics Canada, *Statistical Area Classification: Highlight Tables, 2001 Counts, For Canada, Provinces and Territories*, 2001 Census, Catalogue 97f0024, February 27, 2004.

fact that a high proportion of recent immigrants are very highly educated. Indeed, for the majority of newcomers who are selected by Citizenship and Immigration Canada rather than arrive as refugees or as family-class immigrants, it is almost impossible to get enough points to be selected without either high qualifications or significant work experience in a high-skill occupation. Yet average annual earnings of new immigrants with university degrees ($31,758) fall far short of those of non-immigrants with degrees ($50,306).

■Explaining Pay and Earnings Gaps

It is clear that there is a very fundamental disconnection or contradiction between the skills and qualifications of visible minority workers, at least as indicated by education, and their pay compared to the Canadian majority. One factor at play is clearly the fact that many, though by no means all, minority workers are relatively recent immigrants. It might be expected that it would take newcomers some time to catch up to the Canadian-born, and indeed there has always been an earnings gap between newcomers and the Canadian-born. However, this gap has grown significantly over the past 25 years.

In 1980, male immigrants earned 13% less than the native-born one year after arrival, but the gap is now 31%. The trend is similar for women. Immigrants who arrived in Canada in the 1970s caught up to the Canadian average after 15 years in the country, but newcomers who arrived in the 1980s are still about 12% behind the average (Frenette and Morissette 2003). In the 1990s, the average annual earnings of family-class immigrants and refugees have been only about one-half the national average one year after landing (Grant and Thompson 2001). This may partly reflect the fact that these groups were not selected by immigration officials for their ability to integrate quickly into the Canadian job market and may have limited ability in the English or French language. However, average annual earnings of economic immigrants to Canada who were principal applicants have averaged about one-sixth less than annual earnings of all Canadians one year after landing. About one-half of immigrants entering the labour force are economic immigrants selected for their education, job experience, and language ability. While the gap between economic immigrants and the rest of the population is smaller than for all immigrants, it is still significant and surprisingly large. Economic immigrants actually earned more than the Canadian average in the 1970s and early 1980s when the composition of the immigration population was much more White and European.

The earnings gap has widened and the period of catch-up has grown longer even though the educational gap between immigrants and the Canadian-born has widened in favour of immigrants. Not only are new immigrants and visible minority workers more highly educated than average, their advantage has grown as new immigrants have become even more highly educated than the Canadian-born over the past 20 years (Frenette and Morissette 2003). Part of the reason for the growth of earnings gaps between new immigrants and the rest of the population is the fact that, for much of the 1990s, there was little new hiring into the kinds of workplaces that provide secure and reasonably well-paid jobs. Like young workers, new immigrants have been more likely to find jobs in smaller, non-union workplaces than in large corporations or the public sector. The lack of new hiring excluded many workers of colour from good initial entry jobs and from internal job-promotion ladders. As the economy began to grow strongly in the late 1990s, recent immigrants began to

Box 6.2: "We Are Capable People"

By Marina Jimenez

It is a great irony to many in the immigration field, and to newcomers themselves, a bitter joke. Canada has a shortage of skilled professionals, and yet thousands of internationally trained doctors, engineers, teachers, and nurses are forced to deliver pizzas and drive taxis.

Some immigrants believe that this is intentional, that Canada wants them only for their genetic potential. They may sweep floors and clean offices, but their offspring will be intelligent and creative. Why else would the government accept them and then make it so very difficult to have their credentials recognized?

Citizenship and Immigration Canada bristles at such a suggestion, and advises immigrants to check the ministry's Website, which clearly warns newcomers there is no guarantee they will find work in their chosen profession.

Still, frustration is mounting: This week, a British-trained accountant and his bookkeeper wife launched a lawsuit against the federal government, alleging that they were misled by immigration officials who assured them they would find good jobs here. Instead, the couple—he is originally from Sri Lanka and she from Malaysia—have spent five years in Edmonton shovelling snow, cleaning toilets, and borrowing money to support their teenaged son.

"What angers me is we are capable people. We have the credentials. We just can't get the jobs," complained Selladurai Premakumaran, who feels the government has shattered his hopes and dreams.

Last year, when Canada changed the way it selects immigrants, many were happy to see the end of the old system, which matched newcomers with worker shortages.

Critics had long complained that, by the time the physiotherapists and teachers arrived, those jobs had been filled and the labour shortages were in other fields.

Now, Canada chooses immigrants based not on their occupation, but on their education, skills, and language abilities. Applicants must score 67 of a possible 100 points to be accepted. Ostensibly, being talented and smart should make them more employable.

But it isn't working out that way. Canada is recruiting the right kind of people, but they are stuck in a bottleneck, as the agencies and bodies that regulate the fields of medicine, engineering, teaching, and nursing struggle to assess their qualifications.

"We have a disaster on our hands," says Joan Atlin, executive director of the Association of International Physicians and Surgeons of Ontario.

"There are thousands of un- and under-employed foreign professionals across the country. At the same time, we have a shortage of skilled professionals, especially in the health-care field. We don't so much have a doctor shortage as an assessment and licensing bottleneck."

About 1,300 doctors from more than 80 countries have joined the association she heads, but she estimates there are many more out there. Ontario alone may have as many as 4,000, most of them still trying to get their medical licences.

At the same time, there is a shortage of as many as 3,000 physicians across the country, especially in smaller communities in Alberta, British Columbia, Saskatchewan, and Ontario (provinces that have been forced to recruit doctors from South Africa, whose medical training Canada considers acceptable).

A recent Statistics Canada study of 164,200 immigrants who arrived in 2000 and 2001 found that 70 per cent had problems entering the labour force. Six in every 10 were forced to take jobs other than those they were trained to do. The two most common occupational groups for men were science (natural and applied) and management, but most wound up working in sales and service or processing and manufacturing.

Patrick Coady, with the British Columbia Internationally Trained Professionals Network, believes that far too many engineers are coming—as many as 60 per cent of all those accepted each year. (In Ontario, from 1997 to 2001, nearly 40,000 immigrants listed engineering as their occupation.)

"When they arrive, the Engineering Council for Canada evaluates their credentials, which sets up the engineer to think there are opportunities here," Mr. Coady says. "Then they discover that each province has a body that regulates the industry. They need up to 18 months of Canadian work experience before they will get professional engineering status. And, there isn't a great need for consulting engineers. A lot of the infrastructure has already been built in this country."

Michael Wu, a geotechnical engineer from China, is a classic example of what's happening. Accepted as a landed immigrant last spring, he came here with his wife and child, leaving behind a relatively prosperous life in Beijing, and now works for $7 an hour in a Vancouver chocolate factory.

Back in Beijing, "I had a three-bedroom apartment and took taxis everywhere—the Chinese government sent me to build a stadium in St Lucia," says Mr. Wu, who has a PhD. "Here, no-one will hire me. Many engineering companies think engineers make false documents. They are suspicious of my qualifications. I never imagined I'd end up working in a factory. But I will keep trying. Every month I go to the Vancouver Geotechnical Society lecture."

Susan Scarlett of the Immigration Department points out that regulating the professions is a provincial, not federal, responsibility. "We advise people who are thinking of coming to Canada to prepare by really researching how their credentials will be assessed."

Ms. Atlin says that "Canada has been very slow to change. Our regulatory systems have not caught up with our immigration policies."

But some relief may be on the horizon because the issue has become such a political flashpoint.

A national task force is about to report to the deputy minister of health on the licensing of international medical graduates. And this month Denis Coderre, the federal Immigration Minister, announced that he wants to streamline the process of recognizing foreign credentials, and have provinces announce their inventory of needs so Ottawa can work to fill the shortages.

Source: Marina Jimenez, "We Are Capable People," *The Globe and Mail*, October 25, 2003, F9.

slowly close the large earnings and employment gap, though differences still remain well above the level of the early 1980s.

The evidence suggests that racial discrimination, overt or systemic, helps explain pay gaps between new immigrants and visible minorities as a whole and the rest of the Canadian workforce. The significant income and employment gaps between new immigrants and other Canadians are greatest among the recent immigrants who belong to visible minority groups (Canadian Race Relations Foundation 2000; Galabuzi 2001). As immigrants as a group have become more racially diverse, and as the proportion of minority immigrants has grown, the traditional catch-up period compared to the Canadian-born majority has also become longer and longer. Minority immigrants who came to Canada in the 1980s have still not caught up, and probably will never do so.

Barriers to employment equity for minority immigrants include the fact that many employers and professional associations do not recognize foreign skills and qualifications, and are unwilling to help train even workers who could quickly upgrade their existing skills to meet the requirements of a vacant job. Many employers and professional associations refuse to recognize foreign job experience at all. High unemployment through much of the 1990s has meant that employers have often had a large pool of qualified candidates with Canadian credentials and Canadian job experience to fill openings. Minority workers are likely to be excluded from consideration in such a context, particularly in the private sector where very few employers are covered by employment-equity legislation requiring a formalized, fair, and inclusive hiring and promotion process. Strong job growth and low unemployment do counter racial discrimination to a certain extent by forcing employers to look for hidden skills, and this showed up in a decline in the earnings gaps in very recent years compared to the mid-1990s.

Research by Statistics Canada suggests that employers tend to ignore and discount foreign work experience more than foreign educational credentials (Aydemir and Skuterud 2004). On average, non-minority immigrants from traditional source countries gain a small wage premium for their work experience, but this premium does not exist at all for immigrants from non-traditional source countries. Also, the wage premium for higher education is lower for immigrants from non-traditional source countries compared to traditional source countries. Thus, a new immigrant doctor or engineer or architect from India or China fares much worse than a similarly qualified immigrant professional from the U.S., Britain, or France. While part of the problem may simply be ignorance of the value of work experience in non-traditional source countries, it is hard not to believe that some element of discrimination is at play.

Ignoring foreign skills and experience is very costly. A recent study by the Conference Board of Canada found that 540,000 Canadian workers lose between $8,000 and $12,000 per year in potential earnings because of unrecognized learning credentials, and that the annual cost of the learning recognition gap is between $4.1 and $5.9 billion (Bloom and Grant 2001). The study shows that half (47%) of unrecognized learners belong to visible minority groups, and that 340,000 Canadians have unrecognized foreign post-secondary degrees and diplomas. They provide a striking example: only 56% of engineers who settled in Canada in the first half of the 1990s found work as engineers. Barriers to hiring result in a vicious circle because even highly skilled immigrants are often unable to gain Canadian experience, and then see their skills erode over time. Contributing to this vicious circle, immigrant settlement programs provide only limited language training and little hands-on job search assistance. Many minority immigrants thus find themselves trapped in low-wage, insecure, no-future survival jobs.

The existence of racism as a key factor in pay and employment gaps is often denied, but the existence of racial barriers to employment has been well documented in hundreds if not thousands of complaints to employment equity and human rights tribunals, and in public opinion surveys. People who want to explain away pay and employment gaps based on race claim that differences do not reflect overt or more subtle forms of racial discrimination, but rather hidden differences in job qualifications as well as differences in language skills between immigrants and the Canadian-born. However, as noted above, pay gaps between visible minorities and other Canadians are actually greatest for minorities who are Canadian-born and educated. A recent study has found that graduates from Canadian universities and colleges who belong to minority groups are less likely than other graduates to find jobs after graduation, and are paid less than their fellow graduates when taking their level of qualifications and field of study into account.[4] Minority graduates are more likely to graduate in high-demand fields in the job market, but still experience greater difficulties finding good jobs. *Unequal Access,* a study for the Canadian Race Relations Foundation based on 1996 Census data, similarly made systematic comparisons between workers of colour born and educated in Canada, and other Canadian-born people. The younger generation of minority workers born in Canada (aged 25 to 34 in 1996) were found to be much more highly educated than non-minority Canadians of the same age group. Almost half (47.5%) held university degrees compared to one-quarter (26.6%) of others, and just one in 10 (9.8%) had failed to complete high school compared to 18.2% of others. Immigrants value education, and second-generation immigrants tend to do very well in our educational system.

However, despite far higher levels of Canadian education, the annual earnings of visible minority younger workers born and educated in Canada are no higher than other workers of the same age group. As one would expect, highly educated visible minority workers tend to be employed in skilled and professional jobs, but they have had major difficulties climbing career leaders on a basis of equality with their peers. The Race Relations Foundation study finds that just 36.5% of male, Canadian-born, visible minority workers with a university education were in the top 20% of all income earners in 1996 compared to 49.8% of non-minority, university-educated men. The gap was smaller, but still present, among women.

■Some Implications of the Racial Earnings Gap for Social Inclusion

Canadian population growth and patterns of urban growth have been enormously influenced by new immigration, which now greatly eclipses both natural population growth and internal migration as sources of population change. As urban geographer Larry Bourne notes, "the combination of declining rates of natural increase and highly focused immigration flows has divided the country into declining and growing places more sharply than in the past, and into communities that are increasingly homogeneous or increasingly heterogeneous in social characteristics" (Bourne 2004). New immigrants and racial minorities are highly concentrated in our three largest cities, and lower-income minorities are increasingly concentrated in low-income neighbourhoods in these cities. This gives rise to the disturbing prospect that Canada may be moving in the direction of U.S.-style concentrated urban poverty among racial minorities.

Rates of poverty are disturbingly high among new urban immigrants and visible minorities, largely due to low earnings and larger-than-average families. The 2001 Census found that the low-income rate for all Canadians (percentage with income below the after-tax LICO) was 12.8%, but 27.2% for visible minority people (with little variation by major racial groups); 26.9% for immigrants who arrived between 1990 and 1994; and 33.9% for immigrants who arrived between 1995 and 1999. The Low Income Cut-off for a family of four in a big city in 2000 was $29,163. The risk of poverty among recent immigrants has increased sharply from 1.4 times the national average in 1980 to 2.5 times the national average in 2000, and low-income immigrants are likely to remain in poverty for a considerable period of time. Increased poverty among immigrants, including those who have been here for up to 15 years, has been the major driving force behind the increase in urban poverty among all Canadians over the 1980s and 1990s (Picot and Hou 2003). If anything, Statistics Canada data understate immigrant poverty since low-income lines are set in relation to living costs (including housing) in all large urban areas, while new immigrants and minorities are concentrated in Toronto and Vancouver where rents are well above the urban average.

Over the 1990s, there has been an increased concentration of low-income households in low-income neighbourhoods in our big cities, and many very low-income neighbourhoods have a very high proportion of new immigrant and minority residents (Hou and Picot 2003). In the case of Toronto, this trend has been well documented in reports for the United Way by the Canadian Council on Social Development. Concentrated poverty worsens the already negative impacts of family poverty on individuals, particularly children, and can create very disadvantaged communities, such as inner city ghettos in the U.S. Low income still remains quite widely dispersed in Canadian cities, many immigrants live in high-income ethnic communities as well as in middle-income and diverse communities, and many low-income minority workers move up the income ladder over time. Still, we run a serious risk of creating very low-income communities that are also highly racialized if the labour market disadvantages of visible minorities and new immigrants are not seriously addressed.

Aboriginal Peoples in the Workforce

Self-identified Aboriginal people make up about 3% of the Canadian population and the Canadian workforce. While this sounds low, the Aboriginal population is younger than average and grew very rapidly, by 22%, from 1996 to 2001. Aboriginal workers will make up a much greater proportion of new entrants to the workforce over the next 20 years, particularly in Western Canada.

The category of Aboriginal peoples is quite mixed and includes treaty status Indians on reserves, Métis people, the Inuit, and treaty and non-treaty status Indians living off reserves. Less than one in three (29%) of the Aboriginal population live son reserves, about the same proportion (28%) as those who live in big cities (Mendelson 2004). There is a major ongoing movement to big cities, but big-city residents still account for a relatively small share of the total Aboriginal population, and many people move back and forth between cities, reserves, and rural areas. Most Aboriginal people (43%) live off reserve, but in rural areas and small towns. The majority of the Aboriginal population (62%) live in Western Canada, and the largest urban Aboriginal populations (as a proportion of the total population) are to be found in the prairie cities, notably Winnipeg, Edmonton, Saskatoon, and Regina. That said, other big cities such as Toronto and Montreal also contain significant numbers of Aboriginal residents.

The situation of Aboriginal peoples is incredibly diverse. There are many reserves, especially in rural and remote areas, where the economic base is very limited, very few people have paid work, and incomes are extremely low. The labour force participation rate of the on-reserve population averages just 52% compared to 65% for the off-reserve population. The median income per adult on reserves (half have more and half have less) is just $15,000, and the data for the on-reserve population are not very reliable (some bands refuse to participate in the Census and other surveys). Social conditions on many reserves are appalling, helping to account for a massive difference in life expectancy (seven years for men and five years for women) between Aboriginal peoples and all Canadians. At the other end of the spectrum, there is a small but growing well-educated, urban Aboriginal middle class.

Generalizations are difficult, but Aboriginal people are at a big disadvantage in the job market because many live at a distance from job opportunities, and because average education levels are low. Half (48%) of the Aboriginal population have less than a high school education compared to less than one-third of all Canadians, and just 4% have completed university (compared to 15% of all Canadians). In addition, Aboriginal people often confront discrimination in accessing good jobs, even in resource industries near where they live. The Royal Commission on Aboriginal

Table 6.2: Aboriginal People in the Workforce

	Whole Population	Aboriginal Population	Aboriginal Population as Proportion of Whole Population
Average income of people 15 and over	$29,769	$19,132	0.64
Incidence of low income			
Families	12.9%	31.2%	2.42
Single people	38.0%	55.9%	1.47
Participation rate			
All	66.4%	61.4%	0.92
Men	72.7%	66.8%	0.92
Women	66.4%	56.5%	0.85
Employment rate			
All	61.5%	49.7%	0.81
Men	67.2%	52.5%	0.78
Women	56.1%	47.1%	0.84
Unemployment rate			
All	7.4%	19.1%	2.58
Men	7.6%	21.4%	2.82
Women	7.2%	16.7%	2.32
% of Employed working full-time/full-year			
All	53.9%	40.5%	0.75
Men	59.6%	42.0%	0.70
Women	47.4%	38.9%	0.82
Average employment income full-time/full-year			
All	$43,298	$33,416	0.77
Men	$49,224	$37,370	0.76
Women	$34,892	$28,851	0.83
Average employment income not full-time/full-year			
All	$19,207	$13,795	0.72
Men	$23,370	$16,119	0.69
Women	$15,625	$11,437	0.73

Source: Statistics Canada, *Statistical Area Classification: Highlight Tables, 2001 Counts, For Canada, Provinces and Territories*, 2001 Census, Catalogue 97f0024, February 27, 2004.
Note: Data are for the Aboriginal Identity Population from Aboriginal People of Canada Highlight Series.

Peoples of 1996 identified lack of jobs and discrimination as the main barriers to employment. Good jobs, where they exist, tend to be in public services, in Aboriginal enterprises, and in resource industries that have been prepared to hire and train Aboriginal people.

Table 6.2 provides data for 2000 from the 2001 Census, comparing the Aboriginal and non-Aboriginal population, with separate data for women and men. The average income of Aboriginal people aged 15 and above is just 64% of average, and the low income or poverty rate for families is one in three (31.2%) or 2.4 times the Canadian average. This is due more to low wages and high unemployment than to not working at all. Participation rates are 92% of the Canadian average, while the unemployment rate for Aboriginal people in 2000 was 19.1% or 2.6 times the Canadian average. Aboriginal people are significantly less likely to work full-time for a full year than the general population (40.5% compared to 53.9%) and earn just 77% of the average when they do find such jobs. Compared to the Canadian average, Aboriginal women do slightly better than Aboriginal men, but the incomes of the majority of Aboriginal women who do not work full-time for the full year are, at $11,437, very low.

In sum, Aboriginal people do very badly in the job market, not so much because they do not work, but because they have great difficulty finding permanent, reasonably well-paid jobs. There is some evidence that gaps may be closing with rising educational levels, and as a result of economic development efforts driven by or including Aboriginal people. To a large degree, the job issues facing Aboriginal people are inseparable from the wider economic and social problems facing Aboriginal communities. Community economic development efforts can make a big difference. For example, new mining and resource developments in the North now commonly make efforts to hire Native people, and economic development benefits are sometimes negotiated with Native communities. The federal government supports some Aboriginal-led labour market initiatives, such as the Aboriginal Human Resources Development Council, which was established in 1998.

Box 6.3: What's the Situation for Minorities in My Community?

Statistics Canada have made available on their Web site a wealth of detail from the 2001 Census on employment and incomes of visible minorities, new immigrants, and Aboriginal Canadians on a city-by-city basis. Go to <http://www.statcan.ca> and follow the links from "Census" to "Data" to "Topic Based Tabulations." Enter a search by Census topic—Aboriginal identity or visible minority or immigrants—find the tables you are interested in, and then find data for the city you are interested in on the tables where this level of detail is available.

▉Persons with Disabilities

As proposed by the World Health Organization, people are considered to have a disability if they have a physical or mental condition or a health problem that restricts their ability to perform activities that are normal for their age in Canadian society. Recent evidence (for 2001, from Statistics Canada's *Participation and Activity Limitation Survey*) shows that one in ten working-age Canadians has a disability, of whom about 40%, or about 4% of the whole working-age population, experienced a severe or very severe activity limitation.

Disability rates rise significantly with age, and none of us can be certain that we will never experience a major activity limitation over the course of our working lives. More than one in six older workers (people aged 45 to 64) have a disability, partly because of health risks due to increasing age alone, and partly due to injuries or an accumulated lifetime exposure to unhealthy working conditions. Many older workers experience chronic pain arising from repetitive or heavy work or from injuries. Disability rates are slightly higher for women than for men, and are much higher than average among some marginalized groups, notably Aboriginal Canadians. There are many kinds of disability, but physical disabilities involving limitations in mobility or agility are the most common, followed by chronic pain and hearing and vision limitations. Mental disabilities are less common. Frequently, persons with disabilities have more than one source of activity limitation and multiple health problems. Disability can be relatively mild or severe and can also vary greatly in duration. Roughly one-half of all persons with disabilities experience a continuing, long-term disability, while many more working-age Canadians experience a temporary disability, often as the result of workplace injuries, an accident, or a disease that eventually responds to treatment.

The evidence shows, not surprisingly, that working-age persons with disabilities, particularly long-term and severe disabilities, are much less likely to hold jobs than are other Canadians. As shown in Table 6.3, just 44% of the disabled population aged over 15 are employed compared to 78% of the rest of the population. This compares badly to most other industrial countries, including the U.S. and in Europe, where the gap between people reporting disabilities and the rest of the population still exists, but is not as great. Employment rates are particularly low for women with disabilities. Among the core working-age (aged 25 to 54) group, 38% of men and 46% of women with a disability are not in the labour force compared to just 6% of men and 17% of women with no disability.

Many disabled adults are supported by a working spouse or collect reasonable disability benefits from private insurance, but, for many others, exclusion from the job market means poverty. Canada provides modest disability benefits under the Canada/Quebec Pension Plan to some persons with disabilities and limited financial support through various tax credits, but many disabled persons, particularly those without a long work history, rely on social assistance benefits. These almost invariably fall below the poverty line. In the late 1990s, the low-income or poverty rate for persons with disabilities aged 16 to 64 was 25%, or two and one-half times as high as the general population, and persons with disabilities were more than four times as likely to experience long-term poverty (Human Resources Development Canada 2001).

Even when they find jobs, persons with disabilities are significantly less likely to work full-time for the full year than other workers, and have lower hourly wages. Research by the Canadian Council on Social Development (CCSD) shows that the median hourly wage of male workers with disabilities is about 95% of the median wage of workers without a disability, while women with a disability earn just 86% as much as other women (CCSD 2002). As a result, annual earnings of workers with disabilities are, as shown in the table, lower than for the rest of the population. This pay gap partly reflects lower levels of education. Less than one-half of persons with disabilities aged 25 to 54 (46%) have completed some kind of post-secondary education compared to 57% of people of the same age without disabilities. This partly reflects barriers to education facing children and youth with disabilities. However, workers with disabilities are also older and more experienced, and those who surmount barriers to gain jobs might be expected to be paid better than average. A number of submissions to the recent federal government Pay Equity Commission found evidence of discrimination in pay after controlling for differences between workers with and without disabilities and argued that persons with disabilities should be covered by pay equity laws.

Clearly, some disabilities preclude regular paid employment, even if community and workplace supports were in place. But, in many other cases, lack of employment is due to a failure by society and by employers to address barriers to employment and to accommodate differences (Fawcett 1996). Many persons with disabilities need some help in the home and/or assistive aids and devices, or have special travel needs, or need flexible hours or specially designed and configured work stations. If these supports and services were in place, rates of employment would undoubtedly be higher. The *Participation and Activity Limitations Survey* found that a little more than one-third of adults with disabilities needed more help in daily activities or more help from assistive devices such as wheelchairs and hearing aids than they were able to obtain, and about one in ten had difficulty travelling or could not travel at all.

While the situation of persons with disabilities in the job market is very poor, there is increasing support for positive changes. The federal and provincial governments have begun to advance a more positive agenda through a series of reports with policy recommendations, and funding for community and employment supports is slowly increasing. In part due to a series of far-reaching legal decisions, employers are increasingly obliged to accommodate the special needs of workers with disabilities, which is of particular importance to workers who have stable employment and then become ill or are injured. Disability rights organizations are extremely active in pushing an inclusion agenda, arguing that disability is a social rather than a medical condition. The key point is that there would be many

Table 6.3: Persons with Disabilities, Aged 15 and Over		
	Persons with Disability	**No Disability**
All		
Employed	43.7%	78.4%
Unemployed	4.7%	5.1%
Not in labour force	51.6%	16.5%
Average earnings	$26,760	$32,085
Men		
Employed	47.6%	84.1%
Unemployed	5.1%	5.8%
Not in labour force	47.2%	10.1%
Average earnings	$32,385	$38,677
Women		
Employed	40.3%	72.8%
Unemployed	4.2%	4.4%
Not in labour force	55.4%	22.8%
Average earnings	$20,821	$24,776

Source: Statistics Canada, "Disability in Canada," *A Profile of Disability in Canada, 2001—Tables (2001 Participation and Activity Limitation Survey)*, Catalogue 89-579-X1E, December 2002. <http://www.sdc.ca>.

opportunities in the workforce for persons with disabilities if supports and services were provided, and if differences were properly accommodated.

▌Conclusion

While minority groups are very different from one another, there is a pervasive pattern of labour market disadvantage for new immigrants, workers of colour, Aboriginal Canadians, and persons with disabilities. People from these groups have greater difficulty finding and keeping steady jobs, and receive below-average pay. Specific factors come into play with each of these groups, but discrimination is a common factor as well.

Questions for Critical Thought

1. Women, visible minorities, Aboriginal Canadians, and persons with disabilities are very different groups, but policy makers perceive all of them as vulnerable to discrimination in the job market. To what extent do you think the problems facing these groups have common features?
2. To what extent do the last three groups face very different problems?
3. Employment equity legislation usually requires employers to take steps to eliminate both overt and hidden discrimination in hiring and promotion decisions by adopting formal and transparent procedures, and also to make a commitment to promote greater employee diversity. Do you think this kind of legislation is "fair" in light of the job and pay differences highlighted in this chapter?
4. To what extent do you think that racial discrimination is a factor in the problems faced by many recent immigrants to Canada?
5. Do you think that employers should be required to take special measures to accommodate the special needs of persons with disabilities?

Recommended Reading

Canadian Race Relations Foundation. 2000. *Unequal Access: A Canadian Profile of Racial Differences in Education, Employment and Income* <http://www.crr.ca>. A factual overview of income, employment, education, and earnings of visible minorities and Aboriginal people.

Galabuzi, Grace-Edward. 2001. *Canada's Creeping Economic Apartheid*. CSJ Foundation for Research and Education<http://www.socialjustice.org>. Argues that racism lies at the root of many of the problems facing minorities in the Canadian workforce.

Human Resources Development Canada. Office for Disability Issues. 2001. "Disability in Canada: A 2001 Profile" <http://www.hrdc-drhc.gc.ca/bcph.odi>. A comprehensive profile of persons with disabilities, including their experience in the job market.

Mendelson, Michael. 2004. "Aboriginal People in Canada's Labour Market: Work and Unemployment, Today and Tomorrow." Caledon Institute of Social Policy <http://www.caledoninst.ca>.

The Report of the Royal Commission on Aboriginal Peoples. 1996. <http://www.ainc-inac.gc.ca>. Draws on a wealth of research to describe and analyze the historical origins of the many economic and social problems facing Aboriginal people.

Notes

1. For data from the 2001 Census, see "Ethno-cultural Portrait of Canada," Cat. 97F0010XCB01003, under Census releases <http://www.statcan.ca>.
2. Earnings and income data from the 2001 Census are for the year 2000.

3. Data from Statistics Canada, *Survey of Labour and Income Dynamics* (Ottawa: Statistics Canada).
4. Department of Human Resources Development Canada, *Applied Research Bulletin* (Summer 2001): 19.

References

Aydemir, Abdurrahman, and Mikal Skuterud. 2004. "Explaining the Deteriorating Entry Earnings of Canada's Immigrant Cohorts, 1966–2000." Ottawa: Statistics Canada, Analytical Studies Branch.

Bloom, Michael, and Michael Grant. 2001. "Brain Gain: The Economic Benefits of Recognizing Learning and Learning Credentials in Canada." Conference Board of Canada <http://www.conferenceboard.ca>.

Bourne, Larry S. 2004. "Beyond the New Deal for Cities: Confronting the Challenges of Uneven Economic Growth." Research Bulletin no. 21. Toronto: Centre for Urban and Community Studies, University of Toronto.

Canadian Council on Social Development (CCSD). 2002. Disability Research Information Sheet no. 4. Ottawa.

Canadian Race Relations Foundation. 2000. "Unequal Access: A Canadian Profile of Racial Differences in Education, Employment and Income" <http://www. crr.ca>.

Conference Board of Canada. 2004. "Making a Visible Difference: The Contribution of Visible Minorities to Canadian Economic Growth." Ottawa.

Fawcett, Gail. 1996. *Living with Disability in Canada: An Economic Portrait*. Ottawa: Human Resources Development Canada.

Frenette, Marc, and Rene Morissette. 2003. "Will They Ever Converge? Earnings of Immigrant and Canadian Born Workers over the Last Two Decades." Ottawa: Statistics Canada, Analytical Studies Branch.

Galabuzi, Grace-Edward. 2001. "Canada's Creeping Economic Apartheid." CSJ Foundation for Research and Education <http://www.socialjustice.org>.

Grant, Mary, and Eden Thompson. 2001. "Immigrants and the Canadian Labour Market." Paper based on research by Human Resources Development Canada and Citizenship and Immigration Canada presented to the Tenth Biennial Conference on Canadian Social Welfare Policy, Calgary, June.

Hou, Feng, and Garnett Picot. 2003. *Visible Minority Neighbourhood Enclaves and Labour Market Outcomes of Immigrants*. Ottawa: Statistics Canada.

Human Resources Development Canada. 2001. *Disability in Canada: A 2001 Profile* <http://www.sdc.gc.ca>.

Mendelson, Michael. 2004. "Aboriginal People in Canada's Labour Market: Work and Unemployment, Today and Tomorrow." Caledon Institute of Social Policy. <http://www.caldeoninst.ca>.

Picot, Garnett, and F. Hou. 2003. "The Rise in Low Income among Recent Immigrants to Canada." Ottawa: Statistics Canada.

CHAPTER SEVEN

Older Workers, Pensions, and the Transition to Retirement

▓ Introduction[1]

One of the key transitions in life is that from paid work to retirement. This chapter discusses Canada's retirement income system, the incomes of seniors (which are heavily influenced by their work history), older workers in the job market, and debates over pensions and transitions to retirement.

Until relatively late in the 20th century, the period of retirement was short because most workers died at a much younger age than today's elderly, and had to work until late in life because of the inadequacy of public and private pensions. Old age was very often spent in poverty.

That changed greatly in the latter part of the century as public and private pension systems matured. Today's elderly frequently enjoy long and reasonably secure periods of retirement, and poverty rates among the elderly are very low.

Until very recently, Canadian workers were retiring at much earlier ages than was the norm even in the 1960s and 1970s, typically at about age 60, and most people seem to have been retiring voluntarily. However, some older workers did not fare well in the economic restructuring of the 1980s and 1990s and enjoy only modest incomes, and it is far from clear that the favourable patterns of the recent past will continue into the indefinite future.

Canada has a rapidly aging population. The proportion of all Canadians aged 65 plus has risen from 8% of the population in 1971 to 13% in 2001, and will rise to about 20% by 2020 as the large baby boom generation enters retirement and as the fertility rate (and thus the proportion of children and young people) declines. The prospect of an aging society caused great concern among many policy makers in the 1990s. It was feared that current pension arrangements would be unaffordable and that we could face serious shortages of skilled workers. Some commentators have seen it as undesirable that the proportion of a person's working life spent in the paid workforce should slip so far, from about 74% in the 1960s (for men) to below 50% (Hicks 2003). However, proposals to raise the age of eligibility for public pensions were dropped, mainly because the idea of retirement remains very popular. That said, there is widespread support for the idea of facilitating and supporting more choices for older workers, and increased recognition that paths to retirement can be quite different. Many older workers continue in the workforce even as they begin to draw pension income.

Retirement patterns for the baby boomers, who are now mostly in their fifties, may be different from those of their parents and people now in their sixties. Most significantly, women now entering their fifties and sixties are much more likely to have spent all or most of their lives in the paid workforce than did their mothers, and many will continue to work as they grow older. The gradual shift of employment away from very physically demanding jobs may also lead some workers to want to remain in the paid workforce until a later age than in even the recent past, especially given that both men and women can now expect to live for a good 15 to 20 years in reasonably good health after age 65. Many of today's older workers are well educated, and such workers tend to retire early from their career jobs, but are also more likely than average to pursue second careers.

The economic circumstances of people approaching retirement vary greatly. Some were victims of the economic restructuring of the 1980s and 1990s, while others have been in steady full-time jobs with good pensions for most of their working lives. Another factor at play today is the sharp decline in share prices in 2000, which eroded the retirement savings of some older workers, and had negative impacts on the assets of many pension plans. One can expect even more individualized paths to retirement, perhaps including a rise in the age of retirement after many years of decline, as well as a rise in the proportion of people who combine pension and employment incomes. Looking still further forward, it seems likely that today's young adults will work longer than their parents and grandparents, if only because other life transitions, notably that from education to work and independent family formation, are taking place much later in life. Changes in the job market are also eroding private pension plan coverage, particularly for younger workers.

Canada's Retirement Income System

Canadian workers gain income in retirement from three main sources: public pensions—that is, the Old Age Security (OAS) program, the Guaranteed Income Supplement (GIS), and the Canada/Quebec Pension Plan (C/QPP); private, employer-sponsored pensions; and private savings, including RRSPs. Two of the main sources of income for retirees—C/QPP and private pensions—are provided on the basis of earnings and work experience, and are explicitly intended to replace earnings, while the OAS program provides a flat benefit of just in excess of $5,500 in 2003 to all Canadians over age 65. Higher-income taxpayers now have some or all of their OAS clawed back.

Public Pensions

The GIS, linked to the OAS, is an income-tested benefit. In combination, these two programs provide a minimum income floor for older Canadians. For the single elderly (who are overwhelmingly women), the floor currently amounts to about $12,100 per year, more than $6,500 below the low-income line in a large urban centre as established by Statistics Canada. For an elderly couple, the minimum income guarantee is about $19,400, or $4,000 below the low-income line for a large city. Even so, some very low-income individuals and families experience an income gain when they reach age 65, and most senior families have sufficient income from all sources to push them above the poverty line.

The Canada/Quebec Pension Plan (C/QPP) is a compulsory, earnings-related program, financed from employer and employee contributions, which provides retirement (and disability and death) benefits to the employed and the self-employed and their survivors. The retirement benefit provides 25% of pre-retirement earnings, but only for those earning up to the rough equivalent of average wages and salaries with a steady history of employment. Those earning more than average will get a lower benefit as a proportion of their pre-retirement income, and those with short work histories will get less than 25%. A notable feature of the C/QPP is that allowance is made for periods of time spent by women outside the workforce to care for children. Benefits are indexed to inflation, while pensionable earnings track average wages. The normal age of entitlement to C/QPP retirement benefits is age 65, though reduced benefits are available at age 60, and higher benefits can be obtained by delaying retirement up to age 70. The C/QPP is explicitly designed to contribute to the goal of replacing pre-retirement earnings and is not just an anti-poverty program.

In combination, the OAS and C/QPP replace approximately 40% of wages for an average worker. Because of the offsetting influences of the GIS and the C/QPP, the distribution of public pension benefits among the elderly is actually quite close to a flat amount (Myles 2000; OECD 2001). Compared to many European countries, Canada's public pension programs are quite modest in scale. Few would see an income replacement rate of 40% for an average worker as adequate to secure a comfortable retirement. This is, however, deliberate. In the mid-1960s, when the basic structure of our pension system was put in place, and again after a decade-long debate on pension reform that ended in the mid-1980s, the Canadian government was quite emphatic that it wanted to leave room for privately administered retirement income arrangements (Department of Finance, 1994; LaMarsh 1968). The expectation has been that Canadians should finance part of their own retirement from savings through pension plans or RRSPs, which in turn are an important source of savings in the economy and a key pillar of the financial sector. It is certainly appropriate to finance some part of retirement incomes from savings as opposed to mainly "pay as you go" public pensions, and the retirement savings industry is very influential in public policy debates.

Private Pensions

Employers in the private sector are not legally obliged to establish a workplace pension plan, though pensions for government employees are often established by statute. Private plans are often created to recruit and retain employees. Generally speaking, employers have seen value in such plans since they foster employee loyalty and discourage workers from leaving. Pension plans have also been established, perhaps most importantly, as a result of pressure from unions. Since the end of World War II, the negotiation of workplace pensions has been an important union bargaining priority and remains so to this day. The launching of Canada's modest public pensions in the 1950s and 1960s allowed some shift in emphasis in collective bargaining from the negotiation of benefits starting at age 65 or later to the negotiation of early retirement programs, and it is not uncommon for workers with long years of service to draw a good pension well before age 65. Just under one-half of all workplace pension plans, covering approximately 85% of all members, are of the defined-benefit variety, providing benefits based on prior earnings and years of service. Defined contribution-type plans, by contrast, provide uncertain benefits based on investment returns. Retirement benefits provided by private pension plans vary greatly. In combination with public pension benefits, many provide for very comfortable retirements, while others do not.

Workplace pensions suffer from a number of weaknesses. The most obvious is the partial and slipping level of coverage of workers. In 2001, 43.5% of employees belonged to workplace pensions, down from 48.5% in 1991. Just one in three employees in the private sector is now covered. Traditionally, women workers were less likely to be covered than men, but the gender difference has now virtually disappeared (Statistics Canada 2000). The chances of being covered by a workplace pension plan increase with income, level of educational attainment, and the size of employer. However, aside from working in the public sector, the characteristic that is most decisive is union membership. Overall, 80% of union members belong to workplace pensions compared to just 27% of non-union members. In workplaces of 20 employees or less, 70% of union members belong to workplace pensions compared to just 13% of non-union members (Akyeampong 2002; Lipsett and Reesor 1997).

Very few new defined-benefit plans are now being established, and they are, in some respects, a legacy of the more stable economic conditions of the 1960s and 1970s. However, it also has to be noted that many workers still spend their working lives with a single large employer. Defined-benefit pension plans are best suited to workers who stay for many years with one employer, and have tended to shortchange members who leave their employer before reaching retirement age, whether by choice or because of an involuntary layoff. Further, only a minority of pension plan members have access to even partial adjustments for inflation (Statistics Canada 2000).

The third major source of retirement income is private savings, notably through tax-supported registered retirement savings plans (RRSPs). While of use to the self-employed and those with no or an inadequate pension plan, RRSPs provide most benefits to higher-income earners who are in the best position to save, and very few people use all of their available RRSP contribution room. While some people save enough for a decent retirement and invest funds well, others do not save enough and do not invest well. A key problem with RRSPs is that investment returns are far from certain, and that equity values in particular, while rising over the long term, are subject to large fluctuations in the short term and can stagnate over long periods.

Incomes of Canada's Elderly

The last quarter of the 20th century was a period of very rapid improvement in the incomes of older Canadians. The real incomes of elderly households increased by 50% over the period from 1973 to 1996, and by even more for lower-income seniors. Poverty rates among the elderly fell dramatically from 1980 to 2002, after also falling from 1973 to 1980. Not only did the incomes of the elderly increase in purchasing power, but the incomes of the elderly compared to younger age groups increased as well. From 1973 to 1996, the average income of elderly households increased from 47% to 61% of that of non-elderly households, and the proportion was even higher, at 80%, when the numbers are adjusted for differences in household size (Baldwin and Laliberté 1999; Myles 2000). Over this period from the mid-1970s to the mid-1990s, two sources of income of the elderly grew particularly rapidly—income from the Canada and Quebec Pension Plans, and income from workplace pensions. The C/QPP share of total income of the elderly grew from 2.8% in 1973 to 17.8% in

1996. Workplace pension income increased from 10.4% to 22.3% of the total over the period.

In 1996, almost all elderly households received income from OAS/GIS, and 86.5% received income from the C/QPP, up from only 28.4% only 23 years earlier. Just over one-half (53.2%) received workplace pension income, 57.9% received some investment income (often in very small amounts), and 20.3% received some employment income. Among lower-income senior households, income from public pension programs is of decisive importance. If we divide households into 10 equally sized groups ranked by income, we find that income from OAS/GIS and C/QPP accounts for more than half of all income for all households in the bottom 60%, while only the top 10% receive less than 30% of their income from public pensions. Income from workplace pensions is particularly important for those with above-average incomes, with the exception of those at the very top. Public pensions address the poverty issue, while workplace pensions are the key lever for comfortable retirement incomes and sustained economic well-being in the transition from work to retirement.

There is still a substantial and persistent income gap between older men and women, with the average income of individual women being 62% of men's over the entire period from 1973 to 1996. And, there are striking differences in terms of sources of income of men and women. OAS/GIS and investment income are more important for women and C/QPP and workplace pensions for men. This reflects the working patterns by gender of previous years, and differences may shrink in the future to some degree.

A retirement income system could be judged to be successful if poverty among the elderly is low, and if retirees do not experience a large decline of income compared to their working years. Canada stands out among advanced industrial countries in terms of having a very low level of poverty among the elderly, though there are still major problems for single elderly women (OECD 2001). In fact, using a common definition of poverty (household income of less than one-half the median), the poverty rate of Canadian seniors is just 2.5% compared to 20% in the U.S. and about 10% in most Western European countries. Deep poverty has been all but abolished by the OAS/GIS, but it is important to note that a high proportion of elderly households are still living on incomes that are quite close to the Canadian low-income line, and that single, elderly women in particular are vulnerable to poverty.

Turning to income replacement, in 1996, the average income of the over-65 households had reached 80% of that of younger households after adjusting for differences in household size. However, older households with no earnings had only 65% of the income of younger households. A recent study by Statistics Canada (2001) found that one-third of households approaching retirement (household head aged over 45) had not saved enough to either replace two-thirds of their income or to have an income above the poverty line.

The greatly improved income situation of older households from the mid-1970s to the mid-1990s reflected the maturing of the pension system within a particular set of economic circumstances. Low inflation and high rates of return on financial assets boosted seniors' incomes at a time when most working-age households experienced very slow wage growth. If real wages begin to rise, seniors may begin to lose ground compared to the working population since public pensions are indexed to prices, not wages. Higher inflation and lower investment returns could lower pension income in the future.

Box 7.1: Pension Debates in the 1990s

In the 1970s, there was a major pension debate in Canada in which the major concern was the incomes of the elderly. In the 1990s, the main issue was seen to be the affordability of pensions in an aging society in which workers will live much longer lives after retirement. The debate was initiated by the World Bank and the OECD who have favoured later retirement and more individualized pensions based on personal savings (OECD 2000; World Bank 1994). Despite the success of the pension arrangements put in place in Canada in the 1960s and 1970s, many voices here also called for a return to reliance on individual savings. There was a vigorous campaign by conservative think-tanks in the mid-1990s to abolish the C/QPP in favour of individual retirement accounts (Lam and Walker 1997; Robson 1996).

The federal government forecast in 1993 that expenditures on Old Age Security and the Canada and Quebec Pension Plans would increase from 5.3% of national income in 1993 to more than 8% in 2030. While this caused great anxiety to some, it is striking that OAS and C/QPP expenditures were projected to increase as a share of GDP by only 50% over a period in which the over-65 population was expected to double as a share of the population. One way or another, the costs of aging would have to be borne.

The government claimed that if no changes were made to the C/QPP, those who came after the baby boomers would be asked to pay two to three times more for the same pensions as those who came before them. While true to a degree, this appeal to fairness between generations tended to ignore the fact that there had been a very large income transfer to the first generation to benefit from the C/QPP.

Ultimately, increases in the retirement age and a radical shift to individual accounts were ruled out. Instead, benefits were modestly trimmed and contribution rates were raised from 5.6% to 9.9% of earnings below the maximum amount, with the aim of building up an investment fund to spread some of the cost of future pensions over a longer period. It is now generally agreed that only minor adjustments will have to be made to ensure that the C/QPP is financially sustainable.

The federal government eventually abandoned a proposal to replace the OAS/GIS program with a single Senior's Benefit, which would have been based on family rather than individual income. Opposition arose because this proposal would have deprived many older women of an individual old age pension; would have resulted in lower benefits for higher-income families, and also would, some feared, erode incentives to save for retirement.

Over the period since 1998, there has been little impetus for change in Canada's pension system. The costs of an aging society now seem quite manageable. It will certainly be entirely possible to keep up transfers to a growing elderly population with no reduction in the standard of living of the working-age population if we continue to have steady economic growth. Problems of intergenerational equity are not very important compared to much more pressing inequalities within generations. However, there are some potential sources of disturbance to the current system. On top of declining workplace pension plan coverage, it is possible that these plans could face serious financial difficulties. Plans are required to accumulate assets to match future liabilities, allowing for short-term fluctuations in financial markets. However, as of mid-2003, about half of all pension plans were not fully funded, mainly because of the severe correction to stock market values of 2000. The very high rates of return on financial assets of the 1980s and 1990s are unlikely to return, and we may see more pension plan windups and/or conversions of defined benefit plans to defined contribution plans. Problems with workplace pensions may cause the issue of income adequacy for the elderly to return to centre stage in the coming years.

Older Workers in the Canadian Job Market

Table 7.1 and Figure 7.1 summarize trends in the employment rate of older workers—that is, in the proportion of people in the age group who were working in the year. Participation rates of older workers are a bit higher because some workers are unemployed, but unemployment rates among older workers are well below average due to greater-than-average job security, and because many older workers who lose their jobs leave the paid workforce.

As of the mid-1990s, just 16% of men aged 65 to 69 were still working. The employment rate of men aged 60 to 64 fell steadily from the mid-1970s to the mid-1990s from about 60% to about 40%, while that of men aged 55 to 59 also fell over this period from about 80% to about 66%. This sustained decline in men's workforce participation partly reflected decisions to retire earlier than in the past, at an average age of about 61. This would have been facilitated by the contribution of the pension arrangements described above. However, it also reflected the fact that many older workers lost their jobs in the economic restructuring of the 1980s and the first half of the 1990s.

Older workers who lose their jobs are more vulnerable than their younger counterparts to long periods of unemployment because their skills have often become out of date or devalued, and because many employers would prefer to hire younger workers. About 40% of older workers who lost their jobs involuntarily in the mid-1990s did not work again over the next two years (Pyper and Giles 2002). For some laid-off older workers, early retirement is an unplanned consequence of a layoff (Schellenberg 1994). It has been estimated that planned retirements may account for only 51% of male exits from the labour force and 30% of female exits

Table 7.1: Employment Rate of Older Workers			
	1980	**1996**	**2003**
Age 55–59			
Men	79.8%	65.8%	70.6%
Women	36.8%	44.6%	56.3%
Age 60–64			
Men	60.7%	40.3%	49.0%
Women	23.9%	21.5%	30.1%
Age 65–69			
Men	21.2%	15.7%	20.0%
Women	7.6%	6.7%	9.4%

Source: Statistics Canada, *Labour Force Historical Review 2003*, Catalogue 71f0004, February 17, 2004.

(Rowe and Nugyen 2003). While some workers were pushed out by layoffs in the 1990s, companies that were downsizing also often introduced early retirement incentives funded from pension plan surpluses to maintain jobs for younger workers. Thus a complex mix of push and pull factors can be at play in early retirement decisions.

The pattern for women is different. From the mid-1970s to the mid-1990s, the employment rate of women aged 55 to 59 rose gradually from about 35% to about 45%, while that of women aged 60 to 64 was stable. The difference in the trends between women and men basically reflects the fact that the older women of the mid-1990s had been more likely to spend most of their lives in the paid workforce than were women of the same age in the mid-1970s. In fact, there is a clear break, with women born after the mid-1950s being much more likely to work than those born before. Women do tend to retire earlier than men since couples often retire at the same time, and married women are typically younger than their spouses and because family considerations also influence the work decisions of older women. Retirement from paid work is often determined by the need to care for family members. Such pressures to retire are likely to intensify as publicly provided social services are cut.

It is notable that there was a very pronounced increase in the employment rate of older workers from the mid-1990s to 2003, particularly in 2002 and 2003. As shown in the table and figure, employment rates of both men and women aged 60 to 64 have jumped by about 10 percentage points, while they have increased even more dramatically for women aged 55 to 59. These increases probably represent, in

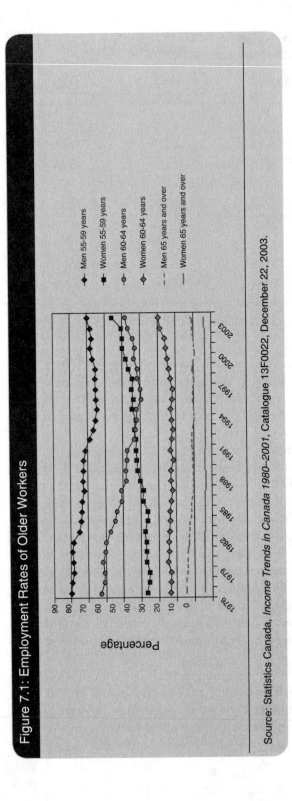

Figure 7.1: Employment Rates of Older Workers

Source: Statistics Canada, *Income Trends in Canada 1980–2001*, Catalogue 13F0022, December 22, 2003.

part, the previous work histories of the current near elderly compared to previous generations, and an increase in individual choices to remain at work, but they are so large that they probably also reflect the impact of the stock market collapse of 2000 on retirement savings. It is impossible at this time to judge how much of the change is voluntary and how much is involuntary. The increased employment of older workers does seem, however, to have been accounted for overwhelmingly by increased hiring, as opposed to a decrease in rates of retirement. In other words, it seems that older workers are staying in the workforce longer, not that they are staying in the same jobs longer.

■The Debate on Older Workers and Retirement

As discussed above, declining fertility and longer life expectancy are increasing the ratio of pensioners to contributors and driving up pension expenditures. This trend has been reinforced by the declining labour force participation rate and the trend among older men to retire early though it has been offset by the rising labour force participation rate of women). Concern about the affordability of pensions and future labour shortages has led to an interest in increasing the age of retirement and in more complete utilization of the labour force in the "near retirement" years. The catalogue of policy responses put forward by the Organisation for Economic Co-operation and Development and others includes raising the age of eligibility for public pension benefits, removing early retirement incentives in pension plans, and ending mandatory retirement.

If pensioners are thought to be claiming too great a share of national income, reducing their relative incomes or relative numbers are the only means of establishing an appropriate balance. And, it is quite true that workplace pension plans do create incentives to retire at or often before age 65. Few workers will choose to work for a modest fraction of their former income if this means deferring a decent pension for very long. When early retirement programs are being valued for actuarial purposes, it is common practice in Canada to assume that the actual age of retirement will fall halfway between the normal retirement age and the date when the right to early retirement without actuarial reduction is established. Access to good pensions is a major reason why public-sector workers tend to retire at an earlier age than private-sector workers, and why the self-employed tend to work longer than employees. In fact, early retirement is, not surprisingly, concentrated in sectors that tend to have good pension plans, such as public administration, utilities, and education (Kiernan 2001). Moreover, Canadian tax rules make it all but impossible for workers to phase in to retirement by combining part-time employment and pension income from the same employer. Thus the mainstream policy prescription to decrease incentives to early retirement to get workers to stay in the paid workforce longer has some elements of truth. It is also true that increasing the labour force participation of older workers could make a potentially important, once-and-for-all contribution to increasing national income.

All that said, the mainstream view ignores what we know about workers' preferences. Public opinion polling in both Canada and Europe suggests that delaying pension eligibility is very unpopular. Huge protests have greeted proposals to raise the retirement age or to cut pensions in many European countries. The short shrift given to the possibility of increasing the age of eligibility for Canada Pension Plan benefits in the mid-1990s likely reflected a fair reading of the public mood. Looking beyond the results of public opinion polls, it is a fair generalization that as societies have grown more affluent over time, working people have shown a desire to take advantage of higher productivity in the form of non-wage compensation, including shorter working hours and pensions. Worker preferences for paid time off may well continue in the face of population aging (Burtless and Quinn 2002).

The preoccupation with early retirement effects of pensions also oversimplifies individuals' retirement decisions and the fact that a wide range of factors influence decisions to work or not to work in the older years. It is interesting to note that there are significant variations in both the trends and levels of labour force participation of older workers from country to country and within countries. Countries with high levels of older worker participation vary a great deal in terms of other labour market characteristics, including their apparent preference for paid time off as opposed to higher incomes over the entire course of working life (Hayden 2003). One key factor at play is the overall strength of employer demand for workers and the level of unemployment. Germany, with a relatively high unemployment rate, has a very low participation rate for older workers. Sweden and the U.S. have very different labour markets, but both have low unemployment and relatively high participation rates for older workers.

It is striking in the case of Canada that provinces with low unemployment rates tend to have high rates of older worker participation in the labour force, while older people tend not to work in provinces with relatively high unemployment rates. Labour force participation rates for people aged 60 to 64 range from just 29% in Newfoundland and Labrador to 44% in Ontario, and to 53% in Alberta. The increase in labour force participation rates of older workers in Canada and some other countries from the mid-1990s provides a reminder of the importance of the overall demand for workers. In short, if jobs are available, many older workers will continue to work. This may be because they are no longer pushed out of work, because they choose to work, or because employers actively seek to have them stay at work.

The preoccupation with pensions' supposed disincentives to work also tends to lead people to ignore negative push factors in the workplace that may play at least as great a role as the pull factor of pensions. As shown in other chapters of this book, for many people, work can involve high levels of stress, long hours of work, discrimination and harassment, poor physical working conditions, lack of training, and lack of control over the work process itself. It is little wonder that many people choose to retire as soon as they are able to do so. However, working conditions could be modified to make work more attractive. To take a concrete example, great concern is currently being expressed about a potential shortage of registered nurses in Canada, given that few new nurses have been hired in recent years while a large share of the current nursing workforce is nearing an age at which pensions can be drawn upon. Nurses tend to retire well before age 65, in part because of pensions, but also in significant part because many nursing jobs can be very physically demanding as well as stressful and involve unsocial working hours. Today, many nurses work very variable shifts due to a shortage of permanent, full-time jobs. Many in the nursing profession say that some nurses might choose to work longer if these negative aspects of the job were modified. It is also probable that some people would choose to shift from full-time to part-time work later in life, especially if they could combine pension and part-time income from the same employer. However, this is generally prohibited under tax law.

Unions negotiate a wide variety of collective agreement provisions that can ameliorate the work experience of older workers (Foursly and Gervais 2002). A seniority-based system for allocation of shifts and access to lighter work, as well as the right to refuse overtime, may persuade some workers to defer retirement. However, the scope for choice is limited by the fact that many workplaces have quite compressed age structures because early retirement programs have led older workers to retire, and there has been no new hiring.

While there is little doubt that good private pension plans do create incentives to early retirement, these may be receding because of poor investment returns. Many plans had large surpluses until quite recently that were often used to finance early retirement, but these surpluses have evaporated or turned into deficits. Workers covered by a defined-benefit plan can usually still count on a secure pension, but government pension guarantees in Canada are weak or non-existent if an employer goes out of business, leaving an unfunded liability in a plan. More importantly, people who draw substantial retirement income from RRSPs or defined contribution plans can be hit hard by negative investment returns, as happened when the stock market fell very sharply in 2000. Wealth and the returns from financial markets do influence retirement decisions, and it seems very probable that the recent rise in employment rates for older workers partly reflects the fact that some people who were dreaming of "Freedom 55" have decided to work longer simply because they cannot afford not to work. A shift to individual retirement savings would likely make it more difficult to forecast retirement decisions since financial returns are so unpredictable. Adding to the affordability issue, older workers are more likely than in even the recent past to still be supporting children in the post-secondary education system.

Finally, the debate over the age of retirement as influenced by pension incentives tends to ignore the complexity of paths out of the paid workforce, and the fact that many older workers combine pension and employment income. Hidden within the overall employment rate numbers for older workers are many transitions from career jobs to second careers. One in five older workers whose career jobs (defined

Box 7.2: The Debate on Mandatory Retirement

During the period of high unemployment that gripped Canada and the U.S. at the end of the 1950s and the beginning of the 1960s, there was a great deal of concern that laid-off older workers faced discrimination based on age. Many jurisdictions adopted human rights legislation that banned employment discrimination on the basis of age, up to age 65. This is specified as the age of retirement in many private pension plan arrangements and employment contracts. While these are private arrangements, they are permitted in most provinces by making them an exception to the general principle of non-discrimination in employment on the basis of age. Contractual mandatory retirement is, however, no longer allowed in Quebec, Manitoba, or the federal public service and, as of mid-2004, was under active discussion in Ontario. (Even where it is generally prohibited, exceptions to the principle of non-discrimination are usually made for some occupations, such as firefighters.)

The key argument against mandatory retirement is that it is discriminatory, and that discrimination in employment on the basis of age is not warranted. It is noted that most workers over age 65 are in good physical and mental health compared to previous generations. Some opponents of mandatory retirement want older workers to stay in the workforce to reduce pension costs and to meet future skill needs, and some supporters of mandatory retirement fear that its abolition could be the "thin end of the wedge" leading to changes in public pensions and longer working lives for all. However, changes to human rights legislation are meant to facilitate an individual choice to stay on at work rather than to modify pension entitlements or the normal age of retirement for all workers.

Supporters of contractual mandatory retirement argue that these are private arrangements that suit the needs of most employers and most workers, and that governments should leave them alone. It is often argued that a fixed age of retirement protects the job security and working conditions of older workers, since employers may be forgiving of lower productivity and poorer performance if they know that an older employee will leave at a fixed date. Getting rid of mandatory retirement could, it is feared, lead to more intense monitoring of work and, perhaps, to disputes over the work performance of older workers. In many unionized workplaces, older, high-seniority workers tend to hold the most desirable jobs, and it is often seen as unfair if they remain past age 65. It is also argued that mandatory retirement opens up jobs for younger workers, though most economists reject the idea that an economy has a fixed number of jobs to be divided up.

Studies have found that getting rid of mandatory retirement has only a limited impact on the age at which most workers will retire, with a few exceptions, such as university professors. As noted, if good pension arrangements are in place, most workers will, in fact, choose to retire well before the mandatory age of retirement. Exceptions may include some individuals who began their career with a particular employer relatively late in life, and thus do not have a good pension at age 65, as well as individuals who have particularly pressing financial needs or derive a great deal of personal satisfaction from a job.

as a job that had been held for more than eight years) ended voluntarily in the mid-1990s continued working in a different full-time job over the next two years (Pyper and Giles 2002). People who continue working after 65 seem to be mainly engaged in second careers. They are much more likely to be working part-time or to be self-employed than are pre-retirement-age workers. In fact, more than 40% are self-employed. They are also much more likely to be well educated. Employment rates of university-educated seniors over age 65 are double those of people with only a high school education (Duchesne 2004). During the period of rapid economic expansion following the recession of the early 1990s, there was a striking increase in the number of people combining employment and retirement income.

There could be broad support for a later average age of retirement if this arose not from the erosion of income security for older workers, but through policies to expand choices, such as more effective adjustment programs for older workers, improvements to social services that reduce the pressure on older women workers to leave paid work to care for family members, and, more generally, improvements in the quality of work that make it less burdensome. Participation rates of older workers could be raised in a positive way not just by recognizing their special needs, but also through more advice and support. Older workers sometimes have difficulty recognizing how their personal work histories might relate to prospects for future employment and training. In some European countries, governments have begun to promote longer working lives more through the use of these kinds of measures rather than the stick of reduced pensions (Foden and Jespen 2002).

Conclusion

In the current discussion on the situation of older workers, the most hotly contested issue is the appropriate age of exit from the labour force. The issue should be approached in a manner that recognizes workers' legitimate need and desires for a financially secure retirement. Looking beyond the concerns associated with pension financing, and bearing in mind that the overall state of the job market will play a vital role in determining the actual age of retirement, there are clearly some contrary pushes and pulls on the age of retirement. Unsafe, unhealthy, and unsatisfying work are likely to drive people to look for a safe haven in retirement. Downsizing of large public and private employers will likely have the same effect. Clearly, though, if work remains attractive to employees, and employers want to pay for them to remain, there will be a growing supply of healthy, older workers to draw upon.

Conflicting views about the appropriate age of retirement will continue to fuel political debate in the years ahead. The range of possible outcomes will be framed, in part, by economic circumstances. Will labour productivity increase at a pace that will allow a growing number of pensioners to receive relative incomes at or above their current level, while also permitting real income growth among the non-elderly?

And, how will people evaluate the choice of using productivity gains to increase incomes today rather than taking paid time off in retirement tomorrow?

No matter how the age of retirement issue is resolved, there are groups of older workers whose work situation should be a matter of public concern, such as the older unemployed and people who have faced discrimination in employment. The situation of older adult immigrants bears particular scrutiny given low earnings, and many older women still have very low retirement incomes. It is also important that the age of exit issue gets resolved in a manner that creates employment opportunities for older workers who want employment and, at the same time, does minimal damage to the employment prospects of younger workers.

• •

■ Questions for Critical Thought

1. How do you think the eventual transition to retirement of the young people of today will compare to that of their parents?
2. Is mandatory retirement a justifiable exception to the principle of not discriminating against employees on the basis of age?
3. To what extent should government policies seek to promote replacement of a high proportion of earnings in retirement?
4. To what extent should pensions be provided by employers, governments, and individuals?
5. Are public pension plans such as the Canada Pension Plan unfair to the young people of today?

■ Recommended Reading

Baldwin, Bob, and Pierre Laliberté. 1999. *Incomes of Older Canadians: Amounts and Sources, 1973–1996*. Research Paper no. 15. Ottawa: Canadian Labour Congress <http://www.clc-ctc.ca>. Details the incomes of Canadian seniors over an extended period. The CLC Web site (policy subsite) contains several other research papers by Bob Baldwin related to pensions, retirement, and older workers.

Country reports on the employment of seniors are available from the OECD Web site <http://www.oecd.org>. See under "Employment" on the subsite "Ageing Society." A country report on Canada should be available (still pending as of Fall 2004).

Duchesne, Doreen. 2004. "More Seniors at Work." *Perspectives on Labour and Income* (Spring): 55–67. A statistical overview of seniors in the workforce today.

Hicks, Peter. 2003. "The Policy Implications of Aging." *Horizons* 6, no. 2 <http://policyresearch.gc.ca>. This paper looks at some of the implications for public policy regarding aging and the changed life-course of younger Canadians compared to previous generations, and favours more varied and later paths to retirement.

Kiernan, Patrick. 2001. "Early Retirement Trends." *Perspectives on Labour and Income* (Winter).

Note

1. This chapter is drawn mainly from Canadian Labour Congress (CLC) research papers written by Bob Baldwin.

References

Akyeampong, Ernest. 2002. "Unionization and Fringe Benefits." *Perspectives on Labour and Income* (Autumn): 5–9.

Baldwin, Bob, and Pierre Laliberté. 1999. *Incomes of Older Canadians: Amounts and Sources, 1973–1996*. Research Paper no. 15. Ottawa: Canadian Labour Congress.

Burtless, Gary, and Joseph Quinn. 2002. *Is Working Longer the Answer for an Ageing Workforce?* Boston: Centre for Research on Retirement, Boston College.

Department of Finance. 1994. *Action Plan on Pension Reform: Building Better Pensions for Canadians*. Ottawa: Department of Finance.

Duchesne, Doreen. 2004. "More Seniors at Work." *Perspectives on Labour and Income* (Spring): 55–67.

Foden, David, and Maria Jepsen. 2002. "Active Strategies for Older Workers in the European Union: A Comparative Analysis of Recent Experiences." In *Active Strategies for Older Workers in the European Union*, edited by David Foden et al. Brussels: European Trade Union Institute.

Foursly, Michel, and Marc Gervais. 2002. *Collective Agreements and Older Workers in Canada*. Ottawa: Labour Program, Human Resources Development Canada.

Hayden, Anders. 2003. "International Work-time Trends: The Emerging Gap in Hours." *Just Labour* (Spring) <http://www.justlabour.yorku.ca.>

Hicks, Peter. 2003. "The Policy Implications of Aging" *Horizons* 6, no. 2.

Kiernan, Patrick. 2001. "Early Retirement Trends." *Perspectives on Labour and Income* (Winter): 7–13.

Lam, Karen, and Michael Walker. 1997. "The Next Step in Changing the Canada Pension Plan." *Fraser Forum* <http://www.fraserinstitute.ca>.

LaMarsh, Judy. 1968. *Memoirs of a Bird in a Gilded Cage*. Toronto: McClelland & Stewart.

Lipsett, Brenda, and Mark Reesor. 1997. *Employer-Sponsored Pension Plans—Who Benefits?* Ottawa: Human Resources Development Canada.

Myles, John. 2000. *The Maturation of Canada's Retirement Income System: Income Levels, Income Inequality and Low Income among the Elderly*. Ottawa: Statistics Canada.

Organisation for Economic Co-operation and Development (OECD). 2000. *Reforms for an Ageing Society*. Paris: OECD.

_____. 2001. *Ageing and Income: Financial Resources and Retirement in 9 OECD Countries*. Paris: OECD.

Pyper, Wendy, and Philip Giles. 2002. "Approaching Retirement," *Perspectives on Labour and Income* (Spring): 5–12.

Robson, William. 1996. *Putting Some Gold in the Golden Years: Fixing the Canada Pension Plan*. Toronto: C.D. Howe Institute.

Rowe, Geoff, and Huan Nugyen. 2003. "Older Workers and the Labour Market." *Perspectives on Labour and Income* 15, no. 1 (Spring): 23–26.

Schellenberg, Grant. 1994. *The Road to Retirement: Demographic and Economic Changes in the '90s*. Ottawa: Canadian Council on Social Development.

Statistics Canada. 2000. *Pension Plans in Canada, 1999*. Ottawa: Statistics Canada.

World Bank. 1994. *Averting the Old Age Crisis: Policies to Protect the Old and Promote Growth*. Washington: World Bank.

PART III

Contemporary Canadian Unions

THIS PART OF THE BOOK LOOKS AT THE ROLE OF UNIONS IN CANADA AND IN OTHER advanced industrial countries, and at the potential future of unions as a force in the modern Canadian workplace. In looking at the role of unions, this part of the book takes up some of the key issues developed in Parts I and II, such as precarious work, growing inequality, and barriers to inclusion.

Unions have historically been a major force for improving the quality of jobs, countering low pay, and promoting greater equality in the job market between women and men, between younger and older workers, and between minorities. However, this role is being undercut by declining union strength, particularly among blue-collar male workers. In Canada, union coverage is stable but very low among private service workers, particularly lower-paid women and minority workers who would gain the most from union representation. Unions can be and are a positive force for better jobs, but a key challenge for unions today is to win support among, and to make gains for, unorganized precarious workers.

Chapter 8, "The Impact of Unions," discusses the role and importance of collective bargaining, describes what kinds of workers belong to unions, and closely examines union impacts on wages, low-wage jobs, benefits, access to training, and other dimensions of job quality. It also discusses how unions affect the way in which the economy and the labour market operate, dealing with the often-heard argument that strong unions may be good for their members, but are a negative for economic performance.

Chapter 9, "Is There a Future for Canadian Unions?," provides a detailed look at the changes in union membership, and some challenges facing unions in attempting to organize and represent workers in today's job market.

There is a major ongoing process of union renewal, but whether it will be enough to ensure a continuing major role for unions in the workplaces of the future is an issue that remains to be determined.

▌Related Web Sites

- The Canadian Labour Congress <http://www.clc-ctc.ca>. The CLC is the largest union federation in Canada, representing almost 3 million workers. The CLC Web site provides access to a wide range of information on unions, and comprehensive links to the Web sites of Canadian and international unions. The largest Canadian unions all maintain Web sites that detail their activities and positions.
- The Centre for Research on Work and Society at York University <http://www.yorku.ca/crws/> publishes research papers and an electronic journal, *Just Labour*, which carries many articles on the theme of union change and renewal.
- The Global Union Research Network (GURN) <http://www.gurn.info/>. GURN was established in January 2004 as a follow-up to the millennium debate of the Global Unions Group, the major international organizations bringing together trade unions around the world. After a request from the international labour movement, the initiative to establish the network was taken by the ILO's Bureau for Workers' Activities (ACTRAV) in co-operation with the International Confederation of Free Trade Unions (ICFTU), the Trade Union Advisory Committee to the OECD (TUAC), the Global Union Federations (GUF), and the ILO's International Institute for Labour Studies (IILS). The aim of the research network is to give union organizations better access to research carried out within trade unions and allied institutions while enabling them to exchange information on matters of joint concern and to develop the capacity to make analyses and take part in debates and policy formulation.
- Rethinking Institutions for Work and Employment in a Global Era <http://www.crimt.org> is the Web site for a major research project on democracy at work and union renewal based at the Université de Montréal. The Web site seeks to stimulate debate and research exchange between researchers working on the project as well as with a broader community of researchers and practitioners interested in the challenge of understanding and developing institutions that promote both equity and efficiency outcomes in the world of work.
- The Workplace Information Directorate of Human Resources and Skills Development Canada <http://www.hrsdc.gc.ca/en/ gateways/nav/top_nav/ program/labour.sht>. This branch of the federal government publishes a wide range of information and studies on workplace and collective bargaining issues, including the quarterly review *Workplace Gazette*.

CHAPTER EIGHT

The Impact of Unions

■ Introduction

This chapter discusses the role of unions in Canada and in other advanced industrial countries. It discusses the role and importance of collective bargaining; briefly summarizes what kinds of workers belong to unions; and examines union impacts on wages, wage differences, benefits, and other dimensions of job quality. Generally speaking, unions are a force for better jobs and greater equality in the job market, and this is shown not to come at the price of economic growth and job creation. However, unions can be a strong force for better jobs only if a high proportion of workers at risk of being in low pay and precarious jobs are unionized. This is not the case in much of the private services sector in Canada, where most low-wage and precarious jobs are to be found.

■ What Are Unions and What Do They Do?

"Unions reduce wage inequality, increase industrial democracy and often raise productivity ... [I]n the political sphere, unions are an important voice for some of society's weakest and most vulnerable groups, as well as for their own members" (Freeman and Medoff 1984, 5).

Unions are organizations that define, promote, and fight for the collective interests and rights of workers or a group of workers, especially in relation to employers, but also in relation to governments, the media, and other social groups. Unions emerge from and are a product of the fundamental difference of interests between workers and employers.

The key defining feature of all capitalist societies—including today's post-industrial societies—is that the great majority of working people gain their livelihood through paid work—that is, by selling their labour to employers. The basic terms of any employment relationship are that workers agree to work under the direction of an employer (with respect to place of work, hours of work, methods of work, etc.) in return for a wage. If it were not for unions, workers would have to negotiate the terms and conditions of their employment (wages, benefits, hours of work, work schedules, conditions of work, etc.) as individuals, protected only by minimum legal standards. And, if it were not for unions, individual workers would be on their own when it came to dealing with arbitrary and unfair treatment by employers, such as dismissal without just cause, harassment, discrimination in hiring, promotion and layoffs, favouritism by employers and managers in setting pay and assigning jobs, and so on. Of course, there are many decent non-union employers, but it is usually only in unionized workplaces that there are formal rules governing what an employee must do and workplace procedures, and a formal process for filing and investigating complaints if the rules are broken.

Unions have been formed out of the fundamental recognition that there is strength in numbers, and that workers are stronger when they unite and bargain together with employers and have a common voice to represent their interests. Individual workers have less power in determining the content of the employment relationship than employers because many workers are capable of doing a given job and can be hired to do so. The bargaining power of individual workers is particularly weak in times when unemployment is high and many workers are seeking any available job. Unfortunately, the norm is for the demand of workers for jobs to exceed the number of jobs that are available at any given time in any particular place. This is particularly true for good jobs with decent wages and working conditions.

Historically, unions have been a major force for humanizing and democratizing capitalist societies by balancing the power of employers, which results from their control over production. Unions are an important source of human dignity in the workplace and a wider force for social justice. Unions promote higher levels of economic equality and, in some ways, also make labour markets work better from the point of economic growth and efficiency.

Canadian unions form a democratic labour movement fighting for better wages and better working conditions, as well as for democratic and human rights and better social programs for all workers. The labour movement has been a central part of the wider social democratic movement to make Canadian society more democratic, both inside and outside the workplace, more secure from the perspective of working people who are vulnerable to unemployment and low income, and more equal in terms of the distribution of income and economic resources between social classes. More recently, unions have joined the fight for women's rights and the fight against racial discrimination. Most big historical breakthroughs in union recognition and in collective bargaining—such as the eight-hour day and the five-day week—have come when many groups of workers were pursuing the same goals at the same time. Of course, unions vary a great deal in terms of how internally democratic they are, and to what extent they are committed to wider social goals and not just the interests of current members. Some of these issues are looked at in the next chapter.

Union strength varies a great deal between countries, including the advanced industrial countries, ranging from collective bargaining coverage of 80% or more of workers in many continental European countries to just 15% in the U.S., and to even lower levels in the formal labour markets of most developing countries. Outside of public and social services, where union coverage is typically high, the key bastions of union strength are usually in larger companies in primary industries, manufacturing, utilities, communications, transportation, and construction. Union coverage typically extends to only a minority of workers in most private-service sector industries, such as finance, retail trade, accommodation and food, and personal services. The main exception is in some European countries where unions and employers sign broader-based agreements covering workers in many smaller workplaces. Unions will clearly be a greater force for equality and for social justice only if union coverage is extended to the many low-paid and precarious workers, many of them women and workers of colour, who are currently excluded from the benefits of union representation. The existence of a large, informal sector in developing countries and of a precarious, secondary labour market in most developed countries poses major challenges for union organization and representation.

As documented in Chapter 9 and summarized in Figure 8.1, union coverage now extends to just one in three Canadian workers. There is a big difference between very high union coverage in the public sector (76%) and low coverage in the private sector (just below 20%). Union representation for men and women is now about equal, but the great majority of union women work in public and social services, while the majority of unionized men work in the private sector.

▉Collective Bargaining

In Canada today, unions are almost always organized on the basis of certification by a provincial labour board, which allows a union or bargaining agent to represent a specific group of workers in a specific workplace. (About one in ten workers is

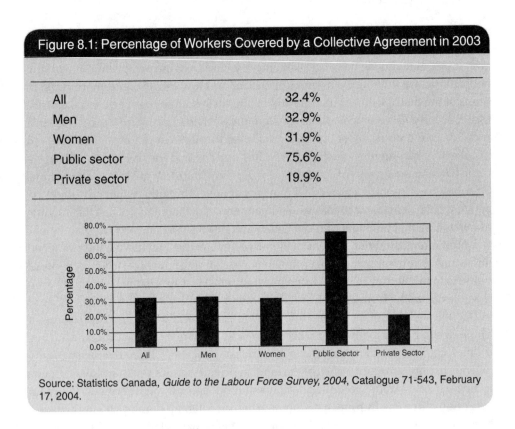

Figure 8.1: Percentage of Workers Covered by a Collective Agreement in 2003

All	32.4%
Men	32.9%
Women	31.9%
Public sector	75.6%
Private sector	19.9%

Source: Statistics Canada, *Guide to the Labour Force Survey, 2004*, Catalogue 71-543, February 17, 2004.

covered by federal labour legislation.) Bargaining units are usually quite narrowly defined, so different groups of workers working for the same employer often belong to different unions and/or bargaining units. For example, at Air Canada, different unions represent and bargain separately for the pilots, customer service agents, baggage handlers, flight attendants, mechanics, and so on. Managers and even lower-level supervisors are typically excluded from these bargaining units, which are meant to represent communities of interest. The norm is for union locals to belong to one of a few major national or international unions, which, in turn, primarily represent either private- or public-sector workers, but are now usually spread across different industrial sectors. These national unions may or may not coordinate bargaining among the locals they represent, and may or may not co-operate with other unions in bargaining.

It used to be the case from the 1940s through to the 1970s that similar kinds of workers in the same industry were represented by the same union. For example, the United Steelworkers of America (USWA) represented workers in the steel industry. Today, most large industrial unions, such as the USWA, the National Automobile, Aerospace, Transportation and General Workers Union of Canada (CAW-Canada), and the United Food and Commercial Workers (UFCW) are the product of mergers between what used to be separate industrial unions, and represent workers in a number of different sectors of the economy. There are often several unions representing similar kinds of workers in the same industry. For example, there are at least two major unions in the mining sector, and employees in long-term care homes belong to different unions in different provinces, and often to different unions in the same province and even municipality. Unions that used to represent mainly blue-collar men in manufacturing have now branched out into different parts of the private sector and even the public sector. For example, the auto workers (CAW) and the steelworkers (USWA) are now general unions. The USWA, for example, represents not only miners and steelworkers, as in the past, but also security guards, clerical and support workers at universities, and retail workers. The CAW represents not only auto workers, but also hotel workers, airline customer-service agents, and fish plant and railway workers, among others.

Most major unions in Canada belong to the Canadian Labour Congress, which tries to make sure that its member unions do not fight each other for members, a practice known as raiding. It is quite rare, but not unknown, for unions to get into fights with each other for the right to represent already unionized workers, and there is certainly a fair bit of rivalry in trying to organize non-union workers.

After a union is certified to represent a group of workers, its central activity is to bargain and enforce a collective agreement covering such issues as wages, benefits, hours of work, and working conditions with the employer. The members of a union local must elect an executive and bargaining committee to take responsibility for bargaining and union affairs, and usually union members also elect stewards to represent members to employers on a day-to-day basis when conflicts arise. Local union officers are typically assisted by full-time, paid union staff, particularly in bargaining, and to help resolve complaints or grievances that cannot be resolved at an early stage of discussions. Unions can and do differ a great deal in terms of the quality of internal democracy and the extent of member involvement, but collective agreements are almost invariably ratified by a vote of members, and a vote will be held before a strike is conducted. Usually members are closely consulted before bargaining begins so as to identify key issues, and most union locals have regular membership meetings to discuss issues that arise during the course of a collective agreement, which typically are in force for two or three years. A great deal of media coverage of union issues focuses on strikes, but these are actually very rare events. In recent years, in all of Canada, there have only been 300 to 400 strikes per year, involving 100,000 to 400,000 workers. One-third of all employees are union members, but in a typical year, time lost due to strikes is well under one-tenth of 1% of total working time.

Most bargaining with employers takes place at the local union level, and some employers bargain with several unions. Industry-wide bargaining was always quite weakly developed in Canada, and has eroded in recent years. This very decentralized bargaining system tends to weaken the bargaining power of Canadian unions compared to unions in countries such as Germany and the Scandinavian countries where bargaining across whole industries is still common, and where there is some coordination of bargaining aims between the different industrial unions at the national level. Fragmented bargaining also reflects the reality of very different issues and economic circumstances in different workplaces and sectors of the economy.

Collective agreements are formal and legally binding documents that can run to many pages. The fact that unionized workers are covered by the terms of a collective agreement means that they have rights. Unions are legally obliged to take up (through a grievance) reasonable complaints by members that the terms of an agreement have been violated, and employers are legally obliged to change their practices if they are found to violate the terms of an agreement. Workers join unions at least as much to ensure due process at the workplace as for the economic objective of higher wages.

Probably the most important aspect of unionization for individual workers is that they have a formal contract of employment that can be readily enforced through the grievance and arbitration process. By contrast, non-union workplaces are usually more informal, which can mean arbitrary and capricious exercise of managerial authority. Of course, minimum employment standards laws do provide for minimum wages, maximum hours of work, and safe working conditions. However, it is striking that very few complaints about wages or working conditions are filed with labour standards officials while an employment relationship still exists. The vast majority of complaints are lodged after a worker has been dismissed, usually for non-payment of wages. Some large non-union employers do adopt formal, written workplace rules and formal complaint processes and procedures, in effect mimicking union workplace rules. These can be effective, but it is also the case that they do not have the binding force of a collective agreement.

Table 8.1 provides information on the proportion of unionized employees covered by selected provisions in collective agreements.

Typically, collective agreements define the following.

Wages
Wages are usually set by the hour, week, or pay period. Sometimes, there is an element of performance pay, but this is much less common than in non-union workplaces where piecework, commissions, and bonuses based on individual or group performance are more common. Wages are usually set for defined jobs and job classifications, so there is a formal system of pay by position.

Non-Wage Benefits
Collective agreements commonly specify benefits, such as employer pension plan coverage, health care, and paid or unpaid time off for family and personal reasons.

Table 8.1: Selected Provisions in Collective Agreements

	% Union Employees Covered
Job security and protection	
Layoffs based on seniority	69.1%
Some restriction on contracting out	64.3%
Advance notice to union of technological change	56.7%
Training to deal with technological change	45.5%
Severance on layoff based on years of service	54.9%
Opportunties for job progress	
Promotion based on seniority:	
Primary criterion	31.4%
Tie-breaker	25.1%
Provision for paid educational leave:	
Specific to job	51.7%
General	12.4%
Apprenticeship program	30.1%
Employer contributes to training fund	34.0%
Deferred salary leave plan	33.9%
Joint committee on training	40.9%
Equity	
Employment equity program	25.5%
Harassment complaint procedure	52.1%
Workplace conditions	
Joint committee:	
Broad mandate	51.8%
Organization of work	36.6%
Working conditions	38.3%
Working-time	
Normal hours of work less than 37.5 hours:	
White-collar	43.8%
Blue-collar	17.7%
Some limit on overtime	24.7%
Paid holidays:	
10 days	14.3%
11 days	30.8%
More than 11 days	34.3%
Annual vacation:	
Four weeks after 10 years or less	70.3%
Four weeks after 5 years or less	27.8%
Five weeks after 15 years or less	30.9%
Provision for job-sharing	16.2%
Provision for flex-time:	
White-collar	21.3%
Blue-collar	9.4%
Compressed work week:	
White-collar	23.8%
Blue-collar	25.1%

Source: Human Resources Development Canada, *Bureau of Labour Information*.
Note: Collective agreement provisions vary widely re the precise content.

Job Security and Protection

Collective agreements formalize the norm that individual dismissal shall only be for just cause, so individual discipline and dismissal can be appealed through the grievance and arbitration process.

There are usually provisions for layoff for economic reasons to be based upon seniority by date of hiring, so long-tenure workers effectively have a high degree of job security. Often agreements have formal provisions to prohibit or limit an employer's contracting out of work, and to provide advance notice of technological and organizational change. Sometimes there are formal no-layoff provisions for the term of a contract, and often layoffs become subject to formal negotiation.

Opportunities for Job Progress

Most, but not all, agreements provide for seniority in promotions, so that a worker who has the skills and abilities to fill an available job will get the job if she or he is the most senior candidate. Job vacancies usually have to be posted, and are subject to formal competitions. Often agreements provide defined opportunities for training. These provisions mean that union members are generally able to access better jobs through formalized internal labour markets. Formal structures for promotion can exist in larger non-union firms, but collective agreements typically provide much stronger rights for workers.

Equity

Only a minority of collective agreements provide for formal employment equity programs (sometimes because legislative provisions exist), but harassment complaint procedures have become much more common.

Workplace Conditions

Many agreements contain provisions—sometimes very detailed—on the content of jobs, workloads, and proper working conditions. Often agreements also set up labour-management committees to informally discuss working conditions. However, almost all agreements also contain management rights' clauses that give management the right (subject to specific exceptions) to assign tasks to workers, to direct work, and so on.

Working Time and Hours of Work

Agreements usually specify regular hours of work, shift schedules, maximum hours, and provisions for overtime pay, as well as provisions for paid time off. Again, this contrasts with informal schedule arrangements (such as variable weekly hours, on-call arrangements, and unpaid overtime) in many non-union workplaces. Unionized workers generally enjoy far more paid time off the job than do non-union workers. (The norm under provincial employment standards is for just 10 days of annual vacation after one year, with no further increase based on years of service.)

■What Are the Impacts of Unions?

Unions Raise Wages, Especially for Lower-Paid Workers

In Canada, as in almost all countries, it is well established that unionized workers earn higher wages than non-union workers. This is referred to as the union wage premium, or union wage advantage. Usually the wage advantage is greatest for workers who would otherwise be low paid.

Table 8.2 provides data on the union wage advantage in Canada in 2003. The median union worker (50% earn more and 50% earn less) earned $20 per hour, $6 per hour more or 43% more than the median non-union worker. The union wage advantage is greater for women ($6.73 per hour) than for men ($5.02 per hour). The difference in average wages between union and non-union workers is less ($4.36 per hour in 2003, representing a union wage advantage of 26%). The union advantage measured in terms of average wages is less because many non-union workers, especially male non-union workers, are very well-paid managers and professionals. The union advantage, measured in terms of average hourly wages, is greater in the private sector than the much more highly unionized public sector, and tends to be highest in relatively low-paid occupations.

Table 8.2: The Union Wage Advantage in 2003			
	Union	Non-Union	Union Advantage	Union Advantage as % of Non-Union
Median hourly wage				
All	$20.00	$14.00	$6.00	42.9%
Men	$21.00	$15.98	$5.02	31.4%
Women	$18.75	$12.02	$6.73	56.0%
Average hourly wage				
All	$21.01	$16.65	$4.36	26.2%
Men	$22.00	$18.69	$3.31	17.7%
Women	$19.94	$14.55	$5.39	37.0%
Age 15–24	$12.66	$9.88	$2.78	28.1%
Public sector	$23.10	$22.09	$1.01	4.6%
Private sector	$18.70	$16.17	$2.53	15.6%
Sales and service occupations	$13.16	$11.28	$1.88	16.7%
Processing and manufacturing occupations	$18.11	$14.76	$3.35	22.7%

Source: Statistics Canada. *Guide to the Labour Force Survey, 2004.* Catalogue 71-543, February 17, 2004.

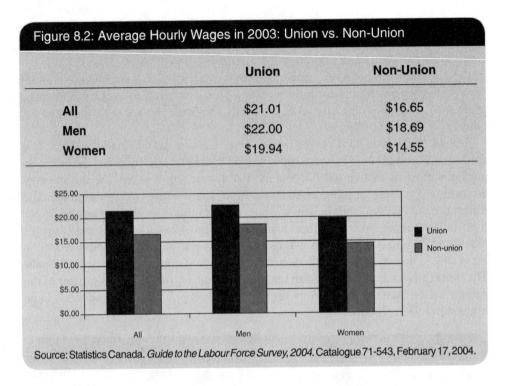

Figure 8.2: Average Hourly Wages in 2003: Union vs. Non-Union

	Union	Non-Union
All	$21.01	$16.65
Men	$22.00	$18.69
Women	$19.94	$14.55

Source: Statistics Canada. *Guide to the Labour Force Survey, 2004.* Catalogue 71-543, February 17, 2004.

It is important to take into account that union and non-union workers are different, and also hold different kinds of jobs. Union members are, on average, older and more experienced than non-union members, and are much more likely to work in public and social services and, if they work in the private sector, for large firms. And, more union members are highly trained and educated. Public-sector wages tend to be higher than those in the private sector, not just because of higher union coverage, but also because of the high proportion of professional jobs. In other words, the apparently very large union wage advantage reflects many factors other than union coverage. Economists have tried to calculate the union wage premium (the difference between the union and non-union wage) for comparable jobs, holding constant all the other factors that determine wages. Calculated this way, the premium has been generally estimated to be in the range of 7% to 14% in Canada in the 1990s (Fang and Verma 2002). Holding everything else constant, unions still have a very significant impact on wages. And, wages are only one part of the union pay advantage, which includes much higher benefits and more paid time off than is the case for non-union workers.

The union wage premium is impossible to determine precisely. It may reflect a compensating differential for more difficult working conditions than those of non-union workers. On the other hand, the union wage premium may be understated to the extent that it takes no account of the positive impacts of unions on the wages of non-union workers. Many non-union employers more or less match union wages in order to avoid unionization.[1]

The union wage premium has been found to be lowest in countries where union density is high, and highest where union density is low. Thus, it is much higher in the U.S. than in Sweden. This is surprising on the surface, but it reflects the fact that non-union employers will more likely be forced to match union wages where unions are very strong. The main impact of unions in countries such as Sweden, where the unionization rate is well over 80%, is to raise wages for lower-paid workers compared to other workers, rather than to raise union wages compared to the wages of non-union workers.

While wages are obviously a key concern in union bargaining, the key goal of labour movements is to expand the range of collective bargaining and to increase union density. The goal is to improve the working conditions of all workers rather than to raise the wages of a small union elite. A very high union wage premium and low union density is likely to promote very strong employer resistance to unions, as in the U.S. On the other hand, widespread unionization, as in Sweden, is likely to promote weaker employer opposition, at least once high density has been established. This is because, in highly unionized environments, wages are effectively taken out of competition since all employers in a sector or region pay roughly the same union wage and benefits. Employers must then compete with each other on the basis of non-wage costs, productivity, and quality.

The union wage premium can be paid for from several different possible sources. Part of it may come from lower management salaries and lower profits than in comparable non-union firms. The major part comes from higher productivity. (Higher output produced per hour worked supports a higher hourly wage.) And, part may come from higher prices that unionized firms charge in order to cover higher wages. The impacts of union wages on jobs and growth are discussed below.

Unions Counter Low Pay and Make Wages More Equal

Economic research has consistently shown that the union wage advantage is greatest for people who would otherwise be lower-paid workers, notably workers with less formal education and skills, younger and less experienced workers, and women and workers of colour who are vulnerable to discrimination. In Canada, unions have been shown to raise the pay of lower-paid workers compared to higher-paid workers, to reduce the incidence of poverty, and to make wages more equal (Chaykowski 1995; Chaykowski and Slotsve 1998). This is partly because unions compress the distribution of wages within unionized firms. For example, highly skilled trades workers in the auto industry make more per hour than regular assembly-line workers, but the difference is not as great as it would be in non-union firms. Because unions bargain for all workers in a bargaining unit, the tendency is to negotiate relatively flat, across-the-board wage increases that benefit all members. Over time, this reduces pay differences in the unionized sector. Unionized establishments have lower wage differentials among workers and probably between union workers and supervisors, and also make less use of performance pay and bonuses, which increase overall pay differences.

Being low paid is often defined as working in a job that pays less than two-thirds of the economy-wide median wage. In 2002, the median wage was $15.65 per hour, so a low-paid worker was someone earning less than $10.42. By this definition, 33.0% of non-union workers were low paid in 2002—including 22% of adult women workers—but just 8.4% of unionized workers were low paid. By raising the wages of traditionally disadvantaged groups the most, unions typically lower pay differences in the unionized sector between women and men, and between workers of colour and other workers.

Unions and Equality-Seeking Groups

Unions have not only raised pay for the lower paid, but have also often attempted to promote pay and employment equity for their members. Many collective agreements contain non-discrimination clauses and some call for formal pay and employment equity procedures above and beyond those mandated by law. In practice, unionized workers are also most likely to benefit from legislated pay and employment equity laws because unions have been prepared to fight long and costly cases through the courts. For example, after many years, the Public Service Alliance of Canada won a landmark, multibillion pay equity settlement for women workers, and in 2004, the Communications, Energy and Paperworkers (CEP) were still seeking a pay equity settlement with Bell Canada.

It is clear that unions play a major role in closing the wage gap between women and men, and in countering low pay among working women.[2] As shown in Table 8.2, the union advantage is greater for women than for men. The pay gap between union men and union women is just over $2 per hour compared to a gap of more than $4 per hour between non-union men and non-union women.

Canadian research (Reitz and Verma 2003) also shows that unionization (controlling for other factors) closes the wage gap between workers of colour and other Canadians, particularly among men. However, the unionization rate for minorities is much lower than for all other Canadians, especially among recent immigrants. Table 8.3 shows the impact of unionization on annual earnings of workers of colour. Here, we compare the annual earnings of employees who are union members to workers who are not covered by a collective agreement. As shown, workers of colour who were unionized earned an average of $33,525 in 1999. This was 29.9% or $7,724 more than workers of colour who were not unionized.

The union wage advantage is greatest for male workers of colour compared to all other workers (28.7% compared to 23.9%). This means that the pay gap by racial status among unionized male workers is smaller than among non-union workers.

Table 8.3: Union Impact on Annual Earnings		
	Workers of Colour	**All Other Workers**
Union member	$33,525	$37,909
Not covered	$25,801	$28,002
Union premium	$7,724	$9,907
As %	29.9%	35.4%
Men		
Union member	$39,675	$43,817
Not covered	$30,819	$35,354
Union premium	$8,856	$8,463
As %	28.7%	23.9%
Women		
Union member	$27,908	$30,875
Not covered	$20,772	$20,362
Union premium	$7,136	$10,513
As %	34.3%	51.6%

Source: Statistics Canada, *Survey of Labour and Income Dynamics—A Survey Overview*, Catalogue 75F0011, May 20, 2004.

Male workers of colour who are union members earn 9.4% less than other male union workers, while male non-union workers of colour earn 12.8% less than other non-union workers. For men, unions make a positive contribution to employment equity. The story is somewhat different among women. Women workers of colour who are unionized earn $7,136 or 34.3% more than non-union workers of colour—a significant pay advantage. Indeed, the union premium for women is greater than for men. However, the union premium is still greater among women who do not belong to racialized groups.

While working-age persons with disabilities are greatly under-represented in the workforce, the unionization rate for the minority of workers with disabilities who do work on a full-year basis is about the same as for the workforce as a whole. This is probably because workers with disabilities are most likely to find jobs in public and social services and in large firms where employment equity programs are most likely to be in place. Again, unionization helps close the pay gap between people with and without disabilities, and has particularly large impacts on the pay of lower-paid women with disabilities (CCSD 2004).

Unions Provide Greater Access to Non-Wage Benefits

In Canada, there are significant gaps in public programs covering health and welfare issues. Public pensions do provide a minimum income in retirement, but maximum benefits from Old Age Security, plus the Canada/Quebec Pension Plan, fall far below what most pension experts see as reasonable wage replacement levels for average- and higher-income workers. Unlike the U.S., doctor and hospital services are covered by public health care, but this still leaves dental care, drugs, and other services to be paid for privately. Only very limited life and disability insurance is provided through public programs. While advocating broader public programs in all of these areas, unions have also traditionally filled the gap by negotiating employer-provided benefits (sometimes on a cost-shared basis). A good benefits package easily makes up as much as 20% of the total compensation package, and this is rising fast with the growing costs of drug plans.

Table 8.4: Benefits Coverage: Union vs. Non-Union

	Medical Plan	Dental Plan	Life/ Disability Insurance	Pension Plan
All employees	57.4%	53.1%	52.5%	43.3%
Unionized	83.7%	76.3%	78.2%	79.9%
Non-union	45.4%	42.6%	40.8%	26.6%

Source: Statistics Canada, *Perspectives on Labour and Income*, Catalogue 75-001, 3(8) August 2002.

The impact of unions on benefits is even greater than on wages, particularly in smaller firms. As shown in Table 8.4, union members are up to three times more likely than non-union workers to be covered by an employer-sponsored pension plan, and twice as likely to be covered by a medical or dental plan. Some 80% of union members have an employer-provided pension plan, which usually provides a defined pension based on salary and years of earning. Only one-third of non-union workers have such pension plans, and pension coverage is rare in the non-union private sector outside very large firms. Unions are associated with higher benefits coverage mainly because this is a priority in bargaining. Of course, union members differ in their priorities, with younger members with children being most concerned with health benefits, and older workers being most concerned with pensions. Workplace pensions mean that younger workers often gain significant pension entitlements long before they start thinking about this as a serious issue. Unions have sometimes facilitated benefits coverage as well by providing the means for smaller employers to join with larger groups.

From the point of view of union members, union jobs are good jobs because they generally provide for a decent pension in retirement, and protection against the costs of ill health and disability. However, it also has to be recognized that private benefit plans come at the cost of foregone current wages, and have to be paid for out of the total employer wage bill. In some ways, bargaining for income and social security at the workplace is a second-best solution to public programs, such as good public pensions and public health care. This is particularly the case when jobs become more unstable.

Job Security and Working Conditions

Unionized workers enjoy greater job security than non-union workers. In 2001, 9.0% of men and women non-union workers experienced an involuntary job separation, meaning that they were laid off or dismissed. Just 5.5% of unionized men and 2.6% of unionized women experienced such a separation.[3] This difference reflects the fact that unionized workplaces tend to be either in the public sector, or are larger and more stable than small businesses in the private sector. Individual union members also have greater-than-average job security because of the norm of seniority in layoffs, which protects workers who have been in a specific job longer. Unionized members are less likely to be dismissed because of formal grievance procedures, and are also much less likely to quit their jobs. Unionized workplaces thus tend to be more stable, though many shut down or experienced layoffs due to economic restructuring in the 1990s.

Only limited information is available on the impact of unions on workplace conditions due to a lack of regular government surveys. One might expect that, other things being equal, unions would help improve conditions at work. However, it is also the case that a higher-than-average proportion of unionized workers are employed in jobs with unsocial work schedules (shift work, night work); in jobs with dirty and dangerous working conditions (e.g., exposure to noise, poor air and fumes, dust); and in jobs that are very stressful in terms of the pace and intensity of work and long hours. Manufacturing, resources, and construction jobs as well as many jobs in social services can be very stressful and demanding. Surveys suggest that there is little overall difference between union and non-union workers in terms of perceived job stress, though unions may well be making some difference in very demanding workplaces.

As shown in Table 8.1, above, many union members now have standard work weeks of less than 40 hours. Union members are much more likely to be paid for overtime hours than non-union members (though unpaid overtime is on the increase in unionized public services). Some union members work a lot of paid overtime, particularly in blue-collar jobs. Because of the nature of unionized jobs, unions have little impact upon the overall incidence of shift work and night work in sectors such as manufacturing and public services. About one-third of both union and non-union workers do not work a regular daytime schedule, but work on evenings, nights, or weekends, or on an on-call basis, but union work schedules are generally more stable and predictable, and there is often premium pay for unsocial hours. More social hours, such as regular day and non-weekend shifts, may be available to higher seniority workers in unionized workplaces even where work is organized on a shift basis.

Box 8.1: Unions and Working-Time

Historically, unions led the fight for the eight-hour day and the five-day work week, which became the standard in industrial jobs only in the late 1940s and 1950s. Since then, there have been only modest reductions in regular working-time, and there has been an increase in overtime and long hours for many workers in the 1990s. For employers, it often makes economic sense to schedule overtime instead of hiring new workers and assuming the cost of training and benefits. Many workers also want higher pay from overtime where there is premium pay such as time-and-a-half and double-time. Long hours are obviously attractive to employers who don't pay for overtime, which is often the case for salaried workers.

In Europe, some unions have seen shorter working-time as a way to avoid layoffs and create new jobs while expanding the quality of life of workers. Some Canadian unions have also put working-time issues front and centre in negotiations. The Communications, Energy and Paperworkers Union has limited overtime in pulp and paper mills, and the Canadian Auto Workers has bargained for more time off the job in the auto sector. These initiatives have helped protect jobs for younger members who might have been laid off. It has also been shown that shorter work schedules can help boost productivity. In many industries, it is cheaper to run a plant for more hours per day with three short shifts instead of two long shifts.

Regardless of weekly hours, union members are more likely to receive much more paid time off the job than non-union members. In Canada, the union norm is for three to four weeks of paid vacation after a year of employment, often rising to six weeks or more after about 10 to 15 years of service. This compares to a legal minimum of just two weeks for non-union workers in almost all provinces.

Unions and Training

Unions commonly bargain education and training provisions, including paid time off the job for training, apprenticeship programs, and provisions for on-the-job training to help workers deal with technological and organizational change. Data from the *Adult Education and Training Survey* show that unionization helps reduce the major gap in available training opportunities between well-educated workers and those with less formal qualifications.

Craft unions, such as the construction trades and some industrial unions, have played a major role in the development and delivery of apprenticeship programs, and some unions provide direct training to their members. A number of unions also participate in joint employer-union sectoral training bodies. Generally, unions promote training that gives workers formal, portable qualifications, as opposed to training that is very narrowly geared to the needs of a single workplace.

The Impact of Unions on the Economy and Labour Markets

To summarize, unions raise wages for union compared to non-union workers, and compress wage differences within unionized firms and sectors. In Canada, research has shown that unions significantly reduce wage inequality among men, and also reduce the gender wage gap. The overall impact of unions is to significantly reduce wage inequality (Card et al. 2003; Dinardo 1997; Lemieux 1993). Research has also shown that wage inequality in Canada is significantly lower than in the U.S. because of higher union density. However, declining unionization has been a source of growing wage inequality in Canada as well as in the U.S.

Studies show that countries with very high levels of collective bargaining coverage have much less pay inequality than lower union-density countries, such as the U.S., Britain, and Canada. In the social democratic countries of Scandinavia and the social-market countries, such as Germany and the Netherlands, collective bargaining coverage is very high (and generally quite stable) because of high union membership in combination with the *de facto* or sometimes legal extension of agreements on a sectoral or regional basis. Wage floors set by bargaining protect the great majority of non-professional and/or managerial workers, including most part-time and even temporary workers. While direct union membership is slipping, bargaining still covers more than 80% of workers in Germany and the Scandinavian and Benelux countries, as well as France and Italy. Also, unions and legislatively mandated works councils mean that there are strong elements of joint workplace governance over such issues as training and working conditions in these countries.

Countries with high levels of bargaining coverage have relatively equal wages and high wage floors, so that the incidence of low pay and earnings inequality are much lower than in Canada (OECD 1996). About one in four full-time workers in Canada in the mid-1990s (23.7%) was low paid—defined as earning less than two-thirds of the median national full-time wage—compared to just one in 20 (5.2%) in Sweden and only one in eight in Germany and the Netherlands. The minimum earnings gap between the top and bottom 10% of workers is about two to one in the Scandinavian countries compared to about four to one in the U.S. and Canada. This is because of institutional differences, notwithstanding common exposure to the forces of globalization and technological and organizational change.

Most mainstream economists see unions as almost exclusively concerned with raising the wages of their members and distorting wages compared to free-market levels, and they see this as damaging to the economy as a whole. In the standard economic model, union wage gains come at the expense of other workers and/or society as a whole, since they are paid for through higher prices or through fewer jobs in unionized firms. In the standard model, higher union wages force union employers to hire fewer workers, pushing more workers into competition for non-union jobs, thus forcing down non-union wages. In fact, the most authoritative surveys of the economic literature conclude that the positive impacts of unions in terms of reducing low pay and inequality and giving workers a voice at the workplace do not come at a significant economic price. Indeed, there is a strong argument to be made that unions promote economic prosperity as well as social justice. A major recent study by the World Bank on the economic impacts of unions (Aidt and Tzannatos 2003) finds that there is no relationship between union density and the economic or employment performance of countries. A major review of economic studies by the Organisation for Economic Co-operation and Development (OECD) also found no valid statistical relationship between trade union membership and the economic or employment performance of advanced industrial countries in the 1980s and 1990s. Union density is, overall, related neither to higher- nor lower-than-average rates of unemployment or economic growth.

The International Labour Organization (ILO 1995) argues that high employment growth and strong economic growth can be achieved in a very wide range of labour market settings. Recent studies by the ILO and others (Auer 2000; ILO 2003; Jackson 2000) have shown that some countries with very high rates of union coverage, notably Denmark, the Netherlands, and Sweden in the second half of the 1990s, have also been able to achieve high levels of employment and strong rates of economic growth. High unionization at the economy-wide level is quite compatible with good economic performance because unions can and do bargain for jobs as well as for wages. Unions and labour movements understand that bargaining outcomes have an economic impact. At the firm level at which most bargaining in Canada (and, increasingly, elsewhere) is conducted, it is also far from clear that the gains of unionization in terms of higher wages, more benefits, and better working conditions come at the price of fewer jobs. A key problem with the standard economic model is that unions do not bargain purely for higher wages with no concern for the jobs of their members. Some elements of the union advantage, such as paid time off the job and restrictions on unpaid overtime, actually increase employment. And, keeping jobs is usually a major priority in local bargaining. Often unions will bargain early retirement provisions for older workers and job-sharing arrangements in order to preserve jobs. Very few unions will raise wages to such a level as to push an employer into severe financial difficulties. Research has found that newly organized firms (in the U.S.) are no more likely to go out of business over the long term than are firms in which unions lost representation elections (Dinardo and Lee 2002), and that unionized firms have similar closure and bankruptcy rates to other firms, controlling for other characteristics (Freeman and Kleiner 1999).

It has to be borne in mind that employers as well as unions have to agree to collective agreements. Wage settlements must and do reflect market realities. In most bargaining situations, both sides understand that the rough limit for increasing total wage costs is set by productivity and employer profitability. Unions can and will push for improvements in real wages if worker productivity is increasing and firms are profitable. This implicit bargain was much more explicit in industry-wide bargaining in the 1960s and 1970s when wages often rose on the basis of an annual improvement factor based on productivity. Sometimes it is argued that this market discipline on wages does not apply in the public sector, but public-sector wage settlements tend to follow the trend that is set in the private sector. (In the 1990s, union wage settlements in the Canadian public sector have, in fact, more or less consistently lagged behind those in the private sector because of statutory or informal wage control programs.)

The union wage premium may be higher than average in highly unionized sectors of the economy. If an industry is highly unionized, such that all employers pay the same union wage and benefit package, the union impact puts no single employer at a significant competitive disadvantage. If union wages are built into the cost structure of all employers, wages are taken out of the competitive equation, forcing firms to compete with one another on the basis of non-cost issues, such as quality and customer service. Indeed, some economists argue that strong unions are a force for positive competition since they force firms to compete with one another on issues that are positive for consumers, but not negative from the workers' point of view. The high road of firm competition on the basis of high productivity, training, and production of high-quality goods and services is often contrasted to the low road of competing on the basis of low wages and poor working conditions.

There are some very tangible and direct links from a union voice in the workplace to higher productivity. The participatory benefits of unions, combined with better wages and working conditions, greatly reduce the incidence of quits in unionized compared to non-union workplaces (Swidinsky 1992). Fewer resignations and much longer job tenure mean that most unionized workers make a long-term commitment to a particular employer, giving an employer the benefit of experienced workers. Long job tenure also means that unionized employers have a major incentive to invest in the skills of employees in the knowledge that they are unlikely to leave the firm, but will use new skills over a long period. Non-union employers can strive to create more attractive workplaces and to retain workers by paying higher than market wages, but it is very difficult for them to give workers the same real stake in the enterprise, which comes from workers having their own voice.

The union voice also gives management greater knowledge of workplace conditions, which can result in more efficient work organization. And, job security means that unionized workers have an incentive to share their knowledge of production and co-operate to increase productivity. If workers know that changes in work organization will not cost them their jobs or lead to poorer health and safety or working conditions, then they will co-operate in workplace change. After all, the existence of a union means that the gains of higher productivity will be available to be shared at the bargaining table. A host of studies have shown that the path to higher productivity lies in the effective combination of new technologies, training,

Box 8.2: Unions and Productivity

The major part of the union advantage in terms of pay, benefits, and paid time off the job is earned through higher productivity or higher output per hour. Higher productivity comes from a firm's investment in capital equipment and technology, as well as investment in worker training and skills. The fact that unionized firms are under constant pressure to pay good wages and benefits and to invest in training may lead them to invest more in new equipment and technologies than would otherwise be the case. Moreover, and most importantly, unionized firms tend to be different from non-union firms in ways that raise productivity.

The important work of Freeman and Medoff (1984) on the economic role of unions emphasizes the importance of voice. Unions provide a collective voice for workers in unionized workplaces, which make them function quite differently than most non-union workplaces. By organizing the internal labour market, unionization can lower the management costs of firms. Formal rules counter discrimination and petty abuses of managerial authority, which can be costly to firms and not just workers. Most importantly, the existence of a union stimulates and facilitates joint management-labour discussion of workplace problems. In this discussion, management listens to the union not just because it is an important source of information, but also because it has some power behind it. Union workplaces have formalized systems in place to govern issues such as promotion and technological change, and work organization and training, which means that there is some joint determination of the work process.

As Freeman and Medoff note, a good labour relations climate is essential to the productivity effect: "the extent to which a union is a liability or an asset depends crucially upon how management responds to it." Good labour-management relations can and do lead to limited workplace conflict and high levels of workplace co-operation. This is enormously important to productivity because production is always a social process and not just a technical process. If individual workers are treated with dignity and respect; if workplace rules are perceived as fair; if workers can raise concerns and issues and have them resolved; and if workers have a say in working conditions, training, and health and safety issues, then workers are likely to work co-operatively with management. True labour-management co-operation is much more difficult, if not impossible, to achieve in non-union environments since labour has no formal voice and no real power behind its voice.

and changes in the organization of work to maximize the use of skills. Many of these studies also show that unions and good labour relations can make a major contribution to the success of workplace restructuring. Far from being inflexible, many unionized workplaces can and have implemented new technologies in a much more effective way than non-union workplaces (Black and Lynch 2000).

▮Conclusion

Unions are an important force for democracy inside and outside the workplace: for better wages, working conditions, and social protections for all workers, and for a more equal distribution of wages. Unions improve workplace conditions for their own members and balance the power between employers and employees. The significant union advantage does not come at the price of fewer jobs or slower growth because unions have significant, positive effects on productivity.

• •

▮Questions for Critical Thought

1. It is often argued that unions may have had a role in protecting workers in the days of large-scale industry, but have limited relevance in today's economy and today's workers. Do you agree?
2. Based on the material in this chapter, what do you think are the major contributions of unions to improving job quality?
3. How do the impacts of unions differ between women and men?
4. Do you think unions are a force for greater equality, or a means of promoting better wages and benefits for a union elite?
5. Do you think unions are good or bad for economic growth and job creation?

▮Recommended Reading

Aidt, Toke, and Zafiris Tzannatos. 2003. *Unions and Collective Bargaining: Economic Effects in a Global Environment*. Washington: The World Bank. A major summary of the economic literature on union impacts that finds little support for the common view that unions have negative impacts upon growth and job creation.

Black, Errol, and Jim Silver. 2003. *Building a Better World: An Introduction to Trade Unionism in Canada*. Halifax: Fernwood Books. A Canadian equivalent to Yates (see below).

Freeman, Richmond, and James Medoff. 1984. *What Do Unions Do?* New York: Basic Books. Now dated, but the introductory chapters are still the classic work on the economic impacts of unions.

Gunderson, Morley, Allen Ponak, and Daphne Taras, eds. 2001. *Union-Management Relations in Canada*, 4th ed. Toronto: Addison-Wesley Longman Publishers Ltd. The standard Canadian industrial relations text.

Yates, Michael D. 1998. *Why Unions Matter*. New York: Monthly Review Press. An introduction to the role of unions from a pro-union, U.S. perspective.

▮Notes

1. For example, non-union Dofasco Steel matches unionized Stelco wages, and non-union Honda matches the Big 3 auto sector wages.

2. For Canadian evidence on the role of unions in closing the gender wage gap, see Doiron and Riddell (1994) and Jackson and Schellenberg (1999).
3. Custom data from Statistics Canada, *Survey of Labour and Income Dynamics* (Ottawa: Statistics Canada, 2001).

References

Aidt, Toke, and Zafiris Tzannatos. 2003. *Unions and Collective Bargaining: Economic Effects in a Global Environment*. Washington: The World Bank.

Auer, Peter. 2000. *Employment Revival in Europe: Labour Market Success in Austria, Denmark, Ireland and the Netherlands*. Geneva: ILO.

Black, Sandra, and Lisa Lynch. 2000. "What's Driving the New Economy: The Benefits of Workplace Innovation." National Bureau of Economic Research Working Paper no. 7479 <http://www.nber.org>.

Canadian Council on Social Development (CCSD). 2004. Disability Information Sheet no. 15 <http://www.ccsd.ca>.

Card, David, Thomas Lemieux, and W. Craig Riddell. 2003. "Unionization and Wage Inequality: A Comparative Study of the U.S., the U.K. and Canada." National Bureau of Economic Research Working Paper no. W9473 <http://www.nber.org>.

Chaykowski, Richard. 1995. "Union Influences on Labour Market Outcomes and Earnings Inequality." In *Labour Market Polarization and Social Policy Reform School of Policy Studies*, edited by Keith Banting and Charles Beach, 95–118. Kingston: Queen's University.

Chaykowski, Richard, and George Slotsve. 1998. "Economic Inequality and Poverty in Canada: Do Unions Matter?" Paper presented to the Centre for the Study of Living Standards Conference on the State of Living Standards and the Quality of Life in Canada, October <http://www.csls.ca>.

Dinardo, John. 1997. "Diverging Male Wage Inequality in the United States and Canada, 1981–1988: Do Institutions Explain the Difference?" *Industrial and Labor Relations Review* 50, no. 4 (July): 629–651.

Dinardo, John, and David S. Lee. 2002. "The Impact of Unionization on Establishment Closure." NBER Working Paper no. W8993 <http://www.pber.org>.

Doiron, D.J., and W.C. Riddell. 1994. "The Impact of Unions on Male-Female Earnings Differences in Canada." *Journal of Human Resources* 29, no. 2: 504–534.

Fang, Tony, and Anil Verma. 2002. *The Union Wage Premium: Perspectives on Labour and Income* (Winter). Ottawa: Statistics Canada.

Freeman, Richard, and Morris M. Kleiner. 1999. "Do Unions Make Firms Insolvent?" *Industrial and Labor Relations Review* 52, no. 4 (July): 510–527.

Freeman, Richard, and James Medoff. 1984. *What Do Unions Do?* New York: Basic Books.

International Labour Organization (ILO). 1995. *World Employment Report*. Geneva: ILO.

_____. 2003. *Decent Work in Denmark: Employment, Social Efficiency and Economic Security*. Geneva: ILO.

Jackson, Andrew. 2000. *The Myth of the Equity-Efficiency Trade-Off*. Ottawa: Canadian Council on Social Development.

Jackson, Andrew, with Grant Schellenberg. 1999. "Unions, Collective Bargaining and Labour Market Outcomes for Canadian Working Women." In *Women and Work*, edited by R. Chaykowski and Lisa Powell, 245–282. Kingston: Institute for Economic Policy, Queen's University.

Lemieux, Thomas. 1993. "Unions and Wage Inequality in Canada and the United States." In *Small Differences That Matter: Labor Market and Income Maintenance in Canada and the United States*, edited by David Card and Richard Freemean, 66–107. Chicago: University of Chicago Press.

Organisation for Economic Co-operation and Development (OECD). 1996. "Earnings Inequality, Low Paid Employment and Earnings Mobility." *OECD Employment Outlook*, 59–108.

Reitz, Jeffery, and Anil Verma. 2003. "Immigration, Race and Labour: Unionization and Wages in the Canadian Labour Market." Mimeo.

Swidinsky, R. 1992. "Unionism and the Job Attachment of Canadian Workers." *Industrial Relations/Relations Industrielles* 47: 729–751.

CHAPTER NINE

Is There a Future for Canadian Unions?

▌Introduction

This chapter looks at some of the challenges facing Canadian unions as a result of economic restructuring and the changing workforce. It analyzes trends in union coverage, especially between women and men and the public and private sectors, and details the sharp decline of unions among blue-collar men, and the much lower but more stable coverage in private services. It concludes with an overview of the process of union change and renewal in Canada.

Unions face enormous challenges in many advanced industrial countries, and are often seen as increasingly powerless, if not irrelevant, in post-industrial societies and the so-called new global economy. There can be little doubt that the power of unions to influence wages, benefits, and working conditions through collective bargaining has been eroded by much more competitive national and international markets. In the 1950s and 1960s, strong industrial unions in North America and Europe were able to take wages and labour conditions out of the competitive equation by ensuring that major employers in a specific sector, such as auto or steel or rubber, provided the same basic conditions of employment. This ability to shape the economics of whole sectors has been greatly eroded by increased international trade and by deregulation and privatization of sectors such as transportation, communications, and health, which were once insulated to at least some degree from the forces of competition. A traditional key bastion of union strength—male blue-collar workers in manufacturing—has been undercut to some degree by the shift to a post-industrial, knowledge-based economy. More recently, public-sector unions have been challenged by the shift to privatized delivery of services.

As unions have declined in numbers, their political influence has weakened compared to that of employers, and the legislative climate has often become much more hostile. In some countries, notably the U.S., unions have been marginalized to a remarkable degree. American unions now represent only one in seven workers compared to about one in three in the 1960s, and it has become extremely difficult to recruit new members due to strong employer resistance and weak labour laws. In Britain, union strength has also declined greatly. Even in continental Europe, where the majority of workers are still covered by collective agreements negotiated by unions and employers, individual trade union membership has tended to decline.

Unions have been forced to confront major changes, not just in the economy, but also in the wider society. The emergence of a more diverse and more highly educated workforce—which is now almost equally divided between women and men and includes many minority workers—has posed challenges for labour movements that were once made up mainly of skilled and semi-skilled, White, male manual workers. Unions were once a powerful expression of tightly knit working-class communities, but old solidarities and forms of class consciousness declined with the decline of heavy industry and the shift of population to the suburbs, which began even in the early days of post-war prosperity. What workers expect of unions has also changed, with quality of work and work-life balance issues becoming more important than the traditional (and still important) emphasis on wages and benefits.

Yet, even if employers and governments have become more hostile and the workforce has changed dramatically, unions can and often do adapt to change. Unions change in order to survive and because of pressures from members and activists. The alternative to union decline is union renewal, and there is no shortage of workers in today's so-called new economy who are still attracted to unions, and no shortage of active and engaged union members who want to build a vital labour movement to address the pressing problems of the workplaces of today.

This chapter documents trends in union strength, in union organizing efforts, and in workers' attitudes toward unions. It makes an assessment of the forces driving union density and briefly flags some of the things that unions could do to turn things around.

◼Trends in Union Density

Union density or coverage refers to the proportion of all employees who are covered by a collective agreement. (Note that a small proportion of workers, usually lower-level supervisors, are not union members but are still covered by a collective agreement.) Canadian unions today represent about one in three workers (32.4% in 2003). This is well above the current level of just 14% in the U.S., and Canadian union strength is often contrasted to that in the U.S. and the U.K. Quite unlike the U.S., the absolute number of union members in Canada has continued to increase. However, while far from marginal and still a powerful force in many sectors of the economy, the best available data suggest that union density in Canada has fallen quite sharply from a peak of about 40% in the mid- to late 1980s.[1] Union density has fallen to below 20% in the private sector, and less than 1% of all non-union workers are currently organized into unions each year. This is probably insufficient to stop future decline. While Canadian union density is much higher than in the U.S., Canadian unions generally see no room for complacency. In opening a major conference in September 2003, Canadian Labour Congress President Kenneth V. Georgetti stressed that the labour movement must greatly expand its organizing efforts if it is to avoid marginalization and remain a major force in Canadian workplaces and in Canadian society.

Table 9.1 provides data on union coverage in 1988 and 2003. (Data in this section of the chapter are drawn from Jackson and Schetagne 2003.) Union density overall has fallen by about 7 percentage points since the late 1980s.

The decline has been gradual rather than sudden, and was concentrated in the recession and slow recovery period of the late 1980s through the mid-1990s when many jobs were lost in already unionized workplaces, particularly in the manufacturing sector. The decline has slowed with the economic recovery. Indeed, density in 2003 was almost exactly the same as in 1999, and union membership has recently grown in absolute numbers.

The decline in union coverage has been much more pronounced among younger rather than older age groups, probably because there was little or no new hiring in union workplaces in the 1990s. As a result, young people entering the workforce have tended to be hired mainly into non-union jobs, while the average age of the unionized workforce has increased. The decline has also been far greater among men than among women. The coverage rate for men is now about one-third, down from a high of almost one-half in the mid-1980s. The rate for women, after rising rapidly though the 1970s and early 1980s, has slipped much less, and the difference in union coverage between women and men has now almost completely disappeared.

Stable union coverage for women compared to the continued decline among men arises mainly from the fact that women are more likely than men to work in public and social services, where the level of union representation is much higher than in the private sector. Coverage is much higher in the public sector (75.9%) than in the

Table 9.1: Trends in Union Coverage

	1988	2003
Total	39.5	32.4
Men	43.2	32.9
Women	35.2	31.9
Public sector	na	75.6
Private sector	na	19.9
Age		
15–24	21.7	15.3
25–44	42.8	32.2
45–54	48.5	43.1
55 and over	44.3	38.4
Full-time	43.1	34.0
Part-time	30.5	25.0
Selected industry		
Manufacturing	45.5	32.6
Construction	35.2	34.4
Transportation	57.8	43.6
Utilities	73.9	71.3
Trade	16.0	14.6
Accommodation and food	13.2	8.1
Finance, Insurance, Real estate	12.2	9.9
Education	75.8	72.8
Health and welfare	61.6	55.6
Public administration	75.8	73.4
Newfoundland and Labrador	45.8	39.6
Prince Edward Island	36.0	29.8
Nova Scotia	37.3	28.6
New Brunswick	39.1	27.8
Quebec	46.2	41.2
Ontario	35.5	28.5
Manitoba	40.0	37.3
Saskatchewan	39.8	35.7
Alberta	38.0	24.2
British Columbia	40.0	33.8

Source: Statistics Canada, *Guide to the Labour Force Survey, 2004*, Catalogue 71-543, February 17, 2004. 1988 data are from the Survey of Union Membership as reported in J. David Arrowsmith, *Canada's Trade Unions: An Information Manual*. Industrial Relations Centre. (Kingston: Queen's University, 1992.)
Note: Industry data are not fully consistent due to change in classifications.

private sector (19.6%), and women in the public sector are even more likely than men to be union members. Union coverage in public and social services (public administration, education, and health and social services) has remained high, and, while perhaps slipping a bit from the mid-1980s to the mid-1990s, has increased in recent years. Two-thirds of union women work in the public sector (defined as direct government employment, plus employment in directly government-funded institutions, such as schools, universities, colleges, and hospitals) and just one-third work in the private sector. By contrast, more than 60% of unionized men work in the private sector.

As shown in Table 9.2, union coverage is very high (above 70%) in both education and public administration, and high (56.5%) in health and social services. These three sectors alone now account for half of all union members. Education and health services make up a large and increasing share of total employment, and jobs in these sectors are predominantly held by women. It is notable that union coverage is quite high, at 28%, even in the private/not-for-profit part of health care and social services. This is because many social services not directly run by governments—such as child care centres, elder care services, and long-term care homes—are often unionized. Union coverage is very high in direct government jobs (public administration). This sector shrank slowly as a total share of employment in the 1990s, though some new hiring began thereafter.

In sum, the large public and social services labour force has continued to be a key bastion of union strength, partly because the direct public sector is now stable in size, and partly because of union strength in private and non-profit, often contracted-out services, such as long-term care, child care, and home care. Public services unions such as the Canadian Union of Public Employees (CUPE) and provincial government workers unions (united at the national level in National Union of Public and General Employees—NUPGE) have actively organized within and outside the formal public sector, and have had notable success among mainly women workers. Some formerly private-sector unions have also organized in this area. It should be noted that the unionization rate is also very high, at 73%, among part-time workers in public services, contrasting sharply to a unionization rate of just 13.5% among part-time workers in the private sector. It was sometimes the case in the past that public-sector unions gained voluntary recognition from government employers, but the overall labour relations climate in public services has become much more like the business sector in recent years.

Unfortunately, there is no consistent long-term data on union coverage in the private sector. Union density outside public services was probably quite close to 30% in the mid-1980s compared to just under 20% today. The process of decline has slowed, but not completely halted, in the economic recovery period since the mid-1990s. This was a period of strong private-sector job growth, but new hiring seems to have taken place more in non-union than in union workplaces. The private-

Table 9.2: Unions and Public / Social Services

	Education	Health Care / Social Assistance	Public Administration
	2002	2002	2002
Total Number	968,000	1,412,000	777,867
% Total workforce	7.4%	10.8%	5.9%
% Women workers in sector	65.8%	84.3%	46.7%
% in public sector	92.3%	56.2%	99.7%
Union coverage			
All	73.8%	56.5%	72.1%
Public sector	78.8%	78.7%	72.3%
Private / Non-profit sector	14.5%	28.1%	na
% All union members in sector	17.0%	19.0%	13.4%

Source: Statistics Canada, *Guide to the Labour Force Survey, 2004*, Catalogue 71-543, February 17, 2004; A. Jackson and S. Schetagne, "Solidarity Forever? Trends in Union Density," Research Paper no. 25 (Ottawa: Canadian Labour Congress).

sector paid workforce grew by 15% between 1997 and 2002, while the union-covered private-sector workforce grew by only 5%. In absolute numbers, the private-sector workforce grew by 1.3 million, while the number of union-covered private-sector workers rose by just 88,000 over this period.

Looking at longer-term changes within the private sector, there has been a marked decline in union density in the traditional bastions of male blue-collar unionism. Density has fallen from about one-half to under one-third of all workers in manufacturing since the mid-1980s. This is a big enough sector for the drop to have had a major impact on overall union density as well as on union density in the total private sector. About one-third of the fall of private-sector union density since the late 1980s is probably explained by the fall within manufacturing.

The decline has been pervasive across most subsectors and occupations within manufacturing and is almost certainly closely linked to a huge turnover in manufacturing establishments since the mid-1980s and the shift of jobs to small and non-union plants. For example, a lot of the job growth in the auto industry has been in non-union Japanese assembly plants, and in small non-union parts suppliers. Widespread industrial restructuring in response to free trade with the U.S. after 1988 and other forces likely drove down union density through a combination of large job losses in union plants because of plant closures and layoffs, and much greater employer hostility to new organizing in a highly competitive environment. Under free trade, workers in Canadian manufacturing have been more directly exposed to competition from mainly non-union American and Mexican manufacturing operations.

There has also been a marked decline of union density in other industries that have undergone similar restructuring—primary industries, transportation, and, to a lesser extent, communications and utilities. Deregulation saw the rise of non-union airlines and telecommunications companies, forcing unions at union airlines and telephone companies on the defensive. By contrast, union coverage in construction has been quite stable and actually increased between 1997 and 2003. The industrial construction sector remains highly unionized in some provinces, and construction union employment has benefited from the housing and commercial building boom in some cities. Construction unions are typically based on crafts or specific occupations, and the union often plays a major role in directing members to jobs and providing training, pensions, and benefits. Craft unions in construction and in the cultural sector (e.g., unions representing actors, writers, and film technicians) can promote better wages, benefits, and access to training for workers who typically move frequently from one job to another. Their resilience in the 1990s suggests that a very old model of union representation remains quite relevant today and one could imagine new craft unions emerging to represent workers in, for example, the software development industry.

Union coverage has always been very low in private consumer services such as stores, hotels, and restaurants as well as in financial and business services, but seems to have held up relatively much better than in the traditional high union-density blue-collar industries since the late 1980s. As shown in Table 9.1, coverage is low (14.6%) in trade, but fairly stable. Many workers in grocery stores and a few department stores are represented by unions. Coverage is very low, but has always been very low, in accommodation and food services (i.e., restaurants and hotels), though some big city hotels and a few restaurants are organized. Coverage is extremely low in business services, though unions have organized some groups of workers such as security guards and building cleaners in recent years. Unions are very weak in the financial sector outside of Quebec, but some insurance offices are unionized. Since the mid-1990s, union density has been quite steady, but at low levels in private services. This probably reflects a combination of stable employment in some traditionally unionized sectors, and some successful new organizing more or less matching job growth. Union organizing is especially difficult in high worker turnover sectors and many unions in private services, such as the United Food and Commercial Workers Union (UFCW), typically organize quite a high proportion of their total membership each year.

Turning to geographical trends in union coverage, Ontario and Alberta, where national job growth was relatively concentrated in the 1990s, experienced larger-than-average declines in density from already well below-average levels. In 2003, as in 1988, the highest union density provinces were Quebec (41.2%), Newfoundland and Labrador (39.6%), Manitoba (37.3%), Saskatchewan (35.7%), and British Columbia (33.8%). All of these provinces, except B.C., experienced below-average declines in density compared to the national average after 1988. This suggests that relative union strength is self-reinforcing to a degree because of the organizational resources it gives to unions, bargaining strength, and, probably most importantly, the union movement's ability to influence governments.

Labour laws in the high union-density provinces were relatively friendly to unions for extended periods in the 1990s, not least because of unions' ties to the New Democratic Party (NDP) in British Columbia, Manitoba, and Saskatchewan, and the Parti Québecois in Quebec. It was more difficult for employers to resist a worker choice for unionization in Quebec than in the rest of Canada, and it was hard for unions to mount successful organizing campaigns in Ontario, Alberta, and much of Atlantic Canada through much of the 1990s. Unions generally benefit if labour law requires employers to recognize a union on the basis of a majority of workers in a proposed bargaining unit signing cards, or on the basis of a genuinely free vote, and operate at a disadvantage if the law allows employers to fight an active anti-union campaign before a vote (Panitch and Shwartz 2003). A lot also hinges on whether a first contract can be won through arbitration, and whether employers can replace workers who go on strike for a first or later contract. It is not uncommon for a group of workers to win union certification, but to fail to get a first collective agreement because of employer resistance. Government attitudes toward unions also matter a lot in terms of representing social services workers. Contracting out services to low-bid, often private-sector providers, as is the case with home-care services in Ontario, works against union representation, as opposed to service delivery through the public or non-profit sector.

Public-sector union density is high across all provinces, while private-sector density is much more variable, ranging from a low of just 9.5% in Prince Edward Island and 12.6% in Alberta to highs of 21.4% in British Columbia and 27.4% in Quebec. Only Quebec, Newfoundland and Labrador, and British Columbia now have private-sector unionization rates above 20%, and private-sector density in Ontario (17.4%) and Alberta (12.6%) is relatively low and falling. Union density is also very variable across cities, but is notably lower than the national average in two fast-growing cities, the huge Toronto Census Metropolitan Area (22.4%) and Calgary (21.5%). It is higher than average in the two other very large urban centres of Montreal (35.3%) and Vancouver (33.5%).

■ Forces Driving Union Density

Canadian union representation is achieved through a labour board's certification of a union to represent workers in a particular workplace. Almost always, unionization is a collective rather than an individual choice, and it continues unless and until there is a vote to decertify the union. Most union members become members by being hired into a job in an already unionized workplace rather than by actively joining or supporting a union campaign to organize a non-union workplace. Most non-union members stay that way simply because there is no active union campaign to certify the workplace in which they work. Changing union density is thus a function of three things: changes in employment in already certified workplaces as a result of closures, layoffs, and new hirings; changes in employment in non-union workplaces; and the rate at which non-union workplaces are organized into unions. Unfortunately, it is impossible to fully separate out these factors.

At a broader level, the growth of union membership will be strongly influenced by structural change in the economy, which influences the relative growth of employment by industrial sector, by occupation, by firm or establishment size, and by form of employment. This is especially true in Canada given that union density varies a lot in all of these dimensions. Union membership is concentrated among full-time workers in larger private-sector firms in resources, manufacturing, transportation, and utilities, as well as in public and social services. Union density will also be influenced by the changing composition of the workforce, especially by age, gender, and race, which is overlaid upon the changing industrial and occupational mix.

Declining unionization has often been associated with the shift to a post-industrial economy, with a shrinking share of male blue-collar jobs and a rising share of private services jobs, especially for women, in growing but low union-density sectors such as business and consumer services. Structural change has brought into question the continued relevance of the labour laws and kinds of unions that emerged in the post-war, so-called Fordist, era when a high proportion of the workforce could be found in large industrial workplaces such as steel mills and assembly plants. Unions, it is often argued, cannot organize workers in small workplaces or in very precarious forms of employment, and win little support from well-educated professionals and skilled workers.

Other forces of change working against unions include the shifting balance of power between labour and employers in workplaces and the job market as a result of fiercer competition, and squeezed profitability in the private sector as a result of globalization and deregulation, as well as restructuring of public and social services through privatization and contracting out to the private sector. Structural social and economic change also influences the balance of power between labour and employers at the political level, and with it the legal and regulatory climate that influences union strength. Studies of Canada–U.S. density differences have often stressed the importance of facilitative labour legislation to new organizing. Finally, density will clearly be influenced by the attitudes of individual workers toward unions, and by the capacity of unions and the labour movement to attract and mobilize the unorganized as well to retain the loyalties and commitment of the already organized. At a broad, cultural level, there has probably been a shift to greater individualism among workers, and less of a sense of working-class identity than may have been the case in the 1950s and 1960s.

The idea that declining union density is strongly associated with the changing industrial and occupational composition of employment is plausible and has some elements of truth given the extent to which deindustrialization, privatization, and the growth of knowledge-based work have eroded former bastions of union strength. However, as was shown earlier in this book, the total employment share of blue-collar men who traditionally supported unions has not fallen dramatically and remains high. Employment in high union-density public and social services has been growing as a share of all jobs, and will continue to do so.

Looking at sectors of traditional union weakness, it is true that sales and service jobs are a big share of employment, but this has been the case for a long time. One big change that has indeed taken place has been the shift of jobs to business services, partly in professional, scientific, and technical services, which employ mainly higher-skilled workers, and partly in administrative and support services, which includes many less-skilled occupations such as building cleaners and security guards.

Without denying the long-term trend toward higher-skilled jobs (at least as measured by education) or the emergence of new economy information technology occupations, it is hard to see why occupational and industrial shifts should have had a big negative impact on overall union density. A technically sophisticated analysis of the decline in union density from 1984 to 1998 indeed finds that shifts of employment by industry and by occupation, taken together, have had only a modest impact on the unionization rate, and that the decline is explained more by downward shifts within industries and occupations (Riddell and Riddell 2001). For example, the decline of unions within formerly strong union sectors such as manufacturing and blue-collar jobs explains more of the fall in density than a shift of jobs away from manufacturing and blue-collar jobs. That said, unions will obviously have to reach out to more highly skilled new economy workers as well as to low-paid private services workers if continued decline is to be halted.

It is often also believed that unions have become weaker because of the decline of large private-sector workplaces and the rise of small business. It is indeed true that the rate of unionization in the private sector is much higher in large rather than small establishments. More than 40% of workers in large firms with more than 500 workers are unionized, and very large industrial operations are still highly likely to be unionized. It is very difficult to organize and represent workers in smaller businesses under the labour relations practices that generally apply in North America. One problem is that union dues from small workplaces make it practically difficult for unions to effectively represent the workers in them. Another is that small- and medium-sized employers tend to be especially hostile to unions, and prefer very informal labour relations practices. Most importantly, it is very difficult for unions to improve wages, benefits, and working conditions in very competitive sectors dominated by smaller firms. High union density in private services in some Northern European countries is made possible mainly by sector-wide agreements, at least at the community or regional level, rather than by North American-style decentralized certification and bargaining. For example, Swedish hotel workers are covered by contracts that are bargained centrally and cover almost all hotel workers, placing no single hotel at a competitive advantage and extending union conditions and protections to workers who are dispersed across many workplaces. Where unions in Canada have gained a foothold among smaller employers, as in the housing construction industry in Toronto, or the child care sector in Quebec, it has often been by developing sector-wide rather than employer-by-employer-by-employer collective agreements and bargaining structures.

All that said, a shift from large to small workplaces does not explain why Canadian union density has declined. In the late 1990s, about 40% of private-sector workers were employed in very small workplaces with less than 20 workers, and about 30% were employed in establishments of more than 100 workers, but this was also the case in the mid-1980s (Drolet and Morrissette 1998). Employment has actually shifted marginally away from small workplaces in the late 1990s. In retailing, for example, there has been a shift from small stores to superstores; in financial services, large call centres have replaced local bank branches; in food services, a lot of food preparation has been contracted out from restaurants to large food processors. And, if anything, recent union organizing successes have been relatively concentrated in small rather than large establishments. Between 1997 and 2002, union density in small workplaces in the private sector actually rose—from 7.6% to 7.9%—while falling sharply—from 47.3% to 40.9%—in private-sector workplaces with more than 500 employees.

Changes in the form of employment have also probably had little impact on union density. Self-employment and part-time employment have become a bit more common, but union density has increased a bit among part-time workers, even in the private sector, since the mid-1990s. The incidence of very low-tenure jobs has not increased since the mid-1980s, and average job tenure has increased. None of this is to deny that many Canadian workers, particularly women, youth, and workers of colour, are employed in precarious and insecure jobs in smaller workplaces, which makes union organization extremely difficult under prevailing labour laws. However, the extent of structural change as a source of union decline can be greatly exaggerated.

◼New Organizing and Union Renewal

Every year, some non-union workers join unions and gain a collective bargaining relationship with their employer through a labour board certification. Much less commonly, some unions are decertified with the consent of the workers involved. Obviously, if union density is to increase, more workers must be persuaded to build and join unions. Indeed, given that many union employers will shrink or go out of business over time and that new businesses will be established, union density will inevitably decline if unions are not organizing many new members. The much slower decline of union density in Canada than in the U.S. in the 1980s and 1990s almost certainly reflects not just more union-friendly labour legislation, but also a greater union commitment to new organizing and movement building. The absolute number of workers organized into Canadian unions each year is, relative to the size of the workforce, probably some five times higher than in the U.S.

Unfortunately, available data from provincial labour boards provide very incomplete information on how many workers are joining unions, and where the new organizing is taking place. From the mid-1970s to the late 1990s, anywhere from between 60,000 and 100,000 workers, or as many as 2% of all non-union workers, were organized into unions through new certifications (minus decertifications) each year (Johnson 2002; Katz-Rosene 2003; Martinello 1996). There has been a downward trend since the high point of the mid-1980s, with some ups and downs, and by the late 1990s, just under 1% of all non-union paid workers were joining unions each year. The organization rate has been consistently much higher than average in Quebec and, until recently, in British Columbia. The content and administration of labour laws clearly make a major difference. In Ontario, more than 30,000 workers were organized into unions in 1994–1995 after the passage of new labour laws by the NDP government, but the total had fallen back to 14,000 by 2002–2003 under new Conservative government laws.

The average size of new bargaining units is small: 50 to 70 members in Ontario since the mid-1990s and just 30 to 40 members in B.C. There is evidence of relative success among women workers and workers of colour, and more new organizing in services, especially health and welfare services (Yates 2000, 2003). In B.C. (where the data are most complete), more than 50,000 workers were organized into unions from 1997 to 2002, of whom just one in six worked in the resource and manufacturing sectors. Large private-sector industrial unions, such as the CAW-Canada and United Steelworkers of America (USWA), have continued to add new members, alongside the Canadian Union of Public Employees (CUPE), the National Union of Public and Government Employees (NUPGE), and other public-sector unions, but many of these new members have been in services rather than in areas of traditional blue-collar industrial jurisdiction. Large unions have also grown through mergers.

In most years, from the mid-1980s to the mid-1990s, union growth from new certifications offset stagnant or declining union membership in already unionized workplaces, accounting for almost all absolute membership growth. Since the mid-1990s, union membership in already unionized workplaces seems to have grown as well. New organizing in Canada has been far from negligible and has made an important difference to union density, but it has been a case of rowing against the tide of forces working against unions in the job market as a whole.

Observers have often drawn a contrast between an organizing, as opposed to servicing, model of trade unionism related to a social movement as opposed to business union model of what unions are about. While overdrawn, the servicing and business union model stands for the bureaucratic, top-down structures, member passivity, and lack of activism and interest in organizing that were often the results of stable industrial relations in long-unionized firms and sectors in the 1960s and 1970s. Some unions were not particularly concerned about an overall fall in union density or building links to the wider community so long as their own membership was stable and members were making gains at the bargaining table. However, falling overall union strength tends to reach a tipping-point, at which time even long-unionized employers will become much more hard line in bargaining or will seek to become non-union because of increased competition from lower-cost, non-union employers. In the U.S., the central labour body, the American Federation of Labor-Congress of Industrial Organizations (AFL-CIO), was quite complacent about union density decline through much of the 1970s and into the 1980s, but this turned to alarm as the absolute number of union members began to fall, and as slipping density began to turn into a downward spiral. By the mid-1990s, almost all American unions recognized that new organizing was absolutely key to survival, and this theme played a key role in the election of new leadership.

The commitment of unions to organizing new members will be strongly influenced, not just by threats to union security in already unionized sectors, but also by whether leaders, activists, and members see themselves as part of a broader labour movement linked to a wider movement for social and economic change. At their best, unions have been concerned about improving conditions for all workers, not just a narrow union elite. Historically, union expansion has come in big waves as a growing labour movement has rapidly expanded into many workplaces over a very short period. In Canada, there were two big waves of union growth. The first was during and just after World War II when hundreds of thousands of blue-collar industrial workers joined unions such as the auto workers and the steelworkers. In the process, they transformed a small labour movement that had hitherto been made up of unions mainly representing skilled tradespeople. Indeed, for some years, there were two rival labour central bodies. The second big wave came in the 1960s and into the 1970s when public services unions grew very rapidly, bringing many women and professional workers such as teachers and nurses into the labour movement. It is notable that both of these big waves of union expansion coincided with periods of major social reform. One of the big questions today is whether unions are fated to experience a slow and steady decline, or if there will be another big wave of union organizing in the future, perhaps on a very different organizational basis than in the past.

Since at least the 1980s, there has been a gradual process of union renewal in Canada (Kumar and Murray 2002, 2003; Schenk 2003; Yates 2000, 2002, 2003). The process of renewal is about much more than just organizing new members, and is much more complex than just turning from servicing current members to organizing new members. Organizing is important, but unions abandon servicing of current members at their peril since active and mobilized members are a necessary base for a growing movement. Most people first hear about unions, about what they are like and what they can do, from family and friends. At one level, renewal has been about making unions more democratic and responsive to changes in the workplace, and to the changed needs and interests of union members. This has involved changes in leadership and staff with an emphasis on making unions more representative of a changing workforce through the inclusion of more women, workers of colour, and younger workers who are better placed to connect with the new workforce both within and outside unionized workplaces. While the shift has been partial, more women in particular have moved into top leadership and key staff positions.

There have been some changes in structures to make unions more accountable to more active and engaged members. There has been a greater emphasis on internal education and on rank-and-file member involvement in union activities, including bargaining, representing members at the workplace, and sometimes in organizing. There has also been at least a limited shift in bargaining priorities and in workplace activities to issues of interest to the new workforce, including training and work-family balance (Kumar and Murray 2002). There has also been a revival of some of the social movement dimensions of unions, which had atrophied to some degree in the days of greater employer and government acceptance of a major union role. Unions have led major campaigns on issues of interest to all workers—such as the need to protect public health care and public services, pensions, employment and pay equity, human rights, and minimum wages and employment standards—and have built stronger links with community organizations and other social movements.

Many unions have changed rather dramatically as a result of declining membership in some sectors, offset by mergers with other unions and expansion into other sectors. The former big blue-collar industrial unions, such as the auto workers and steelworkers, have become much more like general worker unions, representing a very broad range of workers, including more women, while the main public-sector unions have expanded from an original base of direct government employees into the much broader social services sector. Many unions now devote significant resources to new organizing within and outside their traditional areas of jurisdiction. However, resources and staff directed to new organizing are still a relatively small fraction of the total, and many unions still do little organizing outside their areas of traditional jurisdiction (Kumar and Murray 2003). There is often intense union rivalry in organizing and bargaining, which can be counterproductive in terms of building a stronger movement. Organizing practices continue to vary a great deal, with some unions relying on rank-and-file members and activists much more than others. While there is no magic formula for success, the evidence shows that successful organizing campaigns tend to be those in which there is a great deal of rank-and-file member involvement, and close ties to community groups (Bronfenbrenner and Friedman 1998).

A renewal of activism and renewed emphasis on organizing new members helps explain some recent successes, particularly among workers in services who would otherwise be in relatively low-paid and precarious jobs. In recent years, there have been notable successes in organizing security guards, hotel workers, workers in long-term care homes, teaching assistants in universities, and even some workers in retail trade and restaurants. Between 1997 and 2002, the proportion of all union members in low-paid jobs (paid less than two-thirds of the median hourly wage) rose from 7.1% to 8.4%, echoing increased union density among part-time workers, youth, and in small workplaces. Unions have thus had some success in organizing precarious workers. The greater difficulty seems to have been in reaching out to core workers.

Future Prospects for Unions

Union density has fallen slowly in the private sector, particularly in the traditional stronghold of male blue-collar industrial workers. It has held up much better among women than among men, mainly because of union strength in public and social services combined with the impact of organizing efforts among lower-paid workers. Unions are weak in some important parts of the new knowledge-based economy, but are not doomed to extinction because of structural change or the emergence of a new workforce. There is still substantial worker support for unions as a vehicle for improving pay and benefits and, even more importantly, for representation of workers in the workplace.

A factor in union weakness in terms of recruiting new members has probably been the fact that unions have had great difficulty making major gains at the bargaining table for their current members, and have been thrown on the defensive by extensive restructuring in both the private and public sectors. This suggests that, if unions are to grow, organizing strategies must be linked to finding a new economic role.

In the workplace, unions have often actively co-operated in changes that improve firm productivity, especially by promoting more training and business strategies that rely on higher skills. As noted before, unions are not an anachronism just because union employers face much more competitive markets than in the past. Yet, unions will be much more likely to grow in the business sector if they can again find ways to take wages and working conditions out of the competitive equation to at least some degree.

Box 9.1: Do Workers Still Want to Join Unions?

Public opinion surveys and academic studies have found evidence of significant, if qualified, continuing worker support for unions. The Canadian Labour Congress (CLC) has commissioned independent surveys, which find that about two-thirds of current union members are satisfied with their own national union, rising to three-quarters who are satisfied with their local union. In 2003, one in seven non-union workers (14%) would "very likely" vote for a union tomorrow if they had the chance. Another 19% would be "somewhat likely" to vote yes, indicating probable one-third support even before any union campaign for certification. Forty-three percent of non-union workers would be "very or somewhat likely" to join a union if there were no grounds for fear of employer reprisal. Underlying support for unions is even higher among young workers aged 18 to 29 (52%), visible minorities (54%), and women (50% vs. 37% for men), showing that the shift to a new workforce is much more positive rather than negative for the future of unions. Support is somewhat higher from workers in lower-income households and much higher for people from families with a union member.

Workers, both union and non-union, see unions as positive vehicles for workplace representation, protection from discrimination and favouritism, better health and safety, job security, higher benefits and pay, and also support unions that are active in community issues. However, non-union members in particular have concerns about the seniority principle, which gives preference in promotions and layoffs to long-tenure workers, and also have concerns about the degree of member control of unions.

Both union and non-union workers, despite the differences one might expect, are generally quite satisfied with their jobs across most dimensions. One of the big gaps, however, is in terms of worker representation. More than 70% of non-union workers would like to see an association represent them at work. There is strong evidence of a major representation gap in the contemporary workplace, even if workers are divided on whether unions, as they now exist, are the best answer for the future.

Organizing a handful of workplaces in a low-density sector is very hard, given strong employer resistance, and is unlikely to make a lot of difference for workers. Organizing across an economically relevant labour market is likely to result in greater gains and, beyond a certain threshold, less employer resistance. Bargaining of master agreements with groups of employers also makes union representation in small workplaces more viable. Examples in Canada include a handful of master agreements in hotels, restaurants, and the retail sector. In community social services in British Columbia and Quebec, organizing success has been achieved in part by promoting sector-wide bargaining between all employers and unions.

Broader-based organizing and bargaining can also be based on unions working with community organizations. In recent years, notable broader-based organizing and bargaining successes in the U.S. have included large groups of low-paid, predominantly minority group workers. For example, the Service Employees International Union (SEIU) has organized downtown office cleaning services in several cities through community-based Justice for Janitors campaigns. The hotel workforce in Las Vegas is highly unionized as a result of union renewal and new organizing across the sector, and wages and benefits are now well above the industrial average (Meyerson 2004). Broader-based organizing and bargaining are generally hindered rather than facilitated by current labour laws based on the norm of workplace-by-workplace certification and bargaining, but successful union organizing can make change happen in any case. The industrial unions of the 1930s and 1940s forced industry-wide bargaining, and a new legal framework was put in place over what had already happened.

Conclusion

No one can say with certainty that there will be a future big wave of union organizing in Canada, but unions will remain a presence, in one form or another, as long as there are conflicts of interest between employers and workers, and a desire for dignity and respect as well as more democracy at the workplace.

● ●

Questions for Critical Thought

1. Why is union coverage in the private sector so much lower than in the public sector?
2. Why do you think union coverage has been much more stable among women than among men?
3. Do you think young people today are attracted to unions? Why?
4. Would unions do better in organizing workers if they stressed issues of representation and democracy in the workplace, or bread-and-butter issues such as wages and benefits?
5. Based on what you know as well as what you have read in this chapter, do you think Canadian unions will still be relevant to workers 20 years from now?

Recommended Reading

Fairbrother, Peter, and Charlotte A.B. Yates, eds. 2003. *Unions in Renewal: A Comparative Study.* New York: Continuum. This study provides an excellent series of articles on union renewal in the U.S., Canada, Britain, and Australia, with good articles on Canada by Pradeep Kumar and Gregor Murray, Chris Schenk and Charlotte Yates.

Meyerson, Harold. 2004. "Las Vegas as a Workers' Paradise." *The American Prospect* (January). A lively account of Las Vegas's unusual status as one of the strongest union towns in the U.S., and the difference this has made for hotel and hospitality industry workers.

Panitch, Leo, and Donald Shwartz. 2003. *From Consent to Coercion: The Assault on Trade Union Freedoms*. Aurora: Garamond Press. A good account of legal restrictions and barriers to union organizing and union action.

Studies in Political Economy 74 (Fall/Winter 2004) contains a forum on "Reorganizing Unions," with an overview by Andrew Jackson, which is one basis for this chapter, and lively and provocative contributions from Pradeep Kumar, Gregor Murray, Chris Schenk, and Charlotte Yates.

Yates, Charlotte. 2002. "Expanding Labour's Horizons: Union Organizing and Strategic Change in Canada." *Just Labour* 1 <http://www.crws.ca>.

Note

1. From 1962 to 1993, the major ongoing source of data on unionization was the *Companies and Labour Unions Returns Act* (CALURA) return, which was filed annually by most unions with Statistics Canada. CALURA data show that union density in the last year of the survey was, at 32.6%, virtually unchanged from the peak of 33.5% in 1983, giving rise to a general impression of stability. (See Diane Galerneau, "Unionized Workers," *Perspectives on Labour and Income*, Cat. 75-001-XPE [Ottawa: Statistics Canada, 1996] and "Unionization in Canada: A Retrospective," Cat. 75-001-SPE [Ottawa: Statistics Canada, 1999].) However, CALURA data underestimated union coverage due to under-reporting by small unions, particularly prior to the early 1980s, and other sources indicate a decline in density. Labour Canada (now Workplace Information Directorate) data—calculated annually from the reported national membership of unions—show a peak unionization rate of 40.0% of non-agricultural paid workers in 1983 and 1984, falling to 34.8% in 1990 and to 30.4% in 2003. Comparable household surveys by Statistics Canada (the source of the data in Table 9.1) also suggest a significant decline in density, defined as the proportion of paid workers covered by a collective agreement.

References

Bronfenbrenner, Kate, and Sheldon Friedman, eds. 1998. *Organizing to Win: New Research on Union Strategies*. Ithaca and London: ILR Press.

Drolet, Marie, and Rene Morrissette. 1998. *Recent Evidence on Job Quality by Firm Size*. Ottawa: Statistics Canada.

Jackson, Andrew, and Sylvain Schetagne. 2003. "Solidarity Forever? Trends in Union Density." Research Paper no. 25. Ottawa: Canadian Labour Congress <http://www.clc-ctc.ca>.

Johnson, Susan. 2002. "Canadian Union Density 1980 to 1998 and Prospects for the Future." *Canadian Public Policy* XXVIII, no. 3: 333–349.

Katz-Rosene, Ryan. 2003. "Union Organizing: A Look at Recent Organizing Activity through Analysis of Certification across Canadian Jurisdictions." CLC Research Paper no. 26. Ottawa: Canadian Labour Congress.

Kumar, Pradeep, and Gregor Murray. 2002. *Innovation and Change in Labour Organizations in Canada*. Ottawa: Department of Human Resources Development Canada.

_____. 2003. "Strategic Dilemma: The State of Union Renewal in Canada." In *Trade Unions in Renewal: A Comparative Study*, edited by Peter Fairbrother and Charlotte A.B. Yates, 200–221. New York: Continuum.

Martinello, Felice. 1996. *Certification and Decertification Activity in Canadian Jurisdictions*. Kingston: Industrial Relations Centre, Queen's University.

Meyerson, Harold. 2004. "Las Vegas as a Workers' Paradise." *The American Prospect* (January) <http://www.prospect.org>.

Panitch, Leo, and Donald Shwartz. 2003. *From Consent to Coercion: The Assault on Trade Union Freedoms*. Aurora: Garamond Press.

Riddell, Chris, and W. Craig Riddell. 1998. "Changing Patterns of Unionization: The North American Experience, 1984 to 1998." Department of Economics Working Paper. Vancouver: University of British Columbia.

Schenk, Christophe. 2003. "Social Movement Unionism: Beyond the Organizing Model." In *Trade Unions in Renewal: A Comparative Study*, edited by Peter Fairbrother and Charlotte Yates, 244–263. New York: Continuum.

Yates, Charlotte. 2000. "Staying the Decline in Union Membership: Union Organizing in Ontario, 1985–1999." *Relations Industrielles/Industrial Relations* 55, no. 4: 640–674.

_____. 2002. "Expanding Labour's Horizons: Union Organizing and Strategic Change in Canada." *Just Labour* 1 <http://www.crws.ca>.

_____. 2003. "The Revival of Industrial Unions in Canada." In *Unions in Renewal: A Comparative Study*, edited by Peter Fairbrother and Charlotte A.B. Yates, 221–244. New York: Continuum.

THIS PART OF THE BOOK LOOKS AT HOW CANADA'S INCREASING INTEGRATION IN THE global and North American economy has changed the labour market and the world of work, and the extent to which the forces of free trade and global economic integration limit our choices in terms of labour market alternatives.

Chapter 10, "Canadian Workers in a Changing World," focuses upon the impacts of globalization and the Free Trade Agreement (FTA) with the U.S. on Canadian workers and on social programs, arguing that there have been some pressures toward downward harmonization of labour and social standards.

Chapter 11, "Improving Work," compares and contrasts Canada's labour market and workplace institutions to those of some European countries, and argues that the high-inequality and high-insecurity liberal labour market model is not universal, and that there are viable alternatives that Canadians could consider.

■ Related Web Sites

- The Canadian Centre for Policy Alternatives <http://www.policyalternatives.ca> is a left-leaning, labour-supported think-tank that has published many studies critical of the FTA, North American Free Trade Agreement (NAFTA), and the World Trade Organization (WTO).
- The C.D. Howe Institute <http://www.cdhowe.org> is a right-leaning, business-supported think-tank that has published many studies broadly supportive of the trade deals and trade liberalizations, including even deeper economic integration with the United States.
- The European Industrial Relations Observatory (EIRO) <http://www.eiro. eurofund.ie> monitors trends in work in the European countries. Searches can be undertaken by topic or by country. See "Non-Permanent Employment, Quality of Work and Industrial Relations," "Lifelong Learning and Collective Bargaining," "Low Wage Workers and The Working Poor," and "Collective Bargaining Coverage and Extension Procedures."

- The International Labour Organization <http://www.ilo.org> is the UN specialized agency that promotes social justice and internationally recognized human and labour rights. The ILO formulates international labour standards in the form of conventions and recommendations and undertakes and publishes research on many aspects of work.
- The Organisation for Economic Co-operation and Development <http://www. oed.or> is a Paris-based policy think-tank and research centre supported by the governments of member countries, which are almost all advanced industrial countries. The Web site contains numerous statistics on member countries and comparative research studies on labour market and social issues.

CHAPTER TEN

Canadian Workers in a Changing World

The Impacts of Globalization and Free Trade

Introduction

This chapter looks at the impacts on working people that have resulted from Canada's increased integration in the North American and global economy. It sets out reasons why closer trade and investment ties would lead to a process of downward harmonization to lower wages and social standards, and why such pressures have sometimes been exaggerated. The impacts of closer ties with the United States under the FTA and NAFTA on jobs, income inequality, and social programs are examined in detail.

Globalization: A Race to the Bottom?

There have been many important changes in the global economy over the past three decades and more, driven by new communication and transportation technologies, and by trade and investment liberalization agreements. National economies have become more closely integrated as trade and investment flows across borders have grown rapidly, and those flows increasingly take place through transnational corporations. Markets for many goods and services have become much more competitive, and companies facing intense competitive pressures will tend to actively seek lower costs in order to survive and prosper. They will do so in part by trying to holding the line on wages; in part by increasing productivity, with potentially negative implications for hours of work and working conditions; and in part by seeking to operate in jurisdictions that levy low taxes and impose few regulations on business. This often means lower levels of social protection for working families. Many observers see so-called liberal globalization as prompting a race to the bottom in which mobile global corporations play off workers and governments against each other to the detriment of working people. This has undermined the major gains made in the period after World War II of managed, regulated national capitalisms in which unions were strong and comprehensive welfare states were constructed (Teeple 2000).

The basic problem is compounded by the fact that regulation of the economy at the national level to promote the rights and interests of workers has not been replaced by positive regulation at the international level. To be sure, the conventions of the International Labour Organization (ILO) require governments to promote labour rights and standards, and the Universal Declaration of Human Rights ratified by most states protects a wide range of social rights, but no one enforces these commitments. When China recently joined the WTO, for example, the government was not required to recognize the right of workers to form independent trade unions or, for that matter, to hold free elections. The only requirement was to provide free access to its market to foreign imports and investments. Companies can thus effectively choose to operate under one set of social rules in Canada, or another in China, while governments must apply the same set of economic rules to domestic and foreign corporations and investors alike.

Globalization is often associated with especially strong pressures to downward harmonization of wages and labour and social standards because of increased trade and investment ties between the developed and developing, low-wage countries. There are certainly grounds for concern that increased North–South trade has impacted on Canadian jobs and wages. The shift of manufacturing to developing countries in Asia and elsewhere in the Americas has been an important cause of plant closures and layoffs in the manufacturing sector, and there are signs of a growing impact on services as telecommunications technology increases the capacity of developing countries to serve our market from a considerable distance for everything from software to back-office operations to call centres. Wages in developing countries are, at best, only a small fraction of Canadian wages, including for quite highly educated and skilled workers. The average industrial wage even in large export-oriented and foreign transnationally owned plants in China is less than one-tenth of that in Canada.

Box 10.1: "IT Jobs Contracted from Far and Wide"

By John Saunders

Having grown used to buying cars from Japan and South Korea and just about any imaginable consumer item from China, North Americans who work in computer-related fields are seeing some of their own jobs go to faraway places, notably India. This has caused political rumblings in the United States, but not yet in Canada, partly because Canada is at the top end of a cheap-labour pipe draining work from the world's biggest economy.

For the moment, Canada may be siphoning off as much from the United States as it loses to places such as India, where eager computer science graduates are available at a fraction of a Canadian salary.

The process has a name, offshoring, and two categories, nearshoring and farshoring. From the American point of view, anything beyond U.S. borders is offshore, but some locales, chiefly Canada and Ireland, are pitched to cautious clients as nearshore.

Others are farshore—India, China, the Philippines, Russia, even the beach-fringed island of Mauritius.

The mood is no cheerier in the United States. Researchers at Gartner Inc. of Stamford, Conn., predicted $2\frac{1}{2}$ months ago that one in 10 jobs at U.S.-based IT service firms will go offshore by the end of next year. Forrester Research Inc. of Cambridge, Mass., last year projected a loss of 3.3 million U.S. service jobs of all types over 15 years.

An investigation by a U.S. congressional agency is under way and various state legislatures are considering bills to keep work at home, chiefly by blocking use of foreign workers on state contracts. (Politicians expressed shock to learn that help lines for welfare recipients in New Jersey, Missouri, North Carolina, and elsewhere were answered in India.)

Although it has caught a lot of people off guard, offshoring is an extension of a well-known trend. Many companies and governments spent the late 20th century contracting out work to cut costs and shed employees—office cleaners, cafeteria staff, payroll clerks and computer programmers, to name a few.

Fortunes were made in computer services outsourcing, but the work generally stayed in the country. No longer. Now that fibre-optic cables gird the planet and satellites command the sky, anything that can be sent on a data link can be sourced almost anywhere, letting North American companies reach for the next level of savings.

This is happening at a bad time for North American IT workers, who have already watched their job prospects fade in the hangover from the 1990s tech boom. U.S. and Canadian IT service firms are busy setting up operations in India and other offshore spots, partly in response to customer demand, partly to regain former profit margins and partly to meet the threat posed by India's fast-growing Big Three. With about 60,000 employees among them, they are:

- Tata Consultancy Services, a division of **Tata Sons Ltd.,** holding company for one of India's great family-controlled industrial conglomerates, led by fourth-generation chairman Ratan Tata;
- **Infosys Technologies Ltd.,** guided by founder Narayana Murthy, a student Marxist who became one of the country's most admired executives;
- Wipro Technologies, the main business of **Wipro Ltd.** (formerly Western India Vegetable Products Ltd.), headed by Azim Premji, who dropped out of Stanford University to remake his father's cooking oil company and become India's richest man.

None is a household name in the West—even in most households that depend on computers for their livelihoods—but that seems destined to change. All have operations in the United States and Canada (offering U.S. customers a near-shore option) that serve partly as pass-throughs for work going to India.

Richard Baldyga, Infosys vice-president of outsourcing solutions, is eloquent about the benefits of the Indian work force.

"India's a very populous country, over a billion people, highly educated," he said from the company's U.S. headquarters in Fremont, Calif. "English is the predominant language across all education in the universities. Very focused in the engineering area. We hire from some of the top engineering schools in India. Last year, just in India alone, we had over 400,000 applications come to us from college grads. We hired 4,000 people."

About 70 per cent of the company's business and 30 per cent of its employees are in North America, he said. "A good part of my staff is actually based in India, so I do conference calls in the morning and in the evening with my team. While I'm sleeping, they're awake, it's their daytime. With the labour cost advantages, I can hire almost four FTEs—full-time equivalents—or four staff members for the same cost of hiring one here in the United States. And because of the education and the focus on engineering in India, I've got some really bright folks working for me—four times the horsepower that I could have here in the States."

Cheap Labour
Typical salary ranges for computer programmers with two to three years experience (U.S.$)

China	$5,000–$9,000
India	$6,000–$10,000
Philippines	$6,500–$11,000
Russia	$7,000–$13,000
Ireland	$21,000–$28,000
CANADA	$25,000–$50,000
United States	$60,000–$90,000

Source: Neolt.com Inc.
The Globe and Mail

Mr. Baldyga, an American, said Canada offers smaller cost advantages. "We're probably getting about 1.4, 1.3 [Canadian employees for the price of an American]," he said. "It depends on the location you're looking at. If it's Manhattan, I can get a much better saving going to Toronto."

Infosys has what it calls a global development centre in Toronto, although that is not the honour it may seem. The company has similar centres in India, the United States, Britain, Japan, Australia, and Mauritius.

The biggest target in the three firms' sights is Dallas-based **Electronic Data Systems Corp.**, a global gorilla of IT outsourcing with about 135,000 employees. EDS, the brainchild of billionaire political eccentric Ross Perot, was for many years the sole supplier of IT services to **General Motors Corp.**, which owned it from 1984 to 1996. Because GM contracts out all of its IT work, the prize is huge. Under a 10-year separation deal with GM, EDS is steadily losing its lock on the Detroit company's business, giving its new Indian rivals a shot at increasing amounts of work.

Last year, Wipro leased enough space for a staff of 200 on Riverside Drive in Windsor, Ont.—"a dedicated facility ... just across the river from General Motors," Wipro vice-chairman Vivek Paul declared it. Without describing the work being done for GM there, he went on the say that "we are seeing a strong interest on their part to continue to do more work with us."

This may bode ill for employees of EDS Canada Ltd., who are numerous enough in Oshawa, Ont, home of General Motors of Canada Ltd., to have their own corporate softball league. There have been whispers lately of a sizable shift of GM Canada business to Wipro. EDS officials say they are unaware of any major loss, but the car company offers no assurances.

GM Canada public relations director Stew Low said GM does not discuss its dealings with suppliers, but he added that it would be no surprise if Wipro were to win a piece of work.

"The key here is that all our IT is outsourced. We're probably one of the largest [companies] in the world that does that and we've done it for many years. Contracts are let to companies literally around the globe, so one of those may be Wipro," he said.

Even when a domestic firm gets the contract, there is no guarantee the work won't go offshore. EDS and its major rivals, including **Accenrure Ltd.** (formerly Andersen Consulting], **Cap Gemini Ernst & Young**, and **IBM Global Services** (the outsourcing arm of **International Business Machines Corp.**), have outposts in India. So does Canada's home-grown contender, CGI Group Inc. of Montreal, with about 500 Indian employees. They work mainly on U.S. contracts, CGI says.

Chris Howling, director of business development at EDS Canada, says his company runs a trade surplus within the EDS world. That is, it brings more work to Canada from the United States than it sends from Canada to places such as India. "We're fortunate because we're considered an offshore supplier," he said.

The next question is whether the Canadian industry as a whole runs a surplus, whether the nearshore gains exceed the farshore drain. "I think, on the whole, yes, Canada does benefit," says technology analyst Jason Bremner of IDC Canada Ltd., who hopes to assemble data to settle the point.

Frank Koelsch, president of Everest Group Canada, a unit of outsourcing advisers Everest Partners LP of Dallas, said Canada is at least doing better than the United States, which clearly suffers a net outflow of jobs. India's labour-cost edge is narrower if you are paying Canadian salaries, he noted, "but it's certainly there—and certainly, let's say, very attractive to compelling."

He said farshoring is not yet widespread in Canada, perhaps because companies here tend to be smaller and more conservative, but it already has fans in certain groups, including the major Canadian banks, which like the idea of getting their routine computer programming done cheaply. "They are all either doing it or investigating it," he said. He reserved judgment on whether Canada gains or loses jobs on balance.

In one view, Canada's strongest selling point resembles an old Ontario tourist slogan, "Friendly, familiar, foreign and near."

The Offshore IT Race
Who's who (and who's ahead) in offshore information-technology outsourcing.

Leader	India
Challengers	Canada, China, Czech, Republic, Hungary, Ireland, Israel, Mexico, Northern Ireland, Philippines, Poland, Russia, South Africa
Up-and-comers	Belarus, Brazil, Caribbean, Egypt, Estonia, Latvia, Lithuania, New Zealand, Singapore, Ukraine, Venezuela
Beginners	Bangladesh, Cuba, Ghana, Korea, Malaysia, Mauritius, Nepal, Senegal, Sri Lanka, Taiwan, Thailand, Vietnam

Source: Gartner Inc.
The Globe and Mail

In the News
- "Just as China has taken the runaway lead as the factory to the world, India is starting to emerge as the outsourcing capital of the back office to the world, if you will."

  —*The Edge, Singapore*

- "Call centres are the new job haven for the educated women of India ... They are given extensive voice coaching to develop the right British or American identities—Ananya is Alice, Kavita is Kate, and Sashi is Sara ... [Their] eight-

hour night shifts are usually designed to suit the three time zones of the U.S., since it is this country which is serviced by the clients of most call centres."
—*The Hindu Business Line, India*

- Affiliated Computer Services Inc., the world's largest processor of student loan payments, is opening a data processing centre in the South Pacific nation of Fiji. The Dallas-based company has about 12,000 workers in places such as Ghana, Jamaica, and Utah's Ute Indian Reservation to cut contract costs.
—*Bloomberg News*

Toronto lawyer Alison Youngman, who heads an outsourcing group at Stikeman Elliott LLP, advocates a national campaign to promote the country as a nearshore destination for U.S. clients. Canada offers them "a very safe environment," she says. "We've got highly trained people and they don't have to worry about all the security risks that they would otherwise have to worry about in going offshore." The case is already made by IT firms, she said, "but I just don't think it's being pushed and plugged as much as it might be."

Whatever is done, long-term jobs will be fewer as companies feel the shifting winds of world competition, Mr. Fabian, the Toronto consultant, said.

Outsourcing is a natural reaction, he said, "because that, then, makes your people not your people. You've merely rented them, and when you no longer need those people, you rent a new set of people. It's a kind of bloody-minded view of people, but I don't think, given the structure of our economy, there's a whole heck of a lot of options."

Stock Market Darlings
You may not have heard of them, but the stock market likes them, India's IT contractors give North American firms a run for their money.

	Home base	Employees	Revenue	$ million (U.S.) Profit	$ million (U.S.) Market cap*	Exchange
Infosys Technologies	India	17,000	$754	$195	$9,671	Nasdaq
Wipro	India	23,000**	$902	$170	$7,361	NYSE
CGI Group	Canada	20,000	$1,382	$86	$2,355	NYSE, TSX
Electronic Data Systems	United States	135,000	$21,502	$1,116	$10,244	NYSE

* Total value of shares at current market price **including non-IT operations
The business—information-technology and business-process outsourcing—encompasses such things as computer programming services, electronic back-office functions, and call centres. With low labour costs and wide profit margins, the offshore players command higher market values, pound for pound.
Sources: Company documents and Bloomberg Financial Services.
The Globe and Mail
Source: John Saunders, "IT Jobs Contracted from Far and Wide," *The Globe and Mail*, October 14, 2003.

Companies can and do shift production and new investment in search of higher profits, or threaten to do so in order to negotiate lower wages or longer hours or worse working conditions. Canadian unions often face demands for lower wages and other rollbacks at the bargaining table to compete with labour standards in other countries. Most of the industrial exports from developing countries come from foreign affiliates of transnational corporations based in the North, or from subcontractors feeding the global supply chains of these dominant companies. The jobs that are most vulnerable to relocation are those in relatively low-skill and labour-intensive sectors, such as clothing and light-assembly industries. It is now unusual to find an item of clothing, footwear, or, even more so, a toy or a consumer electronics product in a Canadian store that is made in North America or Europe. Developing countries have also built quite sophisticated industries, such as aerospace in Brazil, auto engine manufacturing in Mexico, and software development in India. Even if only a relatively small proportion of workers in India or China have the education and skills needed in these kind of industries, their absolute numbers are large, and the advanced industrial countries have no monopoly on skills or ingenuity.

Box 10.2: Why Can You Buy a DVD Player for under $30?

At Christmas time in 2003, American Wal-Mart shoppers found they could buy a DVD player for U.S. $29, made by the world's fastest-growing consumer electronics company. A report in the *Globe and Mail*, "Employees Boost Earnings with Overtime," June 14, 2004, found that workers at the Chinese plant in Zhenjiang manufacturing the low-price players were earning a basic monthly wage of Can. $74, just enough on which to survive. To bring their incomes up to $135 per month, and to meet rigidly enforced production quotas, most workers were routinely putting in 12-hour days and six-day weeks. One employee reported that he had once worked for 42 consecutive hours.

Limits to Downward Harmonization

All that said, there are clear limits to the logic of the argument that, in a globally integrated economy, production and mobile investment capital will inevitably flow to those countries where investors and corporations find low wages, low taxes, and low social and environmental standards, setting in motion a competitive race to the bottom in terms of wages and labour and social standards. This is certainly true to a degree, and very real forces work in this direction. But, sometimes the critics of globalization tend to exaggerate the power of corporations and the weakness of unions and governments, curiously echoing the often-heard argument of business that concerns for their competitiveness must always take first place in the shaping of public policy. Even in the new global economy, alternative directions are possible.

Despite all the rhetoric of globalization, many areas of the contemporary economy are not very highly exposed to international competition at all, let alone to competition from developing countries. Low-wage McJobs are better explained by high youth unemployment and low minimum wages than by low wages in China. Most service jobs—from health care to hotels, stores, and restaurants, and to business consulting—can be offshored only with great difficulty, if at all. And, while manufacturing production in some sectors has indeed shifted to very low-wage/ low-social standard, brutally exploitative export enclaves such as the *maquiladoras* of Mexico or the coastal zones of China, capital-intensive manufacturing is less vulnerable. For example, the auto industry in North America is gradually shifting toward Mexico, which has won some major new investments in assembly and engine plants as well as in labour-intensive parts manufacturing. But, industrial capacity takes a long time to shift, and companies do not just walk away from the major investments in plant and equipment that they made in the past and remain in place. Even in the 1990s, there was a lot of new investment in the Canadian auto sector even as some kinds of jobs shifted to Mexico.

There is some reality and not just rhetoric to the idea of a knowledge-based economy built on innovation, high productivity, and highly skilled and educated workers. The advanced capitalist countries, including Canada, continue to hold an overwhelming comparative advantage in many major and growing industries, from software development, to entertainment, to aerospace and biotechnology, to the manufacturing of sophisticated machinery and equipment of all kinds. Computers may be assembled in China, but computer-controlled machinery in Chinese factories is imported from Japan, Europe, and the U.S. Mobile phones are assembled in developing Asian countries, but new generations of communications technology are developed and usually first manufactured in Europe, the U.S., and Canada. A lot of manufacturing production in terms of physical volume has shifted to the South, but the higher-valued goods and services are still overwhelmingly produced in the North. Only a handful of developing countries, notably Korea, have built genuinely innovative transnational corporations of their own, as opposed to companies that undertake assembly and other operations at the low end of the supply chain for the transnationals, which maintain most of their research and core operations in the advanced industrial countries. Because of all of these factors, the volume of North–South trade is still hugely eclipsed by trade among the advanced industrial countries. In 2003, the Organisation for Economic Co-operation and Development (OECD) countries (basically the advanced industrial countries, plus Korea) generated more than 70% of both world exports and imports, and most long-term investment flows were also among these countries.

It is also important to bear in mind that, although there is a higher labour content in goods manufactured in the South, almost all of the manufacturing export earnings of the South are recycled in the form of imports of goods and services from the North. As production shifts to the South, living standards and wages should gradually rise, feeding the growth of the global market as a whole. This process is far less automatic than most free trade economists assume. For long periods of time, wages in developing countries can be kept at very low levels because of huge reserves of unemployed and rural workers seeking industrial jobs, and because of government and employer repression of unions. Still, wages have increased in Korea and other developing countries in Asia, and the internal markets of the most successful developing countries have grown more or less in line with exports. If there is a problem with export surpluses for developing countries, it results mainly from very unstable and highly speculative financial markets and the legitimate fear of developing countries that they could face devastating currency crises if they do not bank large foreign currency reserves.

The logic of downward harmonization to the lowest common denominator because of global competitive pressures is also suspect in that highly productive and innovative economies rest on a high level of labour and social standards. In the 1990s, some countries with very high levels of social spending and unionization did very well in terms of productivity and job growth, as detailed in the next chapter. The evidence for OECD countries is that there is no clear link from low taxes, weak unions, and low levels of social spending to higher levels of business investment, job creation, and economic growth as one would expect if it was necessary to win a race to the bottom in order to survive global competition (Arjona 2001; Jackson 2000b, 2001). The U.S., with weak unions and low levels of social spending, turned in a good growth performance in the second half of the 1990s and achieved very low unemployment, but so did some countries with relatively high taxes, strong labour movements, and generous welfare states such as Denmark and the Netherlands (Auer 2000). Despite all the fears of downward harmonization to a minimalist welfare state and deregulated labour markets caused by globalization, the evidence is actually hard to find. OECD data clearly show that public social spending has increased rather than fallen as a share of GDP in the 1990s (Arjona 2001). There has indeed been a trend toward greater income inequality arising from the impacts of high unemployment and more precarious jobs on low-income households, and from the growing market income share of the most affluent. This can be partly linked to globalization. But, not all advanced industrial countries have become more unequal, and there are still huge differences between the social models of these countries, even if they are all exposed in more or less the same way to the forces of international competition (Forster 2000).

∎ The Impacts of Free Trade Agreements and North American Economic Integration

In the case of Canada, at least, globalization has been more about greater economic integration with the U.S. than increased openness to the developing world. Well under 10% of our imports come from developing countries and, for Canadians, globalization as an economic phenomenon is hardly new. From the earliest days of

European settlement, Canada has been very closely integrated with the changing international economy. Economic historians, such as Harold Innis, have seen our national economic development as a process driven mainly by foreign demand for Canadian resources, from fur and fish, to wheat and forest products, to minerals and energy resources. We have always traded a lot with the rest of the world, and relied on foreign capital to finance new investment until very late in the 20th century. Over time, close trade and investment links with Great Britain and the British Empire gave way to gradual incorporation into a North American economy, with the U.S. becoming by far the most important destination of Canadian exports and source of imports and new investment by the 1940s. It is true that Canada built up a manufacturing sector behind tariff walls from the late 19th century in order to create stable jobs and limit dependency upon exports of resources, and that Canadian governments helped shape economic development through policies such as the national energy policy and the auto pact through the 1970s. But, the Canadian and U.S. economies were very closely tied together through trade and major U.S. corporate investments in Canada long before the Canada–U.S. Free Trade Agreement of 1988.

The FTA did, however, mark a further and important stage in continental integration and liberalization. It not only phased out most remaining tariffs and trade barriers, which were modest, but also explicitly prohibited Canada from ever returning to nationalistic economic policies of the kind that had been pursued from time to time in order to actively shape the economic development process. Most notably, the FTA limited the federal government's ability to review, prohibit, or place conditions on U.S. corporate takeovers of Canadian companies, or to block new U.S. corporate investments, or to set up new Crown corporations, or to give favourable treatment to Canadians when it came to pricing our natural resources or giving out government contracts. While subject to numerous exceptions, the guiding principle of the FTA was that Canadian governments would dismantle barriers to the free flow of goods, services, and investment between the two countries, and treat American and Canadian companies in almost exactly the same way. These same principles have been gradually incorporated not just into the NAFTA, which was created when Mexico joined the FTA, but also into the rules of the World Trade Organization, which now govern Canada's economic relations with most of the rest of the world.

NAFTA and WTO rules did not just liberalize trade and investment flows, but also restrict the ability of governments to regulate corporations in the public interest and to maintain a public sphere outside of the market economy. Critics of these agreements such as Stephen Clarkson (2002) rightly point out that they form a new constitution that entrenches not just the principle of non-discrimination against foreign corporations, but also the free market or neo-liberal ideological principle that governments should intervene in the market to only a very limited degree. Trade rules tend to reinforce the currently dominant view that governments should not intervene too greatly in the decisions of business on where and how to operate, and should not insulate large sectors of the economy from the forces of the so-called free market.

The General Agreement on Tariffs and Trade or GATT, which governed liberalization of Canadian trade before the FTA, NAFTA, and the recently concluded WTO agreement, used to be almost exclusively about trade in goods and lowering tariffs, and had few (if any) implications for the boundary between the market and the state outside of a limited set of industrial development policies. But, new agreements such as NAFTA and the General Agreement on Trade in Services (GATS), which is an extension of the WTO, intrude much more deeply into the sphere for democratic choice by restricting the ability of governments to maintain a non-market sector and to change the boundaries between the market and non-market sectors in line with the shifting winds of democracy. Pushed actively by transnational corporations, the fundamental premise of these agreements is that commercial providers should, subject to certain exemptions, have the right to establish in national markets, and be given the same treatment as domestic providers (the principle of national treatment). NAFTA broke new ground by codifying investment rights and extending trade liberalization rules from goods to services such as communications, finance, and culture, and by creating (through Chapter 11) a means through which foreign corporations could directly challenge government decisions outside of domestic legal processes (through investor-state disputes settlement as opposed to GATT provisions for the resolution of state-to-state disputes). While GATS does not have investor-state provisions, it does envisage setting up domestic tribunals to which transnational corporations could turn for redress. Agreements have increasingly effective enforcement mechanisms, usually based on narrow constructions of rules arrived at in private sessions of trade specialists. The central point is that privatization and the erosion of the public and not-for-profit sectors are already being promoted through binding trade and investment agreements to some degree, and that the pressures are mounting.

■The Free Trade Debate

The great national debate in the late 1980s over the Canada–U.S. Free Trade Agreement split the country down the middle. While the Mulroney Conservative government won the 1988 election, which was fought almost entirely on the FTA deal, a majority of voters in fact backed the Liberals and NDP, who opposed the deal. Supporters such as the Business Council on National Issues and many economists and conservative think-tanks argued that there would be significant economic gains from trade and investment liberalization that would be shared with workers in the form of higher wages in better jobs, and that a stronger economy would support and sustain social programs. In line with the economics textbook argument for gains from trade, tariff elimination was expected to lead to higher productivity and a stronger manufacturing sector (Department of Finance 1988). Labour adjustment

Box 10.3: Trade Deals and Public and Social Services

While the underlying presumption of trade and investment agreements is that all sectors should be liberalized and opened up to transnational corporations and investors, exemptions are provided for in general terms and under the specific terms through which states adhere to particular agreements. In the case of GATS, the general exemption for public services is very narrow. Only services "provided in the exercise of governmental authority" are exempt in principle, and this is narrowly defined to make it clear that services provided by governments on a commercial basis, or in competition with private suppliers, are included. Under NAFTA, services such as health, education, child care, income insurance, and welfare services are excluded "to the extent that they are social services established or maintained for a public purpose." The meaning of this phrase has never been definitively established, but the U.S. government's position has been that, like GATS, this excludes only monopoly government services and does not exclude government services delivered in competition with the private sector.

Neither the GATS nor NAFTA general exemption are clear on the potential application of trade and investment rules to areas of mixed public, private, and not-for-profit delivery, yet health care in Canada is a mixed system, with not-for-profit hospitals and private doctors and private laboratories delivering services paid for by governments. The same can be said increasingly of education and skills training, of child care and of many community services, such as home care and elder care. The Canadian social welfare system is a patchwork of public services, private services contracted for by governments or delivered in competition with government services, and not-for-profit services provided on contract to governments or provided with the support of government grants and subsidies. There is a range of means through which government support is provided, from grants and contributions, to subsidies, to exclusive contracts, to contracts awarded on the basis of competitive bidding.

The position of the Government of Canada as of 2004 was that health and social services should be excluded from trade and investment agreements on the still untested NAFTA model. However, the report of the Romanow Royal Commission on Health Care argued that, if privatization advanced beyond a minimal stage, the NAFTA-type exemption would no longer be adequate. For example, if the government of Alberta begins to seriously experiment with delivery of public health care through private hospitals, it will be difficult, if not impossible, for future governments to return to a not-for-profit system without paying compensation to U.S. health corporations that had entered the Canadian market.

was seen as a small, manageable problem because it was assumed that there would be a small overall job gain as workers moved from shrinking to expanding sectors and firms.

For their part, critics such as unions and the nationalist Action Canada Network feared major job losses and argued that closer trade and investment ties with the U.S., and the reduced power of government to control those ties, would increase the bargaining power of mobile corporations compared to workers, unions, and governments. Threats to move investment, production, and jobs to the U.S. would work toward downward harmonization of social standards that add to business costs. Free trade was seen as a threat to the more progressive and more equal Canadian social model of stronger unions, higher levels of income protection, and broader access to public and social services (Cameron 1988; CLC 1987). Critics also argued that the FTA risked freezing the status quo of excessive resource dependency and a relatively weak manufacturing sector. The difference was not so much over whether trade with the U.S. was a good or bad thing as over how much policy space was needed to manage trade and to shape the economy in the interests of Canadian workers and communities.

Structural Economic Change

Canada–U.S. economic integration in terms of two-way trade flows proceeded extremely rapidly in the wake of the FTA, far faster than anyone on either side of the debate had anticipated. Exports and imports both almost doubled as a share of the economy over the 1990s. Most manufacturing industries have become even more strongly oriented to the North American rather than the domestic market to the extent that the U.S. is now a larger market for Canadian-based manufacturers than is Canada itself, and most of the Canadian market for manufactured goods is now met from imports. Some industries, such as auto and telecommunications, are now so closely integrated that components cross and recross the border as they move between different production sites of the same companies.

The FTA was expected to help close the long-standing Canada–U.S. productivity gap, but, at best, the gains were modest in the most heavily liberalized sectors. Many smaller plants went under, but the plants that survived did not necessarily expand. The overall Canada–U.S. gap in terms of output per worker has actually widened since the late 1980s, mainly because Canada has been relatively weak in the knowledge-based sectors where productivity growth has been most rapid.

Canada's healthy export position in the U.S. market through the economic recovery of the 1990s was almost entirely due to the continuing fall of the Canadian dollar rather than to building up a more sophisticated industrial economy. The long-standing structural problems of Canadian industry remain with us: too many small, undercapitalized plants; relatively low business investment in machinery and equipment, research and development, and worker training; and overdependence on production of resources and low value-added industrial materials as opposed to finished goods. Deeper integration of the manufacturing sector in the North American economy has done little to decisively shift the structure of our industrial economy toward the more dynamic and faster-growing knowledge-based industries. Canada certainly has some strengths in high-tech industries such as communications, biotechnology, and aerospace, and our auto industry is large and important, but resources and resource-based products such as oil and gas, lumber, pulp and paper, and minerals still make up more than 40% of our exports. Business investment in research and development is confined to a very few firms and sectors, and is less than half the U.S. level as a share of the economy. Resources are an important and continuing source of wealth and jobs, and help sustain regional economies, but sectors such as mining and energy are extremely capital-intensive and provide very few direct jobs. It will be very hard to raise Canadian living standards and to sustain and create well-paid jobs over the long term if we do not shift production toward more unique or sophisticated goods and services that can command a price premium in world markets and are better placed to withstand competition from producers in low-wage countries.

The labour adjustment costs of the FTA turned out to be much greater than had been forecast, partly because the Canadian dollar was very overvalued against the U.S. dollar just as the deal came into effect. Between 1989 and 1991, more than one in five manufacturing workers lost their jobs through a massive wave of layoffs and plant closures that devastated industrial communities throughout Ontario and Quebec. The adjustment programs that had been promised were not delivered, and many older workers were forced into premature retirement. Other workers found new jobs, but at much lower wages. The lost jobs in manufacturing were, over time, more than offset by gains in the firms and sectors that survived restructuring and eventually began to grow as the Canadian dollar fell against the U.S. dollar after 1992. The scale of change in manufacturing that disrupted the lives of so many working people is underlined by the fact that half of all the plants in existence in 1988—accounting for more than one-quarter of all jobs—had closed by 1997, while 39% of all plants in 1997—accounting for 21% of all jobs—did not exist at all in 1988 (Baldwin and Gu 2003).

Harmonization to the U.S. Social Model?

In the free trade debate of the late 1980s, advocates argued that a stronger economy would support better social programs. However, after the deal was signed, business increasingly argued that high social expenditures, financed from progressive taxes, make Canada uncompetitive in a shared economic space. Competitiveness came to be defined as lower taxes, lower social spending, and more flexible labour markets. Experience has shown that there are indeed downward pressures from North American economic integration on progressive, redistributive social policies that arise mainly from the tax side.

Canada has a very different social model than the U.S., which is highly valued by most Canadians. Among the enduring elements of difference, Canada has a significantly more equal distribution of both earnings and after-tax/transfer (disposable) income. Our more narrow distribution of earnings reflects higher unionization, somewhat higher minimum wages, and a smaller pay gap between the middle and the top of the earnings spectrum. More equal after-tax incomes and lower rates of after-tax poverty than in the U.S. reflect the impacts of a more generous system of transfers, acting upon a somewhat more equal distribution of market income. Until the changes of the mid-1990s, the Canadian Unemployment Insurance system was notably more generous than that of the U.S., and Canadian welfare programs benefit a much larger share of the non-elderly poor. All Canadian provinces, but no U.S. states, provide welfare to singles and families without children, and social assistance benefits, while low and falling in real terms, are generally higher than in the U.S.

In the mid-1990s, the Canadian poverty rate for all people was 10% compared to 17% in the U.S., using a common definition of less than half of median household income, and the minimum distance between the top and bottom 10% of families ranked by income was 4 to 1 compared to almost 6.5 to 1. Comparing Canadian and U.S. after-tax income, the bottom one-third of Canadians are much better off than the bottom one-third of Americans, and the U.S. average income advantage of about 15% goes overwhelmingly to the top one-third or so of the population. In other words, affluent Americans are significantly better off than affluent Canadians, but the gap is very small for middle-income families (particularly if adjusted for out-of-pocket health care costs), and does not exist at all for lower-income families (Wolfson and Murphy 2000). The level of services provided on a citizen entitlement basis is also higher in Canada than the U.S., reducing dependence on market income for some basic needs. Medicare is the key example, but Canada also provides a somewhat higher level of community services, such as not-for-profit child care, home care, and elder care services. Greater equality has sustained better social outcomes in terms of health, crime, and educational attainment (see Table 10.1).

■Economic Integration and Income Inequality

As detailed earlier in this book, there has been a significant increase in income inequality among working-age Canadian families over the past decade, driven by stronger wage growth for high-income earners and cuts in social transfers. Neither can be blamed directly upon North American economic integration and a complex range of factors have been at play. However, there is a link between continental integration and the increased market incomes of the most affluent. Closer trade and investment links and more investment by Canadian and U.S. transnationals on both sides of the border have led to convergence of salary and stock options for highly mobile professionals and managers in the corporate sector. This has driven the increased income share of the top 1%. Interestingly, this has not happened in Quebec, where senior corporate executives are, for cultural and linguistic reasons, much less likely to be tempted to move to the U.S.

Table 10.1: Indicators of Social Development

	Canada	U.S.
Income and poverty		
Poverty rate	10.3%	17.0%
Child poverty rate	15.5%	22.4%
Jobs		
Low paid jobs	20.9%	24.5%
Earnings gap	3.7	4.6
Social Supports		
Health care (public share as % health total)	69.6%	44.7%
Tertiary education (public share)	60.0%	51.0%
Private social spending (as % GDP)	4.5%	8.6%
Health		
Life-expectancy (men) in years	75.3	72.5
Life-expectancy (women) in years	81.3	79.2
Infant mortality/100,000	5.5	7.2
Crime		
Homicides per 100,000	1.8	5.5
Assault/threat per 100,000	4	5.7
Prisoners per 100,000	118	546
Education		
Adults with post-secondary education	38.8%	34.9%
High literacy (% adults)	25.1%	19.0%
Low literacy (% adults)	42.9%	49.6%

Notes and Sources:
Data are from the OECD Social Indicators database.
Poverty is defined as less than half the median income of an equivalent household.
Low pay is defined as employment in a full-time job that pays less than 2/3 the median hourly wage.
Earnings gap is ratio of bottom of top decile to top of bottom decile.

At the other end of the income spectrum, the FTA and NAFTA are associated in a direct way with downward pressures on wages in sectors most exposed to the threat of relocation of production or new investment to the U.S. or Mexico. Increased competitive pressures help explain the very sharp decline in the unionization rate in Canadian manufacturing from 45.5% in 1988 to just 32.4% in

2002. Union decline reflects disproportionate closures of unionized plants and the disproportionate concentration of new hiring in non-union plants, not to mention more restrictive labour laws in some provinces. Real wages in manufacturing have lagged consistently behind productivity in both Canada and the U.S. In fact, output per hour in Canadian manufacturing rose by 18% between 1992 and 2002 while real wages increased by barely 3% over the whole decade. The growing disconnection between wages and productivity has boosted corporate profits as a share of national income. Thus, the promise that workers would share in the productivity gains from free trade has not come to pass.

▌Economic Integration and Social Programs

Closer integration can be linked to the erosion of income transfers to the working-age population and cuts to social programs. Many people would argue that the Employment Insurance (EI) cuts imposed by the Liberal government in 1995, cuts in federal transfers to the provinces for social programs, and provincial welfare cuts were driven primarily by deficit reduction goals, which is true to a degree. However, the Department of Finance, the OECD, and the International Monetary Fund (IMF) have long argued that Canada's supposedly generous welfare state is associated with a stronger tendency to wage-driven inflation than in the U.S. The basic argument is that income benefits strengthen the bargaining power of workers, and their willingness to hold out for better wages if and when they become unemployed. Cuts to transfers, particularly EI, were consciously intended to promote greater labour market and wage flexibility. In short, closer integration made the U.S. model of a more minimalist welfare state attractive to those who worried about the relative strength of Canadian workers (Jackson 2000a).

As noted, competitive pressures to social policy convergence are exaggerated to the extent that progressive and redistributive social models have significant economic pluses. A good economic argument can be made that integration per se does not mean that Canada has to harmonize down to U.S. levels of social spending and public services in order to build a productive economy. Further, Canada–U.S. tax differences in the mid-1990s were quite small, and slightly higher business taxes in Canada were offset by other cost factors for business, such as lower energy prices and lower health costs for workers. Yet, all that said, the operative, endlessly repeated argument of business organizations and the policy mainstream in the era of free trade has been that economic success will go to countries that most closely copy the U.S. model of weak unions, low taxes, and low social spending. Over the 1990s, particularly after the elimination of the federal deficit in 1997, the political argument was constantly advanced that taxes had to be cut to U.S. levels to maintain competitiveness and fuel economic growth and job creation.

The argument was that Canadian business taxes (corporate income taxes and capital taxes) and personal income taxes on higher earners were too high compared to the U.S., making the U.S. a more attractive location for mobile corporations to invest and produce. While many advocates of tax cuts would also argue that lower taxes boost economic efficiency in and of themselves, a great deal of stress was placed on Canada–U.S. tax differences by business lobby groups, such as the Canadian Council of Chief Executives and the Chamber of Commerce, and conservative think-tanks, such as the C.D. Howe Institute. The November 2002 Pre-Budget Report of the Standing Committee on Finance of the House of Commons reported that submissions from business organizations continued to stress that Canadian tax rates—particularly personal income tax rates on high-income groups and business taxes—should be "competitive" with the U.S. and noted that "tax competitiveness is a key component of the federal government's strategy to become a magnet for investment and skilled labour."

The argument for tax cuts won the day after deficits were eliminated. Driven by personal and corporate income tax cuts, the federal government's share of national income has been cut by more than two full percentage points of GDP, or the equivalent of $25 billion, since 1997–1998 (OECD 2003). Provincial tax revenues have also fallen as a share of the economy. The major beneficiaries of the federal government's changes to personal income tax rates and brackets were those making more than $70,000, and the very affluent also won lower taxes on stock options and a major reduction (from 75% to 50%) in the proportion of capital gains income, which is liable to income tax. More than half of capital gains income goes to very high-income people earning more than $250,000 per year. The federal corporate tax rate has been cut by one-quarter, from 28% to 21%. Thus, after the federal deficit was eliminated, much of the growing federal surplus went to the tax cuts that business argued were needed for competitive reasons rather than to reinvestment in social programs.

While Canadian governments still spend significantly more on social programs and public services than U.S. governments, the difference has been shrinking dramatically. Between 1992 and 2001, total Canadian government spending on programs other than defence fell from 42.9% to 33.6% of GDP, while U.S. government spending on non-defence programs remained almost the same (increasing slightly from 27.7% to 27.9% of GDP). Thus, the gap between the two countries fell from about 15 percentage points of GDP in 1992 to just 6 percentage points. We still spend 11.0% of GDP compared to 7.1% in the U.S. on income-security programs, but we now spend a lower share of our national income on public education. We spend a bit less on health, but here we spend much more efficiently (Department of Finance 2003). The key point is that Canada–U.S. differences in the relative priority given to social spending or lower taxes have greatly eroded.

Public opinion surveys show that there was a deep class cleavage over the key issue of tax cuts or social reinvestment after the federal budget was balanced. Polling in 1998 for the Department of Finance found that lower-income groups were most supportive of social spending, but that all but the very highest income groups placed a greater priority on social investment than on tax cuts, and rejected harmonization of Canadian and U.S. tax policies. A survey that regularly charts differences between elite and non-elite opinion found that the former very strongly favoured corporate and personal tax cuts as the best use of the emerging federal surplus (Mendelson 2002).

In the final analysis, corporate elite views were the most influential and the desire of middle- and lower-income Canadians for significant social reinvestment went largely unheeded until the Chrétien legacy budget of 2003. This cleavage between elite and non-elite views has probably been influenced by the cultural and not just the economic implications of North American integration. In an ever-more-closely integrated economic space, corporate executives see their personal prospects and future in continental terms, and make comparisons of their personal well-being to their American peers rather than to other Canadians. Career prospects have been continentalized through transnational corporations operating on both sides of the border. The Canadian trade-off of higher taxes for better services and greater security is less relevant to high-income people who can afford to buy what they need on the market. By contrast, for middle-class and lower-income families, the trade-off of higher taxes for social programs is still relevant, and comparisons to U.S. disposable income are not very relevant. Public opinion evidence shows no loss of broad support for the Canadian social model and, indeed, increasing divergence between Canadian and U.S. values (Mendelsohn 2002).

There continues to be space for autonomy in social policy, and the Canadian social model is not doomed to extinction just because of ever closer trade and investment ties with the U.S. But, there are strong downward pressures on our capacity to finance social spending, which arise from strong pressures to lower business taxes and taxes on high-income earners to U.S. levels. This compounds inequality in Canada, particularly at a time when earnings are becoming much more unequal.

■ Conclusion and Implications

Globalization, the FTA, and NAFTA have significantly increased competitive pressures on Canadian corporations and resulted in erosion of the bargaining power and living standards of working people. The new trade agreements also pose major issues for the future capacity of governments to regulate corporations in the public interest and to maintain a public sphere outside the market. The issues posed by these developments will remain very much with us in the years ahead, given business proposals for still deeper continental integration plus further liberalization of the international trade and investment rules. The services sector will be increasingly affected by liberalization, especially under the GATS, and developing countries, especially China, will become much more important players in the global economy of the future.

In response to these developments, critics have advanced a range of alternatives. The so-called anti-globalization movement embraces a very wide range of views, from supporters of economic nationalism who want democratic national governments to have much greater control over corporations operating within their borders, to progressive internationalists who support a more global economy, but want it to operate under a different set of international rules. The former argue that economic and political space have to be reconnected at the national level to make democracy a continuing reality. The latter argue that globalization is here to stay and that it is possible to build a different kind of global economic order. The international trade union movement, for example, has called for provisions in trade and investment agreements to require countries to respect and enforce basic labour rights, and there have been a number of initiatives to establish binding rules of conduct on transnational corporations in their worldwide operations. In Europe, the ongoing economic integration process has had an explicit social dimension, and there are European Union-wide common standards in a few key areas such as hours of work and health and safety rules.

It is argued in the next chapter that small, open economies such as Canada still retain considerable capacity for political choice at the national level, and countries can certainly work together to shape a different international agenda. In short, globalization is a powerful force, but it remains a force that can be shaped by citizens and governments.

● ●

■ Questions for Critical Thought

1. To what extent do you think that free trade with the United States has benefited or hurt Canadian workers?
2. Based on what you have read in this book, how significant do you think globalization has been in shaping conditions of work over the past 15 years? How big a factor will it be in the next 15 years?
3. Is it inevitable that Canada's more equalizing social model will come to look more and more like that of the United States if economic integration continues?

■ Recommended Reading

Clarkson, Stephen. 2002. *Uncle Sam and U.S.: Globalization, Neoconservatism and the Canadian State*. Toronto: University of Toronto Press. A very detailed analysis of the impacts of the free trade agreements with the U.S. on living standards and on a wide range of Canadian public policies. The author tries to carefully separate out the impacts of what he describes as the "new constitution" of trade rules from other forces for change.

Macdonald, Ian L., ed. 2000. *Free Trade: Risks and Rewards*. Kingston: McGill-Queen's University Press. A collection of papers that are broadly supportive of the FTA based on the first 10 years.

The Report of the ILO World Commission on the Social Dimension of Globalization <http://www.ilo.org/public/english/wcsdg/index.htm>.

Teeple, Gary. 2000. *Globalization and the Decline of Social Reform: Into the Twenty-first Century*. Toronto: Garamond Press. A critique of the impacts of globalization on workers.

References

Arjona, Roman, Maxime Ladaique, and Mark Pearson. 2001. "Growth, Inequality and Social Protection." Draft OECD paper presented to the IRPP-CSLS Conference on Linkages between Economic Growth and Inequality, Ottawa, January 26–27 <http://www.oecd.org>.

Auer, Peter. 2000. "Employment Revival in Europe: Labour Market Success in Austria, Denmark, Ireland and the Netherlands." Geneva: International Labour Organization.

Baldwin, John, and Wulong Gu. 2003. *Plant Turnover and Productivity Growth in Canadian Manufacturing*. Ottawa: Statistics Canada.

Cameron, Duncan, ed. 1988. *The Free Trade Deal*. Toronto: Lorimer.

Canadian Labour Congress (CLC). 1987. *Canadian Labour Congress Submission to the House of Commons Standing Committee on External Affairs and International Trade*, December 4.

Clarkson, Stephen. 2002. *Uncle Sam and U.S.: Globalization, Neoconservatism and the Canadian State*. Toronto: University of Toronto Press.

Department of Finance. 1988. *The Canada–U.S. Free Trade Agreement: An Economic Assessment*. Ottawa: Government of Canada.

_____. 2003. *Government Spending in Canada and the U.S.* Working Paper 2003-05. Ottawa: Government of Canada.

Forster, Michael. 2000. "Trends and Driving Factors in Income Distribution and Poverty in the OECD Area." OECD Labour Market and Social Policy Occasional Paper no. 42 <http://www.oecd.org>.

Jackson, Andrew. 2000a. "The NAIRU and Macro-Economic Policy in Canada." *Canadian Business Economics* (August): 66–82.

_____. 2000b. *Why We Don't Have to Choose between Social Justice and Economic Growth: The Myth of the Equity-Efficiency Trade-off*. Canadian Council on Social Development <http://www.ccsd.ca>.

_____. 2001. "Can There Be a Second Way in the Third Millennium?" *Studies in Political Economy* (Summer): 39–65.

Mendelsohn, Matthew. 2002. *Canada's Social Contract: Evidence from Public Opinion*. Ottawa: Canadian Policy Research Networks. (See charts 56, 118, 119, 123, 124, 149, and 152.)

Organisation for Economic Co-operation and Development (OECD). 2003. *Economic Survey of Canada*, Table 29. Paris: OECD.

Teeple, Gary. 2000. *Globalization and the Decline of Social Reform into the Twenty-first Century*. Toronto: Garamond Press.

Wolfson, M., and B. Murphy. 2000. "Income Inequality in North America: Does the 49th Parallel Still Matter?" *Canadian Economic Observer*, Cat. 11-010-XPB. Ottawa: Statistics Canada.

Improving Work
Could Canada Look More Like Denmark?

◼Introduction

This chapter compares Canada's liberal labour market model to that of some
European countries, and draws on recent European experience to suggest that there
is no inevitable trade-off between job creation and improving the quality of jobs.

◼Labour Market Models

The experience of some European countries shows that low wages and precarious
jobs are not a necessary condition for job creation, and that improving job quality
at the bottom of the labour market does not inevitably come at the price of
unemployment. This is a significant conclusion, since Canadian policy makers' major
objection to labour market regulation aimed at protecting workers in precarious
employment has been that such policies will hurt those whom they are intended
to protect.

The experience of Scandinavian social democracy in the 1990s suggests that a
combination of high employment, relatively equal wages, and real opportunities

for workers in precarious employment is possible. This depends on regulating the labour market to create a wage floor and a low level of wage inequality, achieved primarily via collective bargaining; keeping the non-wage costs of employment low by providing social and economic security primarily through public programs financed from general taxation; providing significant investment in active labour market policies to upgrade the skills of those at greatest risk of engaging in precarious employment; and building a distinct kind of post-industrial service economy based on a large non-market sector and high-productivity private services. Success in securing high rates of employment in good jobs also depends on appropriate macroeconomic policies and good labour relations.

The social democratic labour market model is based on high levels of paid employment for both women and men, high levels of collective bargaining coverage, and universal social welfare programs and public services financed from taxes, which reduce reliance on wages. The model has limited precarious employment by socializing some caring responsibilities of households, such as child and elder care. This has reduced the double burden of household and paid work on women, directly created many jobs of reasonably high quality for women in social services, and reduced the importance of low-wage jobs in private consumer services. However, women still perform a highly unequal share of caring work, and, as in Canada, there is a highly gendered division of paid labour between women and men, with women having only limited access to higher-level jobs in the private sector. In short, the social democratic model is progressive from the standpoint of limiting precarious employment and holds lessons for Canadians, but it still falls short from the standpoint of promoting full equality between women and men.

This chapter is organized as follows. The first section, "The 'War of the Models,'" summarizes the orthodox economic argument for deregulated or flexible labour markets as the key to job creation for workers deemed to be low skilled. It demonstrates that levels of low pay and earnings inequality are high and rising in countries that have embraced this model, but with no evidence of superior job creation performance compared to countries with high levels of collective bargaining coverage. The second section, "Social Foundations of Job Creation," shows that high levels of collective bargaining coverage coexist with other labour market policies that have different implications for the extent of low-wage and precarious employment, notably employment protection legislation, the division of responsibility between the government and employers for financing social programs, and the extent of active labour market policies. The social democratic labour market model is the most employment friendly. The third section, "The Economics of Labour Market Regulation," argues that high labour standards can raise productivity in what would otherwise be low-wage jobs. The final section, "Denmark and the New European Labour Market Model," shows that Denmark, a key example of the new model, has been able to achieve very high rates of good-quality employment with very low levels of precarious work.

■The "War of the Models": Liberal vs. Regulated Labour Markets

In what has been termed the "War of the Models" (Freeman 1998), the Great American Job Machine has often been contrasted to high unemployment Eurosclerosis. The highly influential Organisation for Economic Co-operation and Development (OECD) Jobs Study (1994) argued that more labour market regulation in continental Europe compared to the U.S. and the U.K. was a major factor behind higher unemployment. The orthodox view is that overly generous unemployment benefits create barriers and disincentives to work by leading workers to expect wages that are higher than wages in available jobs, particularly for low-skilled workers who would qualify only for low-wage jobs. Further, it is argued that high-wage floors set by minimum wages and/or collective bargaining mean that low-skilled workers will be priced out of the low-productivity jobs that could otherwise have been created. The ideal labour market is one in which wages rapidly adjust to changing economic circumstances and closely reflect the relative productivity of different groups of workers. The dismal message to governments has been that there is a trade-off between the quantity and quality of jobs for lower-skilled and vulnerable workers, and that protective measures such as generous unemployment benefits, unions, and minimum wages come at the significant cost of unemployment.

The orthodox view has been a major influence on Canadian labour market policy in the 1990s. Employment Insurance and welfare benefits have been substantially cut and entitlements restricted; minimum wages have fallen behind average wages; employment standards have been eroded; and labour laws have generally become much less facilitative in terms of providing access to collective bargaining. The argument has been that a less regulated job market would lead to lower unemployment.

The Canadian policy debate has largely ignored viable alternatives to U.S. and British-style deregulated labour markets. In fact, there are profound differences between the labour markets of advanced capitalist countries: regulated labour markets work far better for vulnerable workers, and there is no clear-cut link between the extent of labour market regulation and employment performance.

As shown in previous chapters, Canada has done reasonably well in terms of job creation since economic recovery began in the mid-1990s. Compared to other OECD countries, the employment rate for both women and men is high, and the long-term adult unemployment rate is very low (see Table 11.1). However, labour market inequality has increased since at least the mid-1980s, and there has been a rise in the incidence of precarious and low-paid jobs. Canada stands out as a low-wage country among advanced industrial countries. In the mid-1990s, about one in four full-time workers in Canada (23.7%) was low paid—defined as earning less than two-thirds of the median national full-time wage—compared to just one in twenty workers (5.2%) in Sweden and only one in eight in Germany (OECD 1996). One in three Canadian women workers was low paid, an even higher proportion

Table 11.1: Incidence of Low-Paid Employment (Mid-1990s)

(% full-time workers earning less than two-thirds of national median wage)

	All	Men	Women
U.S.	25.0%	19.6%	32.5%
Canada	23.7%	16.1%	34.3%
Germany	13.3%	7.6%	25.4%
Sweden	5.2%	3.0%	8.4%

Wage inequality

(ratio of top of ninth decile to top of first decile, i.e., minimum gap between top and bottom 10%)

	Men	Women
U.S.	4.4	4.0
Canada	3.8	4.0
Germany	2.2	2.2
Sweden	2.2	1.8

Source: OECD, Employment Outlook. Paris: OECD, 1996.

than in the U.S., compared to less than one in ten women in Sweden. Further, the minimum distance between the wages of the top and bottom decile of full-time workers is about four to one compared to a little more than two to one in Sweden and Germany. Canadian workers in hotels and restaurants and in retail trade—among the lowest-wage sectors—earn about 60% as much as an average assembly worker in manufacturing compared to 90% in Sweden, where there is a much smaller gap between the bottom, the middle, and the top of the wage distribution. Moreover, upward earnings mobility for low-paid workers is greatest in those countries with the lowest levels of earnings inequality, with Sweden and Denmark performing notably better than the U.S. (OECD 1996).

Labour market institutions—wage floors set by collective bargaining and legislated minimum wages—play a major role in accounting for different levels of low pay and earnings inequality. Advanced industrial countries differ rather little in terms of the big structural forces shaping job markets. All are exposed to increased international competition and technological change, widely believed to be tipping the scales against relatively low-skilled workers. But, there is a strong consensus that labour market institutions still significantly shape outcomes for workers (Aidt and Tzannatos 2003; Freeman and Katz 1995; OECD 1996, 1997). As has been shown, collective bargaining raises the relative pay of workers who would otherwise be lower paid—women, minorities, younger workers, the relatively unskilled—and narrows wage differentials. Due to declining unionization, increases in wage inequality from the mid-1980s have been much greater in liberal labour markets than in the Scandinavian or continental European countries (Freeman and Katz 1995; OECD 1996).

The deregulated or liberal labour market model of Canada, the U.S., and the U.K. differs profoundly from that in most continental European countries. It is common to divide countries into different "social welfare regimes" based upon the level of income transfers, taxes, and public services, as well as the extent of labour market regulation (Esping-Anderson 1999; Pierson 2001; Scharpf and Schmidt 2000). The social democratic countries of Scandinavia and the social market countries such as Germany and the Netherlands differ in terms of the degree of development of public services and the extent of labour force participation by women. But, they are both distinguished from liberal countries by the relative generosity of income-support programs, such as unemployment insurance, and by the fact that the labour market and the workplace are still regulated by the "social partners." Collective bargaining coverage is very high and generally quite stable in the social democratic and social market countries, covering close to 80% of workers, because of high union membership in combination with the *de facto* or sometimes legal extension of collective agreements to non-union workers. Wage floors protect the great majority of non-professional and/or managerial workers, including most part-time and even temporary workers. The more equal after-tax distribution of income and the lower poverty rates in these countries reflect the fact that the distribution of wages is much more equal than in liberal welfare states, even before more generous social transfers are added to the mix (Smeeding 2002).

If the orthodox view of how the labour market works was correct, generous unemployment benefits, high-wage floors, and low earnings inequality would come at the price of jobs. The social democratic and the social market models with their regulated labour markets would lose the "War of the Models" hands down, particularly in terms of employment rates for the relatively unskilled. But, major recent summaries of the research by the World Bank and OECD find that there is no relationship at the country-wide level between collective bargaining coverage and economic or employment performance in the 1980s and 1990s (Aidt and Tzannatos 2003; OECD 1997). Union density is, overall, related neither to higher-nor-lower-than-average rates of unemployment or economic growth. Moreover, evidence of a systematic linkage between other aspects of labour market regulation, such as the generosity of unemployment benefits, and national unemployment rates is lacking (Baker et al. 2002).

To be sure, the larger continental European economies such as France, Germany, and Italy in the 1990s had very high unemployment compared to the U.S., and employment rates for women and young people lag well behind those in North America. But, a number of smaller European countries with high levels of bargaining coverage and still very generous welfare states, notably Denmark and the Netherlands, performed very well in the 1990s. The International Labour Organization (ILO) has recently highlighted the experience of some smaller European economies, particularly Denmark, in a counterattack on the orthodox prescription for jobs (Auer 2000; ILO 2003). The European Commission has also rejected the idea of a job quality/job quantity trade-off for lower-skilled workers, and highlighted the experiences of Denmark and the Netherlands as a desirable alternative to the U.S. model (European Commission 2001, 2002). The fundamental message has been that the liberal labour market gives rise to unacceptable levels of wage inequality and social exclusion, but that a new European labour market model can provide high levels of quality employment with low levels of insecurity.

■ Social Foundations of Job Creation: Labour Market, Regulation, and Social Welfare Regimes

Labour market regulation combines with different key building blocks of social welfare regimes. The social market and social democratic models have similarly high rates of collective bargaining coverage, but differ greatly in terms of the extent of social services and the extent to which women participate in the workforce. The social democratic countries have very high proportions of their workforce employed in social services, have given much more priority to worker training and active labour adjustment programs, and tend to pay for social programs from general taxes rather than by requiring a lot from individual employers. These features all make the model more employment friendly, despite a very high commitment to equality in the job market.

Some countries, notably Germany, France, Italy, and Spain, impose serious restrictions on employers' ability to lay off workers. A high level of job security can perpetuate an insider/outsider labour market, since the incentive is for employers to hire the minimum number of permanent workers and to achieve flexibility by contracting out and hiring temporary workers. But, tight job security has never been a major feature of the Scandinavian countries, which have stressed employment security through active labour market policies and high levels of worker training, as well as generous unemployment benefits as workers move between jobs in a constantly changing labour market. Similarly, some European countries have frowned on the creation of part-time jobs, but others have seen part-time jobs as valuable so long as they are taken voluntarily and provide a decent level of pay and benefits. The very strong job creation performance of the Netherlands in the 1990s owed a lot to part-time job creation.

The more successful European countries emphasize not strong job security regulation or limits on part-time and temporary work, but "flexicurity," striking a better balance between the flexibility needs of employers and the security needs of workers. Part-time work is not seen as undesirable so long as it conforms to certain minimum standards of non-discrimination compared to full-time work. Accordingly, the European Union (EU) has implemented binding directives mandating member countries to legislate non-discrimination against part-time workers (1997) and temporary workers (1999) with respect to pay and access to permanent jobs and training. The directive on fixed-term work requires states to set limits on the maximum duration of contracts or the number of renewals. If Canadian workers were covered by EU directives, significant wage and benefit gaps between otherwise comparable full- and part-time workers would be narrowed.

There are other major differences between the labour markets of advanced industrial countries. The extent to which employers are expected to finance social security through payroll taxes or private pension, health, and other benefits varies greatly. Loading social welfare costs onto employers is common in the social market model, where social security has been primarily financed by employer and employee contributions rather than general taxes. Non-wage costs can also be significant in liberal labour markets such as that of Canada, where modest public programs have been supplemented by bargained health care and pension benefits for core workers, increasing the divide between insiders and precarious workers. High non-wage costs for employers are likely to lead to greater use of temporary and contract workers with no benefits, and perhaps to lower rates of overall job creation. The social democratic model of services for all citizens financed from general taxes lowers these levies on employers.

Countries also differ greatly in terms of the extent to which they invest in public education and active labour market policies to promote labour adjustment and lifelong learning. Training for the unemployed and workers in precarious employment helps equalize access to job opportunities and also creates a base for higher-quality jobs. As shown earlier, training can be a force for better jobs in low-wage private services. Active labour market policies directed to the relatively unskilled have long been a major feature of the social democratic model, but have been much less emphasized in the liberal and social market countries.

Finally, advanced industrial countries differ a lot in terms of the structure of the service sector, depending on the extent to which the caring needs of households, such as child and elder care, and a wide range of community services, such as health, have been assumed by the market or by the state (Esping-Anderson 1999; Pierson 2001). Traditionally, women's low rates of labour force participation in social market countries went hand in hand with the assumption that children and the elderly would be cared for mainly by women in the home. Both social market and liberal countries have less developed social services than the Scandinavian countries. Here, state delivery of caring services has expanded the public sector, enabled women to work, and created new jobs that have gone mainly to women. Jobs in social services tend to have higher skill requirements than private consumer services jobs, and working conditions are usually covered by collective bargaining. Thus, a country's decision to tax and spend on social services has had direct implications for the quality of services jobs. Moreover, higher taxes to pay for these social services means that households have less after-tax income for consuming private services, limiting the growth of low-productivity/low-wage sectors. The structure of services employment differs quite profoundly between social democratic and liberal countries. The ratio of private- to public-sector jobs ranges from 6.0 to 1 in the U.S., to 4.0 to 1 in Canada, to 2.5 to 1 in Sweden and Denmark. One in six of the total working-age population in Canada and the U.S. are employed in the retail trade, restaurants, and accommodation sectors combined, compared to just one in ten in Sweden and Denmark (Scharpf and Schmidt 2000, Data Appendix, Vol. 1; OECD 2000).

It is important to recognize that, while the social democratic labour market model is progressive from the point of view of limiting the incidence of precarious employment among women, it is still problematic from a wider equality perspective. Denmark and Sweden have the lowest gaps in employment rates by gender among OECD countries, and a slightly smaller than average gender wage gap (OECD 2002a). The high level of social services means that children or elderly relatives pose few barriers to women's labour market participation. However, there is an even higher proportion of women employed in women-dominated occupations in Sweden and Denmark than in Canada, and women still perform a very unequal share of work in the home. Glimpses of a more progressive model are to be found in Scandinavian initiatives to share domestic work more equally by promoting longer parental leaves for men, and in the Netherlands model of reduced working-time for both women and men to make a more equal division of both paid and domestic labour possible. The growth of part-time work in the Netherlands has seen the emergence of a new model among some younger families with children, in which both women and men work four-day weeks and men undertake a relatively high share of caring and domestic work.

■ The Economics of Labour Market Regulation: Positive Employment Effects of Labour Standards

As noted, high rates of collective bargaining coverage do not necessarily lead to poor employment outcomes. Denmark, the Netherlands, and Sweden have done well, partly because widespread bargaining has produced wage outcomes that have preserved cost competitiveness for employers and maintained low inflation. Unions in Denmark and the Netherlands have consciously bargained, within a framework of loose national guidelines, to promote job growth. The ILO has underlined the importance of wage moderation in employment success, while noting that this has been consistent with real wage growth and reductions of working-time in line with productivity. By bargaining for jobs rather than just for higher wages for employed insiders, some labour movements have helped counter unemployment and precarious employment.

Many economists argue that relatively high wages for lower-skilled workers destroy jobs that could have been created. However, social democratic countries have tended to think that low-paid jobs should be squeezed out of the system. The famous Swedish labour market model developed from the 1950s through the 1970s featured the negotiation of solidarity wages with the idea that wage differentials by gender, skill, occupation, industry, or enterprise profitability should be very limited. Swedish union economists argued that low-productivity firms and sectors should raise productivity by investing in capital or skills to justify higher wages, or go out of business. Solidarity wages meant that wages would be lower than they would otherwise have been in very profitable firms, which would then hire more workers. The policy of solidarity wages was twinned with measures to retrain workers for jobs in the expanding sectors. The solidarity wage model has been difficult to maintain because it effectively requires higher-skilled workers to lower their wages for the benefit of others, but it still remains quite strongly entrenched in the Scandinavian countries and the Netherlands.

Rather than just destroying private services jobs, high labour standards can raise job quality and pay by raising productivity. Wage floors can lower worker turnover and increase experience and skills, reducing employer costs. A common wage standard can also take wage costs out of the competitive equation. If all employers pay the same wage and benefit package, firms must compete with one another on the basis of non-labour cost issues, such as quality and customer service. There is good evidence that decent wages and high labour standards raise productivity. The fact that employers come under pressure to pay good wages will lead them to invest more in capital equipment and training than would otherwise be the case. Further, high labour standards can raise productivity by improving the social relations of production. If workers know that changes in work organization will not cost them jobs, will not lead to poorer health and safety or working conditions, and that the gains of higher productivity will be shared with them, then workers will co-operate in workplace change.

■ Denmark and the New European Labour Market Model

Denmark has been viewed by the International Labour Organization and the European Commission as a major success story in terms of both the quantity and quality of employment. While it has many distinctive national features, Denmark can be seen as a social democratic model that holds lessons for Canadians as well as Europeans. This section summarizes some key features of the Danish labour market of the 1990s, especially in relation to the issue of precarious employment.

Table 11.2 provides comparative data for the U.S., Canada, Denmark, and Sweden to draw out contrasts between the liberal and the social democratic models. As

Box 11.1: Labour Conditions and Productivity

In a major defence of labour rights and standards, Werner Sengenberger, a recently retired senior official with the ILO, argues that the orthodox view of the labour market is profoundly misleading since it does not take account of the fundamental fact that "labour is not a commodity" or a "factor of production" (Sengenberger 2003). Rather, labour is a productive potential linked to human beings with individual and social needs. Productivity—what a worker delivers in return for a wage—depends upon what the ILO has termed "decent work." "A worker will be more or less productive, co-operative and innovative depending on how he or she is treated; whether the wage is seen as fair in relation to the demands of the job; whether the worker gets equal pay for work of equal value; whether training is provided; whether grievances can be voiced. In short, what the worker delivers is contingent on the terms of employment, working conditions, the work environment, collective representation, and due process" (Sengenberger 2003, 48).

shown, employment rates are even higher in Sweden and Denmark than in the U.S. or Canada, particularly for women. Notably, employment rates for adult workers with low levels of formal education are also significantly higher. If high levels of participation in paid work are seen as key to social inclusion, the development of individual capabilities and gender equity, then the social democratic countries are the clear winners compared to Canada and the U.S. High employment has also been twinned with very low unemployment rates, and, as in North America, by a low incidence of long-term unemployment.

Sweden and Denmark have very low levels of after-tax income inequality and child poverty compared to North America, reflecting much lower levels of earnings inequality and low pay, and also higher levels of social transfers as a share of GDP. Cash benefits (i.e., public pensions, unemployment, welfare, and disability benefits) are almost double the North American level. Taxpayer-funded public services as a share of GDP are, at 16%, far higher than in the U.S. (6.7%) or Canada (9.8%). High levels of spending on public services mean that the share of national income spent on private consumption (i.e., household spending) is correspondingly much lower.

In pure economic terms, the Scandinavian countries have also been very successful. The average annual growth of labour productivity in the business sector was slightly higher in both countries than in the U.S. or Canada (1995 to 2001) and the average growth rate of real GDP per capita (i.e., per person) was comparable. If growth of GDP per capita were adjusted for time worked, Scandinavian performance would look even better because of a lower incidence of long hours and longer periods of paid vacation than in North America. The average full-time Danish worker has a work week of 37 hours; long hours are very uncommon; and all workers now enjoy six weeks of paid vacation per year.

Table 11.2: North America vs. Scandinavia: Key Economic and Social Indicators				
	U.S.	Canada	Sweden	Denmark
1. (a) Average annual GDP growth per capita, 1995–2002	2.3%	2.5%	2.5%	2.0%
(b) Average annual growth of labour productivity in business sector, 1995–2002	1.6%	1.5%	1.7%	1.8%
2. Employment/population ratio 2001				
All	73.1%	70.9%	75.3%	75.9%
Men	79.3%	75.9%	77.0%	80.2%
Women	67.1%	66.0%	73.5%	71.4%
Age 25–64 <Upper secondary education	57.8%	55.0%	68.0%	62.5%
Men	69.6%	66.1%	73.3%	70.9%
Women	45.8%	43.3%	61.6%	55.1%
3. Unemployment rate 2001				
All	4.8%	7.3%	5.1%	4.2%
Men	4.9%	7.6%	5.4%	3.7%
Women	4.7%	6.8%	4.7%	4.8%
4. Long-term unemployment (>6 months) as % of unemployed	4.8%	7.3%	5.1%	4.2%
5. Temporary employment as % total employment 2001				
All	4.0%	12.4%	14.7%	10.2%
Men	3.9%	11.8%	12.3%	8.8%
Women	4.2%	13.3%	16.9%	11.7%
6. Part-time employment as % total employment				
All	13.0%	18.1%	17.8%	14.5%
Men	8.1%	10.4%	7.1%	9.1%
Women	18.2%	27.1%	29.3%	20.8%
7. (a) Net income replacement rate (composite of four family types at two earning levels; short- and long-duration unemployment)	41%	58%	80%	80%
(b) Unemployment compensation as % GDP	0.30%	0.72%	1.19%	1.35%
8. Child poverty rate	23.2%	14.2%	2.7%	3.4%
9. After-tax income gaps (minimum ratio top to bottom 10%)	5.57	4.13	2.61	3.15
10. Public social expenditure as % GDP				
a. Cash benefits	7.8%	8.1%	15.1%	14.0%
b. Public services	6.7%	9.8%	16.0%	16.1%
11. Public expenditure on labour market training as % GDP	0.04%	0.17%	0.30%	0.85%
Unemployed/at risk participants as % workforce	0.99%	1.61%	2.32%	5.76%
Employed participants as % workforce	0%	0%	0.0%	10.15%

Source: Except as indicated, data are from OECD Social Indicators <http://www.oecd.org>.
1. *OECD Economic Outlook*, #73. (Paris: OECD, 2003).
6. *OECD Employment Outlook*. (Paris: OECD, 2002).
9. Timothy Smeeding. Luxemburg Income Study Working Paper #320 (2002) <http://www.lisproject.org>.
11. *OECD Employment Outlook*. (Paris: OECD, 2003).

While in very broad terms a variation of the Scandinavian social democratic model, Denmark differs from Sweden in many ways. It has an economy based much more on small firms in services, food processing, and light industry, and less on large-scale industry. The Social Democratic Party, while in government most of the time until 2002, has been less dominant, and the unions a somewhat weaker social force. Like Sweden and the Netherlands, recent employment success contrasts to experiences of high unemployment, fiscal crisis, and very strained labour-management relationships at various times in the 1980s and early 1990s. Like the Netherlands, crisis led to a renewal of the social partnership model and major reforms.

As noted above, the incidence of low-wage work in Denmark is very low because of the high-wage floor set by collective bargaining. More than 80% of all workers and about 70% of private-sector workers are covered by collective agreements (EIRO 2002). Coverage is almost universal in community and social services, and collective agreements cover the majority of workers even in normally low-wage, consumer services sectors such as retail trade (57%) and hotels and restaurants (50%). Bargaining coverage is stable or even increasing, despite erosion among some higher-paid professionals, and unions and employers have maintained that employee protection legislation is largely unnecessary because of continued high union coverage of potentially vulnerable workers.

Bargaining is conducted on a sectoral basis between employer associations and unions within a loose framework of centrally agreed wage guidelines, with some enterprise flexibility to pay higher wages. The wage determination system has been characterized as centralized decentralization. While wage moderation has been a feature of Danish success, LO, the major union federation of non-professional workers, recently conducted national strikes to win a sixth week of paid vacation and real wages have increased more or less in line with those in Germany (Ploughmann and Madsen 2002). Wage inequality did not increase in the 1990s.

The incidence of precarious employment in Denmark is very low. Self-employment (which is disproportionately, though not universally, precarious) accounts for just 7% of total employment, compared to about 20% in Canada and an EU average of 15%, and has been declining from 9% in 1990 (European Commission 2002). Temporary or fixed-term contract employment accounts for 10.2% of all jobs and is higher for women than for men, but less than one in three temporary workers report that this status is involuntary. The status of temporary workers generally compares very well to other EU countries and to Canada (OECD 2002b). Temporary workers are covered by collective agreements; qualify for paid holidays, parental leave, and sick leave if they have worked for just 72 hours in the past eight weeks; and earn 78% of the hourly wage of permanent employees (more when controlled for other differences in work status). However, they have much less access than permanent employees to training. Similarly, the low incidence of part-time work (at 14.5%) is falling (from 19.2% in 1990), and is generally voluntary (European Commission 2002).

The European Commission judges Denmark to have the highest overall quality of jobs in the EU (European Commission 2001, Chapter 4). Measured by pay, working conditions, subjective job satisfaction, and opportunities for advancement, 60% of Danes are in good jobs (the highest proportion in Europe), 20% are in jobs of reasonable quality, and just 20% are in jobs of poor quality (of which less than half qualify as really bad dead-end jobs). There are also very high rates of transition from lower-quality to higher-quality jobs, with 35% of workers in low-quality jobs moving to better jobs one year later, and 50% in better jobs three years later (compared to 35% in the U.K.) (European Commission 2002, 93). Subjective job satisfaction is the highest in the EU. Data from the *European Survey on Work Conditions* also suggest that jobs in the Danish services sector are, on average, much better than elsewhere in the EU in terms of levels of work autonomy and the incidence of monotonous work (OECD 2001). It seems probable that the high level of social services jobs and high incidence of training have militated against dead-end (very low-skill/low-productivity) consumer services jobs.

The Danish labour market is remarkable in terms of its high level of labour mobility. Annual worker turnover is as high as 30%. About one-half of annual job turnover is due to job destruction, but the level of voluntary resignations to seek or take new jobs is also very high (Madsen 2003, 64; Ploughmann and Madsen 2002, 21). Only about two-thirds of workers have been in their current job for more than two years, the lowest proportion in the EU, and one-quarter have been in their current job for less than one year, the highest proportion in the EU (European Commission 2001, 72). There is a very low level of job protection by law or collective agreement. On the OECD scale of strictness of employment protection, Denmark ranks very low, just above Canada. Collective agreements typically specify two to three months' notice of layoff for long-tenure workers. The main union central, LO Denmark, has not called for stronger job protection, arguing that generous unemployment benefits and access to training serve workers better.

Despite quite high rates of entry into unemployment, perceived employment security is very high. A 2000 survey found that only 9% of Danish workers were afraid of losing their current jobs, the lowest in the EU (Ploughmann and Madsen 2002, 12). By contrast, one-quarter to one-third of Canadian workers have reported fear of job loss in recent years, according to the Canadian Council on Social Development's Personal Security Index.

The annual incidence of unemployment is as high as one in four workers, but, for the majority, unemployment is very short term (less than 10 weeks). Madsen, who has written extensively on the Danish model for the ILO, talks of the "Golden Triangle" of the Danish labour market. As in liberal labour markets, there is a very low level of job protection, which has encouraged job creation. However, in line with the principle of flexicurity and the traditional social democratic model, unemployment benefits replace a high proportion of wages, and there is much more emphasis on training and active labour market policy to promote employment security.

The great majority of unemployed workers belong to an Unemployment Insurance Fund administered by the unions, and are eligible for benefits if employed for one year in the last three. The OECD calculated the relative generosity of benefits for unemployed workers for different family types and earning levels and found that the Danish and Swedish systems are by far the most generous. The income-replacement rate for an average production worker is at least 70%, rising to 90% for relatively low-paid workers (Madsen 2003, 74). For an estimated one-third of unemployed men and one-half of unemployed women, benefits just about match prior earnings (Benner and Vad 2000). As shown in Table 11.2, expenditure on so-called passive unemployment benefits was 1.3% of Danish GDP in 2001, almost double the Canadian level despite similar unemployment rates.

Reforms to the unemployment insurance system in the mid-1990s very modestly trimmed benefits and introduced individual employment plans. It is now mandatory for beneficiaries to participate in an active labour market program after one year, and after six months for younger workers. While this has been seen as akin to North American-style workfare in some critiques and is deliberately intended to counter dependency, the carrots of good benefits and meaningful training opportunities are much more important than the stick of potential sanctions. Moreover, unemployed workers are clearly being trained for jobs at decent wages.

As shown in Table 11.2, public expenditures on labour market training are, at .85% of GDP, much higher in Denmark than in Sweden, and five times higher than in Canada. The main focus is on training for the unemployed, and about two in three unemployed workers or 6% of the total workforce receive some public training each year. This can be in private firms with a wage subsidy, with a public-sector employer, or in training or educational programs to fill future labour market vacancies. In addition, about 10% of the Danish workforce benefit each year from government training programs directed to employed workers, compared to almost zero in Canada. There has been skepticism in Canada about the effectiveness of skills training for unemployed and vulnerable workers, but Danish studies judge their programs to be effective in job placement and raising skills (ILO 2003; Madsen 2003). Credit has been given to the decentralization of public training to the regional level since the mid-1990s, where it is run by the social partners.

In addition, the Danish system features high levels of education and training for the currently employed. On top of a strong base of universal public education and high participation in post-secondary studies, the rhetoric of lifelong learning in a skill-based economy has been translated into reality through rights to individual educational leaves, and opportunities to take education leaves funded by unemployment benefits. These were quite popular when used to address high unemployment in the early to mid-1990s. Unions bargain access to training, and help run employer-sponsored training. Denmark has recently ranked very high among OECD countries in terms of the extent of adult participation in training and equality of access for women (OECD 1999). Average hours spent in training per worker are double the OECD average. Such training extends to workers in private consumer services, with participation rates of 70% in hotels and restaurants, and 49% in retail trade (European Commission 2001, Table 9).

In the discussion above, emphasis was placed on the importance of public and social services as a source of quality employment for women. Such services account for about one-third of Danish employment, and fully one-half of employment for women, but private services employment has grown faster since the mid-1980s, and two out of three new jobs created between 1993 and 2002 were in the private sector (Madsen 2003). The importance of not loading too many non-wage costs onto employers was also noted. In Denmark, tax reform in the mid-1990s trimmed already low payroll taxes, and sharply reduced employer responsibility for funding active labour market programs. According to Madsen (2003, 60), "[t]he direct costs of protecting the employee are borne to a large extent by the state and not by individual firms." Workplace pensions play a modest role compared to universal state pensions and the state-run, work-based pension system. As a result, the proportion of social expenditures financed by employers is the lowest in the EU—8.7% compared to 46.5% in France and 37.4% in Germany (ILO 2003, 58) and the percentage of non-wage costs in total labour costs is just 6.3% compared to 31.8% in France and 20.7% in the U.S. (ILO 2003, 61).

The Danish model is not without flaws. In common with other socially homogeneous small countries, the values of social solidarity tend to be racially and culturally defined. Unemployment is relatively high among recent immigrants from developing countries, and the recently elected (conservative) government has limited immigrant access to full welfare benefits. As noted, occupational segregation of women and men is high.

■ Conclusion and Lessons for Canada

The central conclusion to be drawn from this chapter is that it is possible to have high levels of employment at decent wages and with decent working conditions. There is no inevitable trade-off between job quantity and job quality, even at the low end of the job market. Several European countries have achieved very high employment rates and low unemploymen even with generous welfare benefits and wages that are extremely equal compared to Canada.

The Danish example is unique in some respects, but has wider lessons. First, a wage floor and the virtual elimination of low pay do not preclude job growth in private services. Good labour standards can raise productivity, though a high-wage floor probably works best when combined with training policies that raise the skills of workers. The Danish example also suggests that high levels of public services, financed from general taxes, can make a positive contribution to high-quality, post-industrial employment.

Though it is assumed that it is easier to pursue solidaristic policies in very homogeneous countries, Canada is clearly more ethnically and culturally diverse than Denmark, and at the same time there is a fairly broad concensus on some core values. Canada is also highly integrated with the deregulated U.S. economy. This poses limits on policy, particularly with respect to the level of taxes as was noted in the last chapter, but the experience of Denmark and Sweden strongly suggests that precarious work is not a precondition for success in today's changing international economy.

● ●

■ Questions for Critical Thought

1. Do you think the U.S. is often held out to Canadians as a social model to be copied if we want to create a lot of good jobs?
2. What positive lessons for Canada can be drawn from the way in which European labour markets and workplaces operate?
3. Is it reasonable to argue that strong unions and high minimum wages can be good for the economy?
4. Are European models relevant to Canadians given the high degree of economic integration with the U.S.?

■ Recommended Reading

Aidt, Toke, and Zafiris Tzannatos. 2003. *Unions and Collective Bargaining: Economic Effects in a Global Environment*. Washington: The World Bank. This overview of studies on the economic impacts of unions—from an organization that is not usually seen as pro-labour—generally finds unions not guilty of undermining economic growth and job creation.

Auer, Peter. 2000. *Employment Revival in Europe: Labour Market Success in Austria, Denmark, Ireland and the Netherlands*. Geneva: ILO. This study by the International Labour Organization draws on the experience of four smaller countries to suggest that improving the quality of jobs can be consistent with high levels of job creation.

Esping-Anderson, Gosta. 1999. *Social Foundations of Post-Industrial Economies*. Oxford: Oxford University Press, 1999.

Pierson, Paul, ed. 2001. *The New Politics of the Welfare State*. Oxford: Oxford University Press. Both Esping-Anderson and Pierson provide good accounts of the major differences in labour markets and social programs between the advanced industrial countries, and how this affects their relative performance in terms of meeting economic and social goals.

■ References

Aidt, Toke, and Zafiris Tzannatos. 2003. Unions and Collective Bargaining: Economic Effects in a Global Environment. Washington: The World Bank.

Auer, Peter. 2000. *Employment Revival in Europe: Labour Market Success in Austria, Denmark, Ireland and the Netherlands.* Geneva: ILO.

Baker, Dean, Andrew Glyn, David Howell, and John Schmitt. 2002. "Labor Market Institutions and Unemployment: A Critical Assessment of the Cross-Country Evidence." Centre for Economic Policy Analysis Working Paper 2002-17 <http://www.newschool.edu/cepa>.

Benner, Mats, and Torben Bundgaard Vad. 2000. "Sweden and Denmark: Defending the Welfare State." In *Welfare and Work in the Open Economy: Vol. II Diverse Responses to Common Challenges,* edited by Fritz Scharpf and Vivien Schmidt. Oxford: Oxford University Press.

Esping-Anderson, Gosta. 1999. *Social Foundations of Post-Industrial Economies.* Oxford: Oxford University Press.

European Commission (Employment and Social Affairs). 2001. *Employment in Europe.* Brussels: European Commission.

_____. 2002. *Employment in Europe.* Brussels: European Comission.

European Industrial Relations Observatory (EIRO). 2001. "Annual Review for Denmark" <http://www.eiro.eurofund.ie>.

_____. 2002. "Annual Review for Denmark" <http://www.eiro.eurofund.ie>.

Freeman, Richard B. 1998. "War of the Models: Which Labour Market Institutions for the 21st Century?" *Labour Economics* 5, no. 1: 1–24.

Freeman, Richard B., and Lawrence F. Katz, eds. 1995. *Differences and Changes in Wage Structures.* Chicago: The University of Chicago Press.

International Labour Organization (ILO). 2003. *Decent Work in Denmark: Employment, Social Efficiency and Economic Security.* Geneva: ILO.

Madsen, Per Kongshoj. 2003. "'Flexicurity' through Labour Market Policies and Institutions in Denmark." In *Employment Stability in an Age of Flexibility,* edited by Peter Auer and Sandrine Cazes, 59–105. Geneva: International Labour Office.

Organisation for Economic Cooperation and Development (OECD). 1996. "Earnings Inequality, Low Paid Employment and Earnings Mobility." *OECD Employment Outlook,* 59–108. Paris: OECD.

_____. 1997. "Economic Performance and the Structure of Collective Bargaining." *OECD Employment Outlook,* 63–90. Paris: OECD.

_____. 1999. "Training of Adult Workers in OECD Countries." *OECD Employment Outlook,* 133–175. Paris: OECD.

_____. 2000. "Employment in the Service Economy: A Reassessment." *OECD Employment Outlook,* 79–126. Paris: OECD.

_____. 2001. "The Characteristics and Quality of Service Sector Jobs." *OECD Employment Outlook,* 89–127. Paris: OECD.

_____. 2002a. "Women at Work: Who Are They and How Are They Faring?" *OECD Employment Outlook,* 61–125. Paris: OECD.

_____. 2002b. "Taking the Measure of Temporary Employment." *OECD Employment Outlook,* 127–183. Paris: OECD.

Pierson, Paul, ed. 2001. *The New Politics of the Welfare State*. Oxford: Oxford University Press.

Ploughmann, Peter, and Per Madsen. 2002. "Flexibility, Employment Development and Active Labour Market Policy in Denmark and Sweden in the 1990s." CEPA Working Paper 2002-04. New York: Centre for Economic Policy Analysis, New School University.

Scharpf, Fritz, and Vivien Schmidt, eds. 2000. *Welfare and Work in the Open Economy: Vol. I From Vulnerability to Competitiveness*, and *Vol. II Diverse Responses to Common Challenges*. Oxford: Oxford University Press.

Sengenberger, Werner. 2003. *Globalization and Social Progress: The Role and Impact of Labour Standards*. Bonn: Friedrich Ebert Foundation.

Smeeding, Timothy. 2002. "Globalization, Inequality and the Rich Countries of the G-20: Evidence from the Luxemburg Income Study." Luxemburg Income Study Working Paper no. 320 <http://www.lisproject.org>.

Copyright
Acknowledgements

Tables

Table 2.1: "Labour Market Trends," adapted from the Statistics Canada publication *Labour Force Historical Review 2003*, Catalogue 71F0004, February 17, 2004. Copyright © Statistics Canada. Reprinted by permission of Statistics Canada.

Table 2.2: "Family Income Trends in the 1990s," adapted from the Statistics Canada publication *Income in Canada 2001*, Catalogue 75-202, June 25, 2003. Copyright © Statistics Canada. Reprinted by permission of Statistics Canada.

Table 3.1: "Canadian Job-Related Training in International Perspective," adapted from the Statistics Canada publication *Adult Education Participation in North America: International Perspectives*, Catalogue 89-574, September 7, 2001. Copyright © Statistics Canada. Reprinted by permission of Statistics Canada.

Table 3.2: Valerie Peters, "Participation in Formal Employer-Supported Training in 2002," adapted from the Statistics Canada publication *Working and Training: First Results of the 2003 Adult Education and Training Survey*, Catalogue 81-595, 2003, no. 15. Copyright © Statistics Canada. Reprinted by permission of Statistics Canada.

Table 3.3: "Proportion of Employees Participating in Employer Supported Training in 1999," adapted from the Statistics Canada publication *Guide to the Analysis of Workplace and Employee Survey, 2001*, Catalogue 71-221, August 2003. Copyright © Statistics Canada. Reprinted by permission of Statistics Canada.

Table 4.1: "Unionization and Fringe Benefits," adapted from the Statistics Canada publication *Perspectives on Labour and Income*, Catalogue 75-001, vol. 3, no. 8. Copyright © Statistics Canada. Reprinted by permission of Statistics Canada.

Table 4.2: "Physical Work Environment," adapted from the Statistics Canada publication *The General Social Survey: An Overview*, Catalogue 89F0115, March 15, 1991. Copyright © Statistics Canada. Reprinted by permission of Statistics Canada.

Table 5.1: "Employment by Broad Occupation," adapted from the Statistics Canada publication *Labour Force Historical Review 2003*, Catalogue 71F0004, February

Figures

Figure 6.2: "Distribution of Annual Earnings: Visible Minorities Compared to Non-Visible Minorities," adapted from the Statistics Canada table *Statistical Area Classification: Highlight Tables, 2001 Counts, For Canada, Provinces and Territories*, 2001 Census, Catalogue 97F0024, February 27, 2004. Copyright © Statistics Canada. Reprinted by permission of Statistics Canada.

Figure 7.1: "Employment Rates of Older Workers," adapted from the Statistics Canada publication *Income Trends in Canada 1980–2001*, Catalogue 13F0022, December 22, 2003. Copyright © Statistics Canada. Reprinted by permission of Statistics Canada.

Figure 8.1: "Percentage of Workers Covered by a Collective Agreement in 2003," adapted from the Statistics Canada publication *Guide to the Labour Force Survey, 2004*, Catalogue 71-543, February 17, 2004. Copyright © Statistics Canada. Reprinted by permission of Statistics Canada.

Figure 8.2: "Average Hourly Wages in 2003: Union vs. Non-Union," adapted from the Statistics Canada publication *Guide to the Labour Force Survey*, 2004, Catalogue 71-543, February 17, 2004. Copyright © Statistics Canada. Reprinted by permission of Statistics Canada.

Boxes

Box 1.1: "Young People and the Transition to Work," adapted from the Statistics Canada publication *The Daily*, Catalogue 11-001, June 16, 2004. Copyright © Statistics Canada. Reprinted by permission of Statistics Canada.

Box 1.2: Swartz, M., "Work: The 21st Century Obsession," *The Toronto Star*. Copyright © Mark Swartz. Reprinted by permission of the author.

Box 1.3: Jencks, C., Perman, L., and Rainwater, L., "What is a Good Job? A New Measure of Labour Market Success," from *American Journal of Sociology* 93(5), 132–1357. Copyright © American Journal of Sociology. Reprinted by permission of American Journal of Sociology.

Box 2.3: Galloway, G., "The Rich Get Richer," *The Globe and Mail*, August 4, 2004. Copyright © The Globe and Mail. Reprinted with permission from The Globe and Mail.

Box 4.3: Immen, W., "'Role overload' makes workers sick," *The Globe and Mail*, October 22, 2003. Copyright © The Globe and Mail. Reprinted by permission of The Globe and Mail.

Box 6.2: Jimenez, M. "We Are All Capable People," *The Globe and Mail*, October 25, 2003. Copyright © The Globe and Mail. Reprinted by permission of The Globe and Mail.

Box 10.1: Saunders, J. "IT jobs contracted from far and wide," *The Globe and Mail*, October 14, 2003. Copyright © The Globe and Mail. Reprinted by permission of The Globe and Mail.

Box 11.1: Sengenberger, W. 2003. "Globalization and Social Progress: The Role and Impact of Labour Standards," from *Globalization and Social Progress: The Role and*

Impact of International Labour Standards. Copyright © Friedrich Ebert Foundation. Reprinted by permission of Friedrich Ebert Foundation.

■Photos

Cover: *Health Canada website and Media Photo Gallery,* Health Canada, <http://www. hc-sc.gc.ca>. Reproduced with the permission of the Minister of Public Works and Government Services Canada, 2004.

Photo 1.1: Peter Hostermann, "Hanomag 01" from stock.xchng, <http://www. sxc.hu>. Copyright © Peter Hostermann. Reprinted by permission of the photographer.

Photo 2.1: *Health Canada website and Media Photo Gallery,* Health Canada, <http:// www.hc-sc.gc.ca>. Reproduced with the permission of the Minister of Public Works and Government Services Canada, 2004.

Photo 3.1: Matt Williams, "Cybertruck 1," from stock.xchng, <http://www.sxc.hu>. Copyright © Matt Williams. Reprinted by permission of the photographer.

Photo 4.1: *Health Canada website and Media Photo Gallery,* Health Canada, <http:// www.hc-sc.gc.ca>. Reproduced with the permission of the Minister of Public Works and Government Services Canada, 2004.

Photo 5.1: *Health Canada website and Media Photo Gallery,* Health Canada, <http:// www.hc-sc.gc.ca>. Reproduced with the permission of the Minister of Public Works and Government Services Canada, 2004.

Photo 6.1: *Health Canada website and Media Photo Gallery,* Health Canada, <http:// www.hc-sc.gc.ca>. Reproduced with the permission of the Minister of Public Works and Government Services Canada, 2004. Reprinted by permission of Health Canada.

Photo 7.1: *Health Canada website and Media Photo Gallery,* Health Canada, <http:// www.hc-sc.gc.ca>. Reproduced with the permission of the Minister of Public Works and Government Services Canada, 2004.

Photo 8.1. Joe Sarnovsky, CAW Local 222. Reprinted by permission of the photographer.

Photo 9.1: *Health Canada website and Media Photo Gallery,* Health Canada, <http:// www.hc-sc.gc.ca>. Reproduced with the permission of the Minister of Public Works and Government Services Canada, 2004.

Photo 10.1: *Health Canada website and Media Photo Gallery,* Health Canada, <http:// www.hc-sc.gc.ca>. Reproduced with the permission of the Minister of Public Works and Government Services Canada, 2004.

Photo 11.1: Source: *Health Canada website and Media Photo Gallery,* Health Canada, http://www.hc-sc.gc.ca. Reproduced with the permission of the Minister of Public Works and Government Services Canada, 2004.

Index